The Barnsley Whale

For my mother and father: true tykes

The
Barnsley
Whale

The true story of the world's first inland whale hunt

Steve Deput

MAINSTREAM
PUBLISHING
EDINBURGH AND LONDON

First published in Great Britain in 2003 by
MAINSTREAM PUBLISHING COMPANY (EDINBURGH) LTD
7 Albany Street
Edinburgh EH1 3UG

ISBN 1 84018 749 2

A catalogue record for this book is available from the British Library

Typeset in Garamond, Helvetica and Trixie
Printed and bound in Great Britain by
Mackays of Chatham, Kent

In the lands of the north
Where the black rocks stand guard over the cold sea
In the dark night that is very long
The men of the northlands sit by their great log fires
And they tell a tale . . .

From *The Sagas of Nogin the Nog*

Contents

Tykes

Many say that the first to take on this adventure must
have been fanatic-eccentrics and dare devils . . .

Jules Michelet on whaling, *La Mer*, 1856

The Vision

I AM A TYKE. I WAS BORN AND BRED IN THE TOWN (OR 'TARN', IF you say it in our accent) of Barnsley. And before you start, like all tykes, I've heard it *all* before: flat caps, black pudding, Geoff Boycott, whippets, miners, Parky, slag heaps, pits, pigeons 'n' trouble at t'mill. Oh aye lad. We're known for all these things and more besides – but a whale? As far as sea life is concerned, the odd cod (with chips 'n' mushy peas) is usually as far as it goes.

Was there ever a whale in Barnsley: a *real* whale? Tarn's 70 miles from the coast! How did it get there? What was it doing there? All I know is that one morning as I trudged along the road to work I was struck by a vision; a revelation. I've no idea where it came from or why, but the image was clear enough: the sad eye and gaping mouth of an enormous whale. Some fragment of a memory from a long, long time ago.

From the moment he popped into my head I knew I was in trouble. After all, life can sometimes be easier if you don't talk about what you've seen, or *think* you've seen. UFOs, little green men, yetis, fairies, ghosts and the like. Instinctively, I knew that a huge whale in a northern mining town fell into the same category. My new companion proved troublesome; he just wouldn't go away. Day and night he cruised through my mind. I needed back-up on this, but who to ask? Fellow tykes obviously, but it wasn't that simple. That summer I was completing my 20th year of exile in an alien world far, far from tarn.

Board Games

LONDON 2000: THROUGHOUT THE CAPITAL, MILLIONS OF EYES were glued to glass screens. Mine were no exception. I worked in an office at the time – it doesn't matter which one, they're all the same – and whatever my job title was, my job was much the same as yours: a shoveller of e-mails. Every morning I found my in-box stuffed with urgent enquiries to be sifted, sorted and sent on a never-ending cycle of communication. On a good day I actually bothered to read some of them.

But that day I was distracted. Ungluing my eyes and peering across the floor, all around silent heads were thrust into computers.

'*You know, when I was a kid I saw a whale in Barnsley . . .*'

Well, I formed the statement in my head but it got no further. No use broaching this bizarre subject with those around me. The corporate animal has often struck me as particularly unadventurous. Rarely venturing beyond the rolling steel fortress of the M25, the rest of the country is regarded as a vague hinterland shrouded in mystery. I knew that the mere mention of my marine mammal would be met by the time-honoured mantra: '*Miners, strikes, black pudding, mushy peas . . .*'

Strangely enough, it was my mouse I had to thank for showing me the way that day. Now, I don't really like computers. I don't have even a vague grasp of how they work, yet I have to admit they're tremendously useful tools in the office. Like every other earnest e-mail shoveller, I'd perfected the art of whiling away entire days mailing friends, passing the porn, playing games and aimlessly surfing the Internet. And it was on one of these idling cyber-strolls that I chanced upon my tarnspeople.

A few days before, my mouse had sniffed out the Barnsley Football Club website. All clubs have websites and boards that fans can visit and post their questions, opinions or whatever. Naturally, many postings revolve around football, but with Euro 2000 long finished and the new season still weeks away, there wasn't much new football talk to talk. Everyone found themselves drawn to reminiscences of the previous season, though: a true roller-coaster ride of emotion crowned by one glorious day.

After 48 hard-fought First Division battles, the 'Reds' had secured a place in the Division One play-offs. A jubilant 4–1 thrashing of Birmingham City bounced us into the final showdown. Just one more victory and we would regain our rightful place in the Premiership! Our clash with Ipswich Town at Wembley was one of the most emotionally charged matches in Barnsley Football Club's history. Although we'd won the FA Cup way back in 1912, the game hadn't been played at the national stadium. It would be another 88 years, the early summer of 2000, before a red wave of tykes rolled up Wembley Way. This, our very first visit, was to be one of the last competitive games under the Twin Towers' shadow before the stadium was redeveloped. It was an epic encounter; a riot of red-and-blue flags, banners, painted faces and end-to-end football. But we lost, 4–2. There were tears, of course, but all agreed it had been a fantastic day for every single fan crammed in the ground. We'd still lost though – and it hurt. We tykes now finished licking our wounds and eagerly anticipated the coming season.

'Regulars' whiled away dog days of summer with transfer speculation and comment: good riddance to our defecting, kebab-eating captain; gnashing of teeth at the loss of our top goal-scorer; fretting about how much our manager would be prepared to spend in order to launch our next campaign for promotion. Over the previous few days, football news had worn thin, so other stuff cropped up: 'Where did you drink your first pint and how much did it cost', joke-of-the-day contests, anything really. If anyone could confirm my vision it would be these invisible tykes far beyond my glass screen. I would ask them. I would ask them about the whale in tarn.

By 11 a.m. my day was clear. I'd done four coffees, thirty-six e-mails, *The Sun*, *The Guardian*, one Cup-a-Soup, five cigarettes and nine minutes' work. Five meetings were posted in my electronic diary, three of them at the same time. I was confident the company's electronic diary coordinator would resolve that little problem. Four would be cancelled, the fifth labelled 'urgent' and rescheduled for last year.

My mouse scurried to the site. This was it. I tapped out my question. All I wanted was for someone to confirm my vision of a whale in Barnsley. That was all.

It's best to visualise 'the board' as exactly that – a public notice board. At any time, night or day, people come along and post messages for anyone to read. The only difference is that this is a bulletin board the world can look at. The messages on the board come from anybody, anywhere.

Replies can come almost instantly, in minutes, or hours or even days later – and those replying? I wouldn't know who they were. Respondents give only their 'handle'. Other than that, they could be male, female, of any age, background or denomination. I've never met any of the people on the board. I have no way of knowing whether their characters are real or invented.

Why I rechristened myself 'StatisTYKE' I'm not quite sure. Lots of people on the board used 'tyke' or 'red' in their names; I'd noticed postings from 'tyketanic', 'tykethat' and, memorably, a mysterious 'sparTYKEus'. I think mine was some feeble distortion of 'statistic'. I meant to change it. Little did I know that my very next posting would establish me as StatisTYKE forever.

11.01: There it was on my screen. A simple, daft question about a whale in tarn, along with the only other fragments of memory I could be sure of. It would probably be ignored or someone would slate me for being mad. After all, I didn't know too many football fans preoccupied with marine mammals, but it was worth a go. At most I might get a few replies before things moved on. As far as I knew, the greatest number of replies to a single posting was about 30 and there was *no* way I was expecting *anything* like that.

11.01 My finger pressed the key and the question disappeared into cyberspace.

> **BIG WHALE ON A LORRY**
> in t'tarn. Does anybody else remember this or have I lost it altogether? I were only a nipper and I think it were in t'60s. It was a whale pasted up in brown creosote stuff abaht 50 ft long, and they brought it to tarn on a lorry. There were crowds flockin' to see it. Sumdi must remember it.
> StatisTYKE

> **RE: BIG WHALE ON A LORRY . . .**
> The '60s . . . what were they like? Tad before my time chief . . . I reckon you were hallucinating any road mate. Whale on a lorry indeed.
> Pablo

> **RE: BIG WHALE ON A LORRY . . .**
> Its true Pab, also a pink elephant was seen walking up Pontefract road and a cow jumped over the moon.
> Ish

> **RE: BIG WHALE ON A LORRY**
> Too many beers in the Stables and the Changes maybe one or two in the Penny Farthing, Elephant and Castle and the Three Cranes!!!!
> Derby Red

F.UCK ME! YES. GOOD SHOUT.
Mad or what! It was on that car park near what's
now Old Courthouse pub. Big blue whale. That's
the first time I've recalled seeing that since seeing it
and I must have been a reyt young un then. What on
earth was that all about? Big bloody blue whale on a
lorry! It's true honest! I saw it with me
grandmother.

I'd get her to back me up but she waint remember
and she dunt go on bulletin board.
Big 'n' Daft

YES! YES! YES! TOP MAN BIG'N I AM NOT ALONE!
A blue whale, but it had gone brown with age,
creosote or whatever! There were THOUSANDS
turned out to see it!
StatisTYKE

That is mad! Remembering that after all these years.
Big 'n' Daft the man who recalls a blue whale in
t'cooert house car park.
Big 'n' Daft

RE: BIG WHALE ON A LORRY . . .
Christ!!! I'm glad tha remembers that, I thought I'd
dreamt it!!!! Can't remember much abart it, I think it
wor on show in t'old market place.
norman

Re: F.UCK ME! YES. GOOD SHOUT
Bloody hell lads thought I'd dreamt it 'n' all – any
details? I remember it near the level-crossing bus
station area. I'm gonna phone mi mum, she'll know.
Casper

Yes! There had been a whale! Big 'n' Daft, norman and Casper's enthusiasm was more than enough for me. That should have been the end of that. The banter would no doubt move on to other stuff. I'd posted my original question almost an hour ago: an old posting quickly sinking further down the board would often be ignored as most tykes tend to concentrate on the cut and thrust of conversation bubbling at the surface. But none of us had set sail in search of a whale before; little did we know the adventure had only just begun. Fifteen minutes past midday I almost fell off my chair, spluttering Cup-a-Soup across my computer as a tale of horrific death exploded from the screen.

> **THAT WHALE IN T'TARN**
> Me and Sed had a drunken conversation abart it last year and both confirmed it – the beer monkeys agreed as well. This has made me laughy loads.
> **Casper**

> **YES! MORE WHALE BELIEVERS**
> This topic merits further discussion when I gatecrash Bubbas on Setdi.
> **Big 'n' Daft**

> **AND DO YOU KNOW WHAT HAPPENED TO IT?**
> In 1968, weatherbeaten and colour fading fast, hence the s'tty brown colour from the original sky blue, the Borough Engineers department had it broken up and incinerated in a furnace which belonged to the NCB at Soot Hill just outside Wakefield. I know because my old dad was the Borough Engineer. I was taken to see it burn. Because of the paint and plastics as well as paper the fire raged out of control for about an hour and you could see the dense black smoke for miles. A right f'king to do. NCB went ballistic and

never gave out any contract work again with the Council.
Franco tyke

Franco tyke's news seared through my mind. A whale destroyed in Yorkshire! Was this the same one? Then again, how many whales had there been in tarn? The date itself threw others into confusion. News flooded in thick and fast, but rather than help solve the mystery, it deepened further still.

MORE WHALE NEWS BREAKING
I have just phoned me mother about the whale and SHE CAN'T REMEMBER IT. Even though she took me and usually remembers everything. I'm worried. Am goin to phone R Kid.
StatisTYKE

1968. That would have made me two years old or less. Are you sure it wasn't later? I definitely remember it though or am I going crackers?
Big 'n' Daft

It must have been later. I remember – it's one of my first memories and I wasn't born til the end of '67. I think it may be early '70/'71. But where did it come from – Cawthorne Park, Tinkers Pond? With the meeting of great minds at the Cheap Ale Kings Palace we should crack it – Johnny Bummer is bound to have an opinion on it!
Casper

****URGENT WHALE NEWS****
I have just spoken to R Kid who remembers it as well!!!!!
JONAH – TOP TARN WHALE OR WHAT?
StatisTYKE

BUT WHERE DID IT COME FROM?
Maybe a phone call to the *Chronicle* might help? Does
Keith Lodge* know about Whales? Or maybe Parky –
he must have mentioned it on telly? Dickie Bird will
know cos I remember him roaarin over its rancid
corpse!
Casper

Exactly! Questions need to be asked.
WHERE did it come from? WHY the f.uck was it in
tarn in first place?
    HOW did it get ter tarn? On a lorry I presume but
imagine overtekin that on A64 from Scarboro. I've e-
mailed the *Chronicle*.
Big 'n' Daft

Big 'n' Daft and Casper were right: newshounds from Barnsley's
local paper missed nothing. They were famous for bringing us all
the news that was news. Any paper that could run a story
headlined 'Shed Found in Wood' had to have the answer to the
whale.

Good work Big Fella. We'll crack this and probably
give them a front-page story that will be much better
than the usual 'One Pound Coin Stuck to street in
Wombwell' – true story that 'n' all. Lets soooort it
aht lads then maybe sort out some other tarn myths
like – Tinkers Pond having no bottom and Big 'n'
Daft's dad managing Mud!
Casper

It must have made front page of *Chroni* at the time.
There can't have been anything more exciting

* Sportswriter for the *Barnsley Chronicle*.

happened that week. In fact from the way that we're going on, it's the most exciting thing to have happened ever. I'm buying the bastard if they've got a back edition anyway.
Big 'n' Daft

I was stunned. The whale question jammed the board all morning. What was happening? I'd been pleased that my 'big whale on a lorry' posting hadn't been ignored – I was more than happy that somebody had confirmed this vague memory – but others had joined the cause with surprising enthusiasm. So far it seemed there were four of us; me, Big 'n' Daft, Casper and norman (not to mention Casper's friend 'Sed' and the 'beer monkeys'), who were prepared to swear by the memory of a whale, and Franco tyke who'd witnessed an exploding whale in Wakefield. A few doubters had revealed themselves, but I knew there would be other tykes following the debate. How many more 'whale believers' would rally to our cause?

By now we'd passed the one o'clock cut-off point where the board fell silent as most people drifted off for lunch. The office too had emptied, all except for my fellow e-mail shoveller. Dear Boy twitched and muttered, nodding at the world outside. We unshackled ourselves from our workstations and headed for the usual place.

The River

AT BATTERSEA, TO BE PRECISE. ALL SUMMER LONG I'D BOBBED around that sleepy backwater west of London's oppressive heat. Despite what I said about all offices being the same, the one I found myself in now had a big plus. After years in Soho's rat-runs, I took to my new workplace in a slim glass tower perched directly on the Thames, at the south side of Battersea Bridge.

From my fourth-floor desk I had a panoramic view of an evolving city. Anchored by my PC, I could gaze north over Chelsea, the towers and turrets of the Victoria & Albert Museum. Scanning east, the Telecom and Nat West towers, a hazy Canary Wharf and a new London landmark, the Millennium Wheel. On the river to the west, I witnessed the birth of another: Foster's Montevetro Tower, a glittering triangular mountain of glass dwarfing the drab concrete towers of 1960s Battersea. Overlooking Chelsea harbour on the north bank, its crystal penthouses in the clouds offered accommodation to anyone with £3 million to spare. Below me, traffic congealed in the summer heat, inching bad-temperedly over the bridge into town. Underneath, dredgers and container barges ploughed back and forth, skirting tourist-crammed riverboats turning back from the western extreme of their Thames tour. To the south, commuter trains shuttled back and forth through Clapham Junction, sleek grey-and-yellow bullets of Paris-bound Eurostars occasionally whistling between them. On a rail bridge just beyond Montevetro, the Shuttle's forefather, the Orient Express, often rumbled over the Thames like some ghost of a bygone era.

Overhead the sky was packed. Battersea Heliport, the feeding station for scores of chattering helicopters, whisked executives to and from the city over snarled-up traffic. Higher still, an aerial armada whined west on final approach to Heathrow; I'd watch them shrink to dots between the chimneys of Lott's Road power station on the north bank. With this Victorian powerhouse generating electricity for London Underground as a near neighbour, I imagined I could peer straight into the tube's subterranean labyrinth. I stood at the hub of every form of transport, the centre of a child's giant toy set.

But the river was my favourite spot. Most lunchtimes myself and Dear Boy broke free from our moorings and drifted below the bustling city into the cool, damp air of low tide. Here another London revealed herself.

Dear Boy had a name of course, but no one used it much. His habit of referring to everyone as 'dear boy' led to him being re-christened. A strange fenland creature – part rusting conquistador, part shambling chimpanzee – he'd shuffled south from Peterborough around the same time as I'd left Barnsley. A childhood spent on windswept flatlands had equipped him with an uncanny ability to sniff the rise and fall of the river.

Ducking under hulls of paint-flaking barges, he'd scuttle bent-backed along the water's edge, splashing through the grey clinging film of a disposable world. To most, the low-tide river was a morass of pebble and rubbish; to Dear Boy it was a treasure trove. Muttering and wheezing through a roll-up, his bony fingers pointed out how tidal swirls and eddies carefully sifted the tangle of flotsam and jetsam by weight – islands of coconuts, credit cards, tennis balls, plastic lighters, watches (some still ticking), teddy bears, crabs and, deeper still, bending even further, the most prized of all: fragments from a lost city. Prodding through pebbles Dear Boy plucked out brittle ivory stems and fragile bowls. Clay pipes decorated with leaves, birds and buffalo horns: faint echoes of a living river of Empire. Bustling wharfs and quays and air laced with cocoa, oranges, hemp and tobacco. Long ago these pipes had fallen from the lips of lightermen and sweating stevedores – and whale hunters perhaps?

Was it during these riverside forays that my mind quietly dredged through the silt of a deep subconscious? All I knew for sure that humid afternoon as we kicked along at low tide was that a childhood memory had drifted unbidden onto the shores of my waking mind: the gaping mouth and sad eye of a huge whale. A vague image but deeply imprinted nonetheless. No more than two hours before, I'd tossed this pebble from the past into the cybersea. Even now the ripples were spreading. But how far would they go?

I mentioned the whale to Dear Boy. Distracted by his need to collect enough of the polished 'river stones' he regularly took back to the office in an attempt to restore its karma, he couldn't give the matter his full attention.

'A whale, dear boy? Ummmm . . . ummm . . . ummm . . . er . . .'

Skirting the muddy pool containing a sunken pram and grey traffic cones, he crabbed out further along the shoreline, much to the consternation of a couple of paddling geese. Given time, he would come up with something profound, but more often than not it took a very, very long time. I didn't idle on the shoreline as long as usual and left him to it: the call of the whale was strong. We were onto something big. As Big 'n' Daft quite rightly put it, 'the biggest thing to happen in tarn ever'.

A bloody big blue whale on a lorry.

Laikin

JUST BECAUSE A NUMBER OF PEOPLE ALL BELIEVE THE SAME thing doesn't actually make it true, at least not to anyone listening to their story. Some swear by the Yeti; most Americans claim to have been abducted by aliens at some time or another; I've heard of people who actually believe what's printed on railway timetables. True, I was no longer alone on the whale issue, but I had merely drawn a handful of fellow nutters to me, or that's the way it looked to new tykes clambering aboard.

Admittedly, I too began to have vague concerns. R Kid stood by me and with almost magical powers of recall grasped at a name: Jonah. Yet if we'd seen a whale as children it must have been with our parents. My mother was adamant: neither she nor my father knew anything. On putting down the phone was she sitting even now, pondering her offsprings' mental state? E.I. Addio certainly thought so.

Oh aye, I can just imagine that phone call . . .
StatisTYKE – Mam, can you remember tekkin me
to see a big f.uck-off whale back in '68?
StatisTYKE's mam – No luv, whereabouts was it?
StatisTYKE – In t'tarn centre . . .
StatisTYKE's mam – 'Ev you had your medication
today?'
E.I. Addio

So it's not a cult it's 'Tarn Whale Believers'. That's a
relief. Too much sickly sweet sugar sweets in the '60s
– sends folk mad and buggered my teeth.
pepsi exley

Yeeeeees, riiight . . . So the average drug intake of the
four whale believers is?
Munich tyke

Of course I knew 'Tarn Whale Believers' would be accused of
being off their heads on something or other. But I felt sure the
Chronicle would soon silence the likes of Munich tyke. One
phone call, then a quick search through the archives and we'd
have our whale. That afternoon the phone rang and rang and
rang and rang in the editorial office of the *Chronicle*. No reply.
Even my e-mail wouldn't send. In frustration I called out to a
fellow drug addict.

Can't e-mail the *Chroni* for some reason. Also tried
givin' 'em a call but there's no bugger in the editorial
dept. Munich thinks Tarn Whale Believers are on
drugs. Can you believe that?
StatisTYKE

Course not! . . . ahem . . . Yes, I read that accusation
further down. Anyway I wasn't when I was an

innocent young lad, staring open-mouthed in wonder at the carcass of Moby (or Findus) rotting on the back of a lorry. I've heard nowt from the *Chronicle*. Probably the editorial staff have all rushed out to check out a pound coin superglued ter road again. I've e-mailed *Watchdog* as well. Got a rather snotty reply about whales in Barnsley having nothing to do with consumer affairs and Charlotte Hudson will not be investigating it let alone complying with my sordid requests. Sara Cox hasn't replied either.
Big 'n' Daft

They'd be straight onto it if somebody bought it and found out the bloody thing couldn't swim.
Munich tyke

Our investigations were getting nowhere. I remained unconcerned and more than happy that others had taken up the cause with such enthusiasm. Then came a change in the air – or rather a change in dialect. Beyond my screen, tyke minds began trawling back through time; back to a long-gone tarn of markets, owd money, chippies and tap oils as they spun tall tales in an old tarn tongue. But the following light-hearted exchange between E.I. Addio and the mysterious 'Bill Smurthwaite' was no mere diversion. It would set us on a new and terrifying heading . . .

Mitchell's fish stand on 'towd May Day Green. I used to sell f.uckin' gret lumps of it for one and three, that's reight it was one and three a f.uckin' gret lump. Now most Barnsley folk used to gently sauté it in butter with a Bernaise sauce, mange tout and baby corn, or flambéed in Napoleon cognac with a vegetable roulade and champagne sauce.

Personally I preffered it fried wi' a bit o' pig bag.

You heartless bastard! He wor mi friend, a true red
'n' all.

He wor oni red on t'inside!

Ah could on tellt thee that wi'art thee 'avin' ter cut
'im open. Poor old Findus, tha nars ar allus beeat 'im
at t'dominoes cos 'e couldn't 'old 'em. Mind 'e nivver
went in t'pub, 'e dint like it when they were laikin
darts.

Now Bill Smurthwaite's claims that the whale shunned taprooms
for fear of puncture by a stray dart and that he was less than
dextrous with the 'doms' were no surprise. It was his use of a
dogged fragment from long ago that caught my eye: 'laikin'.
How long was it since I'd heard that word? No one around me
would have had the faintest idea what it meant, but to a tyke its
use is as natural as breathing. Smurthwaite said 'laikin' and in
that breath sent us plunging back through time. For the
birthplace of us tykes lies farther back than flat caps, mushy peas
and mythical whales . . . far further back than any living
memory.

My mind slipped away from the glass tower above the
Thames to a time long ago. A dark, dangerous time to be sure,
but go there we must if anything of this tale is to be understood.
In the blackness of centuries rolling by I kept a sharp lookout for
yet another exiled northerner. Although born not far from tarn,
he's the only Yorkshireman I've heard of who cannot claim the
title 'tyke', yet his story holds the secret of the invisible crew now
assembling to hunt the whale. Like me, he was far from home;
like me his hands flickered over the latest technology; like me he
was looking for clues. But for him time was running out.

Fire Dragons

ALCUIN HEADED UP THE CENTRAL INTELLIGENCE UNIT
attached to the world's military high command, a big job by
anybody's standard. And to say that Alcuin was a worried man
would be a massive understatement.

Even at the best of times the world was a very messy place
back then. The Dark Ages aren't called 'dark' for nothing. When
empires collapse it's usually a prelude to a coming terror. When
the Romans pulled out and left us to our own devices, the world
descended into a chaos that makes the wars in Bosnia after the
collapse of Communism look like a tea party. Death became a
way of life. Tribal warlords, local chieftains and continental
invaders slugged it out with anyone and everyone. Existence was
day to day; any idea of a future would have been laughable.

But in long winter evenings safe in their wooden halls, as the
warlords stuffed themselves on oxen and chicken, deep within
even the most savage heart, there must have been doubts. Minds
addled by buckets of mead must have contemplated what lay in
store come dawn: another bout of chopping, slicing and dicing
the neighbours? Scuttling around under a hail of arrows – an axe
in the face? Even the greatest of warlords sensed he was no more
than the sparrow that flew into the great hall, felt the brief
warmth of the fire, then flitted out once more into the freezing
night. Life was a flash that ended in eternal oblivion at the hands
of the fearsome twin hags, Hel and Weird. There had to be more
to it than that, surely?

That's when Alcuin and his network came in with a new idea.
They were men on a mission and that mission was to change the
world. The world as it existed back then was roughly defined by

the boundaries of the old Roman Empire, from Spain in the west to a fuzzy frontier round about Germany, from Britain in the north to the Mediterranean coast in the south. Beyond was a void of the unknown. As this world could scarely be called civilised by any stretch of the imagination, Alcuin's predecessors set sail on their quest across safe sea channels with their great story.

They told the story of a great warrior chieftain more powerful than Hel and Weird, a lord who could offer life everlasting. To prove this, he'd sent his son to earth with the news. And here was the best bit, the bit that really got the warlords interested. *He wasn't tooled up to the eyeballs!* Like them he knew there was no tomorrow on earth, but he just wandered around talking to people rather than slicing their heads off. Of course he'd been strung up in the end, but what did that matter? Even now he was sitting at his father's right hand . . . *forever!* No fighting, no struggle, just a cushy cloud.

The warlords were intrigued. Standing before them were Alcuin's predecessors, men dressed only in sackcloth and sandals bearing a funny little cross. They could have taken these guys out with one flick of a sword. But what did that matter? They were going to live forever. Warlord after warlord decided this was a chance too good to miss. More and more signed up for everlasting life as the years went by. Of course, this new idea was quite tricky to get hold of. Even the mighty Charlemagne, who'd plucked Alcuin from the Anglo-Saxon capital of Eboricum to sit at his right hand, thought nothing of slaughtering a thousand prisoners from time to time. His representative in Britain, King Offa, gouged out the eyes of a rival without too many qualms. But hey, you've got to start somewhere.

Throughout the world, holy places sprang up under the protection of newly converted kings, who must have thought that life everlasting was a fair exchange for taking care of a few peaceable sandal-wearers. Slowly but surely, Alcuin and his soldiers were putting down the roots of Christianity. Steering clear of potential trouble spots, they criss-crossed the seas lighting beacons of civilisation in the darkness, remote islands where they could get down to developing their new technology. On these outposts at the edge of the world guarded by the sea, they spent their lives in contemplation and churning out the operating manuals for a new world: illuminated, gold-covered, bejewelled manuscripts that held all the secrets of the new way of life.

Now it was all going wrong. The world had been placed on a war footing; the top brass were looking to Alcuin for answers, and quickly. What had been predicted for years now appeared to be coming true and he was the last hope. Alone by candlelight he flicked backward and forward, looking for clues, a solution, a way out. All he found were fearful warnings that confirmed what was happening. Yes, yes, it was all there: a comet in the sky both day and night meant unending destruction – famine . . . plague . . . the wearing of jewellery and fancy hairstyles among the learned . . . corruption in our very midst! The scriptures made it clear. This was the end of the world. *Alcuin was witnessing the very end of mankind!*

Had not the beast from the sea whose name was Blasphemy already risen up? With flashing scimitars thousands of heathen horsemen were storming in from Africa and the East. A cry of holy war! Unstoppable Islamic hordes flooded into Gaul and Spain. Even now the hated crescent flag flew from the Pyrenees. Charlemagne's forces were doing their best, but it was little more than a holding action. Soon the defences would be breached and Christendom, the light of the world, would be snuffed out forever.

If ever there was a time to pray to his Lord it was now. But if there was one consolation for Alcuin in this desperate situation, it was when his thoughts and pen turned to home. Far away in Gaul he may have been, but Alcuin is the first recorded proof of the saying: 'You can take the boy out of the north, but you can't take the north out of the boy.'

He reflected with pride and relief that his 'North Humber Land' could rightly claim to be the home of Christianity. From there the learned Bede had contributed so much from his Jarrow cell, the great St Aiden, St Hilda – the great-great-great grandmother of 'girl power' – from Streaneshalch, where she'd founded a coastal abbey. And greatest of all was St Cuthbert and his 'cult of saints' on the island of Lindisfarne: the David Beckham, Manchester Utd and Old Trafford of Christianity. Shielded from trouble on land by the imposing north-east coastal fortress of Bamburgh, Lindisfarne lay a good way offshore in the protective bosom of the North Sea. Here rested Christianity's greatest work: the glittering Lindisfarne Gospels. With lavishly illuminated pages it was the code, the operating system, the very beating heart of civilisation. No matter how fast heathen forces ravaged their way north, Alcuin knew the Gospels would be safe. Should Armageddon strike, his men would have warning enough to spirit their operating system away.

Little did Alcuin suspect that a new terror was gathering, a terror beyond the fringes of all human imagining. The Gospels had been right all along, but Alcuin had been looking for threats in the wrong direction. Across the world's northern frontier people cowered as lightning flashed over storm-tossed seas and monstrous fire dragons snarled and roared through the thunderclouds. It's easy for us to dismiss such warnings as the fanciful imaginings of a primitive people; but they weren't. The dragons were the shape of things to come.

Alcuin sank into a troubled sleep as his candle spluttered and died. Far out in the void, the aliens made their final course corrections: a guided missile coming in at sea level and aiming straight at the heart of civilisation.

Berserk!

THE FIRST STRIKE SENT SHOCK WAVES AROUND THE WORLD. What was this missile? Who were these creatures from hell? Alien savages spewing from the belly of a great dragon set upon the gentle monks of Lindisfarne. The island screamed and died in an orgy of violence.

Some have tried to play up the point that these sea-raiders, or Vikings, have been a little misunderstood over the years. Good farmers and excellent craftsmen they may well have been, but you don't invade a country by offering tips on growing asparagus and setting up stalls to sell pretty silver earrings.

A landing craft crammed with stormtroopers, slashing, burning, slaughtering all in their path struck the island. *Bearshirts*: the special forces of the Nordic war machine! The fact that our word 'berserk' derives from 'bearshirt' gives some indication of how they went about their business. Yet savage as they were, the berserkers had developed the hardest-hitting military technology on earth. The guidance system for their missile was in their very bones. Generations had navigated the fjords of Norway and struck out on exploratory voyages west. The many names they had for what we call 'sea' — ever-lying salt, overhang, empty one, flood and surf, engulfer, sparkler — reflect their understanding and ability to read its moods. Their missile was the longship, a craft with speed and stability on the open ocean, which also doubled as an amphibious landing craft: the first roll-on, roll-off fighting ferry. With its dragon-prow the longship bore down on the Lindisfarne monks as living evidence that the devil himself had come to earth. Clambering ashore, the berserkers began their work with the fearsome two-handed war axe; one stroke could cleave a man in two.

The holy men were slaughtered or carted back to the landing craft as slaves, the monastery torched, holy images trampled underfoot. Breathless messengers delivered the news to Alcuin, who dispatched frantic, weeping letters home. What had any of them done to deserve this? Was it the fancy hairstyles God was punishing them for? Then again, what about that shower of blood that had rained down from a clear sky in York some time ago? It must have been a warning! If Lindisfarne couldn't defend itself against this attack, what hope was there for the rest of the churches? The short answer was 'none'. With the score standing at 1–0, the Vikings had tasted blood and treasure and they were up for more.

Fearsome *jarls* (earls) like Skullsplitter and Bloodaxe weren't interested in hearing about this namby-pamby, peace-loving Christ. They hadn't even worked out a way of writing down their own language yet, and as far as the after-life was concerned? Well, their special forces, chewing dementedly on their shields, screamed into battle shouting 'Bring it on!'

Every berserker knew that death was an honour. Their great Lord Odin up in the hall in the sky, Valhalla, sent out the berserkers' Jordans and Caprices – the Valkyries – to choose the lucky ones. At death it would be they who would leave this earth to live it up forever at Odin's right hand. More wine, supermodels and song than you could shake a two-handed war axe at. Now that's what I call heaven!

Further blitzkrieg raids followed, on Iona, Jarrow and Skye. St Hilda's abbey was reduced to ruins. Inroads were made into Ireland; massacre after massacre. Through forest and glen the berserkers carried their landing craft to trash places other invaders hadn't reached. Alcuin was beside himself with grief. Nowhere was safe. Correctly judging that Anglo-Saxon and Irish kings who'd spent too long fighting each other were about as much use as a chocolate teapot, the 'Great Host' stormed ashore.

Swarming across the sea, these armies were no hit-and-run

raiders. Working in close cooperation they made sure the war axe ruled the east from Scotland to Sheppy. Towns, monasteries and centres of learning were sacked from London to the lands north of the Humber. Alcuin's home, Eboricum, was razed and his precious libraries burnt. Thankfully he didn't live to see it. Across the land, 'O Lord deliver us from the fury of the northmen' was offered up in hopeless prayer.

Victorious in every battle, they showed no mercy to the defeated. Fallen kings became guests of honour in a charming little ceremony known as the 'blood eagle'. This involved being speared to a tree and repeatedly hacked before your ribs were torn apart to form . . . well, a sort of . . . 'eagle's wings' arrangement. Please don't try that one at home.

The Anglo-Saxons were finished. The country would be defeated. All that remained was to polish off one pathetic prince from the West Country. The Great Host bore down on its prey and inflicted another crushing defeat. Staggering away into the sanctuary of southern marshes, the tattered freedom fighters knew the game was up. Even the leader of the rebel forces, the prince, knew there was nothing more he could do. What he didn't know was that even at that moment Superman was speeding to his aid.

Saint in a Box

ST CUTHBERT HAD NEVER BEEN ONE FOR GETTING OUT AND about. He spent most of his life in isolation on a barren outcrop on the rain-lashed Farne Islands with only the seals and puffins for company. Even the monastery on Lindisfarne, a few miles north and the forbidding refuge for a handful of monks and a smattering of windblown sheep, was more action than he could handle. When King Egfrith requested that Cuthbert pop in to

Lindisfarne for a bit of holy work, he had to sail to the Farne Islands and drag the reluctant saint from hiding himself.

Cuthbert was around when that Viking missile struck. But in the midst of the murder and mayhem, the saint lay back and took it in his stride. Not surprising, as he'd been dead for almost 100 years. Though the Vikings destroyed or looted virtually everything, they gave the old saint's bones a miss; as it turned out, this would be a very costly mistake. After a lifetime of solitude, Cuthbert was about to zip around all over the place.

As the years went by, the holy men were slaughtered on a frighteningly regular basis, but they didn't just sit back and take it. Churches may be burnt and manuscripts destroyed, but the earthly remains of saints (revered as a connection between this life and the next) were treasured above all else. They had to be saved at any cost.

We shouldn't underestimate just how important these last earthly remains were. The holy men themselves were prepared to indulge in some pretty unholy practices to secure them. Take St Oswald for instance, a warlord who converted to Christianity. While trying to impress his faith on a heathen Celtic rival he came off worst. Oswald's soul drifted up to meet his maker from the aptly named 'Heavensfield', while his head and arms were stuck on battlefield spikes. Swiftly these holy body parts were recovered: his head was deposited on Lindisfarne while his arms were kept safe in a chapel of St Oswald's Bamburgh fortress – but not safe enough. During a spot of ecclesiastical stocktaking the Bamburgh monks noticed something was missing. At that very moment, a group of Peterborough monks who'd just visited the north-east were excitedly exchanging high-fives as they hotfooted it back to their abbey with St Oswald's right arm tucked safely beneath their cassocks. A fantastic away win for the fenlanders – an arm was worth a good few points in their push to get into the ecclesiastical Premiership.

With repeated Viking attacks raining down the coastline, however, such treasures could never be allowed to fall into the clutches of alien invaders. On Lindisfarne the bishops and monks drew up a quick checklist of the holiest of the holy. St Cuthbert (whose body had miraculously not rotted over the years) was the most important, followed by the head of St Oswald. After rummaging around they also came up with a few ribs from St Aidan and assorted bits and pieces from various bishops. Packing a portable altar – a kind of laptop to keep in touch with the man on high – the convoy of the 'Cult of St Cuthbert' was ready to roll.

And what a journey it was! Almost immediately the dead saint (who'd naturally predicted all this) took command. The sea off Lindisfarne miraculously parted; not one monk got their sandals wet as they hurried onto the mainland. Danger loomed almost immediately, but Cuthbert was more than a match for it. Sea haar, a dense mist that often rolls along the north-east coast, was summoned to hide his followers from the savages. As if guided by a force on high (or in a box), the convoy criss-crossed northern England, always one step ahead of the rampaging Vikings. The monks carted Cuthbert over treacherous Cumbrian Fells, intending to head for safety in Ireland. The saint objected and capsized the boat. It was back over the grim, unyielding Pennines. Guiding and protecting his flock might have seemed a full-time job, but the saint had time and miracles to spare. And anyone who's seen *Star Wars* knows what comes next.

In the depths of the southern marshes the young freedom fighter was at the end of his tether. Running for cover from flashing axes and ever mindful that he was next in line for a session of eagle-inspired rib-reshaping he dodged, exhausted, into a hut for a bit of a think. And now some woman was giving him a hard time for singeing a few bloody cakes!

'King Alfred burnt the cakes!'

Yes, it must have been a reporter for '*Ye Sun*' huddled in a far corner who scribbled that headline down. No matter that the future of the country hung in the balance – a woman's buns made a better story even then.

Now cakeless, starving rebel fighters left the camp to scour the land for food, leaving Alfred alone in this, the darkest hour. Then something quite remarkable happened. A frail stranger chanced upon Alfred's deserted encampment and asked if he might have some food. The King, although having next to nothing, shared what little he did have. The stranger thanked him and left. That very night he returned, all Obi-Wan Kanobi-like, in shining robes to the young rebel fighter. St Cuthbert (for it was he) told Alfred that if he truly believed in the 'force' the evil empire could be defeated.

Next morning Alfred woke with new purpose and with three blasts on the horn summoned his troops for a confrontation with the Great Host. After many battles and great adventures the young king won the day, stopped the Vikings and saved Britain.

The end.

And what, you're probably asking yourself by now, has all this got to do with whales and tykes? Patience, my friend, patience.

Blood and Land

LEARNED MEN HAVE LONG STUDIED AND ARGUED OVER THE Vikings, reading between the lines of letters of men like Alcuin and plucking fragments from earthworks. Who were they? What did they do? Does their influence live on? A few things can be said with some certainty. Many more battles would follow King Alfred's establishment of peace with the invaders, but the 'Danelaw' (established to the east of a rough diagonal line running from the Wash to Merseyside) was a place where many northmen hung up their war axes once their terrible fury was spent. Little did he know it, but Alfred had marked out a north/south divide of the country that lives on to this day.

With the Anglo-Saxon capital taken, the northmen began to

redefine their North Humber lands. Alcuin's Eboricum was rebuilt and renamed Jorvik, now known as York. The wooden capital city was a wonder to behold – the equivalent of New York today – and proved the northmen could indeed do more than just fight. And so the shape of a county began to form. From York, three administrative 'ridings' were decreed (north, east and west), 'thriding' being Norse for a third.

Though further Danish armies were defeated and York eventually given up, the influence and blood of the settlers mingled with Anglo-Saxon to give birth to the young shire. Nordic farming prowess came to the fore when victorious *jarls* rewarded their men with land on eastern flatlands and dales. Warlords had their own settlements named after them: Torkil Scarthi's name lives on in the coastal resort of Scarborough, and the map of Yorkshire is dotted with towns and villages indicating their origin in Old Norse *by*, meaning farmstead; after demolishing her abbey, St Hilda's Streaneshalch was renamed Whitby. *Thorpe*, meaning 'enclosure', and *thwaite*, 'clearing' or 'meadow', also speak of that time. All would eventually find their way into surnames, as in Bill Smurthwaite's case.

Further west, scattered settlements were established on the Pennine foothills, possibly by traders who braved the dark cloud-swept peaks, journeying to Jorvik from Ireland and Cumbria. Crouching in a valley from wild Pennine weather, the terrain must have reminded the settlers of fjords far away. Here they established Denby, literally meaning 'farmstead of the Danes'. No doubt on dark winter evenings they'd sit around the fire and retell old tales of Iona and Ireland and perhaps stories that were stranger still.

'You know when I was a child . . . I . . .'

'Yes, Sven?'

'Well . . . when I was a child I'm sure I saw . . . a saint . . . in a box . . .'

'You mean in a monastery?'

'No . . . out there . . . the monks were carting it over the hills . . .'

'Think you're hallucinatin' chief . . . saint in a box indeed . . .'

Just a little way east, where bleak moor dropped into dense forest valleys, northmen like Thogeirr and Keptr laid down their war axes as they finished carving out their own forest clearings alongside older settlements, the great wooden hall and cultivated land that offered refuge against harsh winters for four Saxon lords; Wryc's stronghold or 'burgh' high on the southern side of a broad wooded valley; Beorn's woodland clearing on the northern side. It was an area peppered with settlers hoping to scratch out a living, perhaps no different to most of the country. But this was the embryo of tarn: the birthplace of tykes now scattered to the four corners of the world.

And if anyone keeps the memory of those wild northmen alive today it's us. Forget those baggy-shorted lads from *Time Team* scrabbling around for fragments of bone and silver, and reminders though they are, forget even the Selbys and Smurthwaites. Because while some Norse words have been lost or smoothed out (old Thogierr's land is now the village of Thurgoland), others cut through the centuries as cleanly as a war axe.

'Are you laikin out today?' translates as 'Are you playing out today?' Generations of runny-nosed tykes banging on their mates' doors have kept the Norse word *laik* (to play) alive to this day. And even if it were 'siling' it down (Norse verb *sil* – to pour) a tyke would still manage a game of footy.

Which brings us onto 'tyke'. Now, anyone born in Yorkshire can claim to be a tyke by birthright, although it's a matter for individual choice; originally it was intended as an insult. The dictionary defines 'tyke' as a 'low, objectionable fellow'. Over the years it's been variously applied to scruffy mongrels, old men in mufflers walking Jack Russells, wayward children and disreputable or obstinate folk. Perfect! Tarn embraced this Norse word (from 'tik', meaning bitch) to such an extent that Barnsley

Football Club naturally adopted it as their nickname, a name we wear as proudly as our red shirts. And, by the way, if you think Valhalla belongs to ancient myth and legend, then try tarn centre on a Friday or Saturday night.

So, could it be that out on the black cybersea a crew were gathering; a crew with more than a few drops of wild Viking blood running through their veins, disreputable descendants of those wild northern raiders? I may not have met any of them, but as I peered into my glass screen I knew I couldn't have found a better crew. Because I knew one thing beyond doubt – once tykes set their obstinate minds on something, they aren't laikin. As far as this mythical whale was concerned we wouldn't be surfing . . . *we'd be hunting!*

The Whale Hunt

To strive, to seek, to find and not to yield.

Alfred Tennyson

All Aboard!

PERHAPS OUR LONG VOYAGE THROUGH TIME WASN'T QUITE what you expected? Well, this was my first whale hunt and I couldn't say where we'd be going. Yet before we set sail, our voyage so far highlights at least one other thing.

The Viking invasions took place some thousand years back, in a time when little was written down and much is still unclear. Even so, remarkable events were recorded, though often by people who were assembling notes from long-dead witnesses and word of mouth. If old scribes could document the trans-Pennine 'saint-in-a-box' episode, then surely the *Barnsley Chronicle* would supply us with full details of a whale on a lorry. By comparison, the visit of a whale to tarn looks like only yesterday.

On that first afternoon I remained focused on the whale and its imminent capture. The bulletin board lit up like a Christmas tree in a torrent of whale-inspired postings. Although many regarded the story with guarded suspicion, it became clear that just beneath day-to-day minds lurk mysterious animals waiting for their chance to emerge once more. Other mammals, buried deep in the tyke subconscious, leapt to the surface:

> Anybody remember them dolphins that came to Wakefield? It was about 1976/'77, really hot summer, and we'd bin to the Isle O' Man for our holidays. We got back on the Saturday and then are mam took us shopping to Wakey on the Monday. In them days the Ridings Centre wasn't there, just a road up to Queen's supermarket (which became ASDA). We were stood on the side of the road and then we

could hear a band playing. We stood and waited (as
you do when you're in the town centre and you hear
a band playing, especially when you're only eight or
nine years old) and then along came a procession.
Majorettes, bands, jugglers, you name it, they were
there, then, at the back was a big lorry with a big glass
fish tank on the back and in it were two dolphins,
swimming around and jumping in and out of the
water. Amazing! We stood there with our mouths
open for about five minutes as they headed up the hill
towards the Bull Ring and then down Westgate. Then
we went to Hagenbachs for a sausage roll.
Toby Tyke's Golf Clubs

I like it! It is true abart that whale though.
Big 'n' Daft

Porpoise in Don. I think it was in the early '80s when
a porpoise swam up the Don as far as Doncaster
where it stayed for abart two weeks until local kids
started throwing stones at it, so the NRA took it
back to sea.
Ish

Giant chameleon lizards are rarely found in these
temperatures. However one day in Beverley I
remember them simply falling out of the sky. Bit hard
to see 'cause they changed colour to look like
raindrops . . .
pepsi exley

Important whale news. Full skeleton of massive whale
suspended from the ceiling in the Manchester Museum.
Apparently donated by an 'anonymous' vendor some
years back . . . hmmmm . . . They've also got a stuffed

elephant that used to belong to Belle Vue Zoo – they couldn't afford to put it on a train when its time was done at the zoo, so this geezer walked all the way to Edinburgh with the elephant to sell it. There's a great old picture there of the actual elephant and the geezer having an argument somewhere in Newcastle for the correct price for an elephant to pass thru the toll gates.
WHALES, ELEPHANTS AND OWT BIG'LL DO ME
Pablo

First there was the whale but who has seen that monster pike down in the Fleets. Now that is a story worth talking about. Legend has it that it's over 5 ft long and weighs over 15 stone. It eats calves and whole sheep and leaps out of the water to take crows and bigger birds just for a snack.
Satan 666

I heard many a tale bart that pike and lost many a lure trying to catch the bastard. All I ever caught was a few roach and a nasty skin rash. Anybody heard the story about Tinkers Pond being bottomless?
E.I. Addio

What abart that elephant? Ave asked mi fatha and his mate abart that whale but they can't remember ought, but they can remember that elephant that escaped frum a visiting circus and ran amok rarnd Sheffield Road area. Anybody remember that?
norman

Alligators in Derwent. In Derby city centre noticed a gret crowd on the bridge on Derwent St. When I looked down I couldn't see owt and wondered wat crack wor when suddenly this massive f.uck-off

> alligator leapt out o' Derwent and seized this
> wildebeest that wor evin a drink theer like. What
> next? Blue whales in tarn probably!
> Big 'n' Daft

Big 'n' Daft's enthusiam for whale hunting spilled over into
manufacturing new legends. This was a dangerous move: I
swiftly reprimanded him.

> Aye. Soz. We need to keep the story straight, there's
> enough people thinking we're mad as it is. I would
> have hoped for more back-up. Mebbe the evening
> shift are more 'whale aware'. SAVE THE WHALE – It
> could be as good as the Hartlepool Monkey.
> Big 'n' Daft

And so, early evening on the first day, the hunt became
becalmed. Casper reasserted his faith as a 'Tarn Whale Believer'
and Big 'n' Daft slunk away to attack the rum ration.

Dusk fell as I left the river and journeyed back to my solitary
cabin to ponder the day's events. Was the Manchester skeleton
the last remains of Jonah? But what kind of anonymous
desperado would hump a whale across the Pennines? Then
again, it would have been no weirder a journey than a saint in a
box. But it couldn't be Jonah; he'd been burnt, according to
Franco tyke . . . unless that was a wind-up . . .

By nightfall I half dozed through the Shipping Forecast's
soothing waves lapping from my radio, Ruby and Millie, the ship's
cats, curled peacefully on my lap. Although, as I've said, I have no
great love of computers, I found myself staring into the glass screen
well past midnight. Despite Big 'n' Daft's hope of more 'whale
aware' regulars, the night proved empty of further speculation. Yet
we had sailed far in that 12 hours: a handful of confirmed
sightings, a possible date – surely we were close. Ship-to-shore
communication with the *Chronicle* had failed but we were mere

novices, just learning the ropes. Tomorrow the paper's investigative beam would sweep through tarn history, cutting through unreliable memories and pick him out in the depths.

In the early hours the last of the crew turned in; I tapped out a reassuring message to him. A reply echoed back across the black cybersea . . .

> Played Statis. The whale out. And it carries on till termorerr. U know it. I know it, at least three others know it. THE WHale story is TRUE.
>
> Ps cheers statis 4 that. If they only knew.
> Big 'n' f.uckinpissed

Outside, fat chameleon raindrops pattered across the street. What other strange legends were out there in the darkness? My mind drifted off course as I mulled over Big 'n' Daft's earlier words.

It could be as good as the Hartlepool Monkey . . .

Unbidden, our sleeping vessel leaves the estuary and follows a compass heading north as I keep solitary watch over our ship of dreams. True north. Yorkshire's east coast looms on the port bow of my imagination. Wind strums our rigging: a coming storm. Out on the black mainland a torch flares, a beacon crackles orange, then another, then another. Urgent drumbeats rap out the warning.

He is coming. He is coming!
War boys! This is war!

H'Angus

BEACONS BLAZED ON AND ON INTO THE HEART OF ENGLAND.
Pitchfork and needle were thrown aside in a scramble for musket
and bayonet. The whole country was in trouble, big time. For
endless nervous months, musket and cannon had been trained
seaward. OK – so we've never actually been invaded. Well, not
since 1066 and all that. But we've had a fair few near misses.
And if you were there at the time, things must have looked very
dodgy indeed. Word flashed from town to town, village to
village, mouth to mouth faster than any e-mail. You couldn't
read the word but you didn't have to. You just listened to horror
stories shouted from the trembling leaflets that were doing the
rounds: from a war-torn continent there would come an evil to
plunge the country into a living hell. The bloodstained devil
stood at our very shores!

He promises to enrich his soldiers with our property; to glut
their lust on our wives and daughters; to incite his hell-hounds
to execute his vengeance . . .

He would come by battleship, balloons – why, it was even
rumoured he was digging a tunnel through which his
bloodthirsty army would march.

Napoleon Bonaparte, the conquerer of Europe, is upon us!

This was an England now well used to the threat of invasion;
everyone knew what to do. Vigilance was the watchword, for the
enemy's spies were everywhere. Every man knew his duty. Every
man knew that when the time came he would have to play his
part in a terrible fight to the death.

For a small band of Hartlepool fishermen one wild December
day, that time had come. The fishermen huddled on the gale-

blasted beach of Fish Sands, brushing sleet from their sou'westers; no one but a fool would put out in that storm. But as they stared out across a heaving icy sea they were struck by a sudden horror. The fishermen shivered inside their beards. Someone was out there, and it wasn't the village idiot.

Rearing up through the North Sea, plunging straight at them with sails outstretched like some deadly bird of prey, was a French frigate – the *Chasse Maree*. The invasion was on! A few poor fishermen pitted against the might of the French navy. You could only liken it to facing a Stealth bomber armed with only a butter knife.

But aboard the *Chasse Maree* few French soldiers or sailors were thinking of being in London by nightfall. Not only was the storm too much for fishing boats, it was more than a match for a warship. The crew knew they were in desperate trouble. Such a storm could break the stoutest warship in two. Glad eyes on Fish Sands realised her end was imminent too. The enemy would be vanquished!

Dashed helpless onto rocks, the *Chasse Maree's* timbers tore apart, spilling her human cargo into the vortex. Even if the fishermen had felt pity for their foe, rescue would have proved impossible; all would perish.

For the fishermen, this was a bit of a double victory. Not only had they avoided a set-to with the French army, they knew the pounding seas would carry ashore rich pickings from the wreck. Braving the weather, they scurried along the beach, keeping a sharp look-out for spectacular Christmas presents: cannon, coins, cognac, croissants or whatever. But there was something washed up they hadn't counted on finding – a soldier, and to their horror he was still alive. *A Frenchman!* The first they had ever seen, one of Napoleon's fearsome hell hounds. The fisherfolk gazed on the sorry figure. Not so hellish now, but dangerous nonetheless. A spy no doubt! That was why he had survived . . .

The situation was growing desperate. The man was clearly an

enemy and in weather like this there was no chance to alert the military. Besides, who knew what was going on elsewhere? The *Chasse Maree* had foundered, but along the coast there could have been successful landings; even now thousands of troops could be pouring ashore.

They interrogated him there and then, but the wretch gave away nothing. How could he? Jabber though he did, the crofters assumed it was some strangled form of French. In this time of national emergency there was nothing else for it: he would be given a fair trial right there on the beach. It proved a rather one-sided affair. The accused understood nothing he was accused of, while his manic gibbering in a strange tongue amounted to a pretty shambolic defence. The solemn verdict was passed: guilty. Hastily the fishermen erected a makeshift scaffold and lowered a rope around the poor man's neck.

Or should I say *monkey's* neck.

For it was indeed a monkey, possibly the ship's mascot, a pet chimpanzee in a soldier's uniform. How could the crofters have known? They'd never seen anything as exotic as a foreigner or a monkey before. And, after all, didn't its bizarre behaviour and appearance fit with the wild descriptions of their hated enemy?

It might seem a bit bizarre that anyone would mistake a monkey for a man. But is it? Put yourself on that Hartlepool beach 200 years ago. Like just about everybody else, the fishermen were born, grew up and worked in the same place. No one travelled. The next town was a far-distant land. You couldn't read, for books and learning were for the rich and powerful. There's no way you'd have any idea what a monkey was, never mind what it looked like. As for a Frenchman, well, you'd never seen one of those either, and who knew what sounds came from a Frenchman's mouth? You didn't have a clue what the enemy might be.

Or perhaps you did. Remember the leaflets and the wild stories going around? Hadn't you been told what to expect . . . hadn't you been told what the French looked like? 'Bloodthirsty devils', 'beasts' . . . and 'hell-hounds'. What the hell does a hell-hound look like anyway? Ever seen one? So there you face a beast in enemy uniform screeching and spitting like the very devil, because that chimpanzee must have been less than impressed with his brush with death. Sodden, terrified, snarling in defiance . . .

'Hell-hound? Mad monkey? Hell-hound? Spy? Mad monkey? Frenchman? Spy? Hell-hound? Mad monkey? War boys, this is war! Are you sure . . . quite sure?'

'HANG HIM!'

The storm blew over, leaving a monkey lifeless on a gibbet while the crofters drifted off to down a few in celebration of their defence of the realm. Napoleon's threatened invasion never came though: it had all been yet another false alarm.

And so this sad little story might well have faded into history. In fact, from Scotland to Cornwall there were various shady tales of monkey-hanging doing the rounds. The good people of Boddam in Aberdeenshire are said to have found a monkey, the only survivor of another shipwreck. As the law stated that 'wreckers' could only salvage cargo if all the crew were dead, the survivor was swiftly dealt with Hartlepool-fashion. Word of mouth might keep such stories alive for a little while, but fate had picked out the Hartlepool Monkey for bigger things.

Some 50 years on, top north-eastern entertainer Ned Corvan took the stage to riotous applause in a Hartlepool music hall. It was a full house and, as an expectant silence fell, the entertainer belted out his latest single . . .

> In former times, when war and strife
> The French invasion threatened life
> An' all was armed to the knife
> The fishermen hung the monkey oh!
>
> The fishermen with courage high
> Seized on the monkey for a French spy
> 'Hang him!' says one, 'he's to die!'
> They did and they hung the monkey oh!

> They tried every means to make him speak
> And tortured the monkey till he did speak
> Says yen 'That's French' says another 'It's Greek'
> For the fishermen had got drunky oh!

Although he probably didn't admit it at the time, Ned Corvan wasn't being completely original. He'd ripped off an older song, 'The Baboon', which told of a monkey, again in French uniform, that escaped from a travelling menagerie only to be pursued by miners who were convinced he too was a spy.

No matter: Corvan's tale of monkey mayhem brought the house down and went straight in at Number One around Hartlepool. A legend was born. Local poets and songwriters swiftly latched onto the new craze and the town's Lord Mayor became immortalised in local song for his meeting on the sand with a little chap, banana in hairy hand.

Old Hartlepool had once been a prominent port, but at the time of the hanging its population had dwindled to under 1,000. By the time of Corvan's performance the area was being reborn. This Hartlepool was fast becoming a different place to the stormy fishing village of the Napoleonic wars. Dock Street music hall nestled among the thriving dockyards of West Hartlepool; newly arriving West Dockers took up the song with enthusiasm to taunt their simple fisherfolk neighbours across the river.

'Who hung the monkey . . . who hung the monkey?'

Although he would remain a source of local amusement for 100 years, a miniaturised monkey eventually escaped the town tucked into the kit bag of Hartlepool Rovers Rugby Club. Throughout the country spectators must have held their breath as their forwards booted the ball toward the Hartlepool posts. How many must have wondered, as play resumed, what exactly was the small creature hanging from their opponents' crossbar?

The Rovers unfortunately ran into financial difficulties and folded, so the small toy monkey found himself on a free transfer to Durham. It proved to be a good move. During a match between

Durham and Cornwall, the monkey got his big break. Swinging merrily from the bar, he caught the media's attention. Claims from Cornish players that they too had a monkey came too late: the Hartlepool Monkey kicked all his rivals into touch. His photograph was rushed to the papers and nationwide fame assured. The legend of the 'Hartlepool monkey hangers' began to weave its way into the folklore of Britain. Maybe you've never heard of him, but don't think he's finally been dumped in the wastebin of history; I have to tell you he's alive and in the very best of health.

On 31 October 1999, Hartlepool FC's Victoria Ground witnessed a rebirth of monkey mania. Before Millwall and Hartlepool emerged from the tunnel for their first-round FA Cup tie, a new signing left the dressing-room having exchanged his French naval uniform for the blue-and-white home strip and scampered onto the pitch to roars of approval not heard since Ned Corvan's days. For years previously, chants of 'who hung the monkey' had often been employed by away fans to taunt the home crowd. They responded in turn, by waving inflatable bananas. But now the main monkey was back!

H'Angus is a mascot once more, well loved by his new crew for his antics before every Hartlepool match. With over 200 years' experience, the old campaigner knows just how to handle himself. They say if you pay peanuts you get monkeys, but in H'Angus's case it's a lucrative banana deal. He also knows how to grab the media spotlight, having been banned from Scunthorpe FC for making 'suggestive' comments to a female steward, and Blackpool's ground for being on something stronger than fruit juice. He is an animal after all.

But when all's said and done, no one's quite sure whether the Hartlepool Monkey story is true or not. Children employed on ships to prime cannons with gunpowder were often referred to as 'powder monkeys' . . . but hey, never let facts interfere with a fine legend.

Tarn Whale could be as good as the Hartlepool Monkey, Big 'n' Daft had said. But he was wrong.

It would be better . . . because the simple fact was . . . *we'd seen it!*

The Whirlpool

'YOU KNOW, A FEW YEARS AGO, I THINK I SAW FLYING SAUCERS over Barnsley. Only about 30 or 40 silver cigar shapes . . . you know the kind of thing . . . but a few of them landed and these green slimy things with bug eyes squidged out and ate some sheep. I'm sure I saw that . . .'

Now if I'd decided to sell that story to the *Barnsley Chronicle*, I might just have got a result.

'*Really?* Where exactly? We'll get someone on it right away. *Hold the front page!* We'll run an appeal. See if anyone else remembers that. Thanks for the story.'

But trying to tell someone you've seen a big blue whale in tarn is quite another thing: that really *is* beyond belief. On finally making contact with the editorial department that Friday, I felt sure Paul would whip the pencil from behind his ear and start scribbling down details in his notebook. Hanging on the phone, dubious silence at the other end told me otherwise.

'A . . . a . . . *whale* . . . in . . . in . . . *Barnsley?*'

I remained adamant. Eventually he agreed to check the archives for 1968. Job done. I relayed the great news to the crew, whose enthusiasm for the hunt had not been dulled.

> Land that motherff@ker big boy!
> Cap'n Ahab

> Excellent news Statis. The whale existed. We need more whales in tarn.
> Big 'n' Daft

But will it knock the pound coin stuck to pavement in Wombwell off the front page or nudge out 'Man steals joint of beef'?
Casper

Whale I'll be damned, just mailed the favva-in-law (architect in Barnsley) and he seems to know summat abart all this . . . he too is on the case and is seeking answers to questions. I'm just bewildered by the gravity of this whole situation.
Pablo

Good work Pabs. Nice to see you've got Barnsley connections as well.
BIG 'N' DAFT – ON THE WHALE TRAIL

At this point I should mention that not all crew members were tykes. Pablo from Manchester had become a regular when City and the Reds were neck and neck for promotion. In the virtual world of football, anyone can drop in to anyone else's home ground any time. Verbal skirmishes with taunting away fans were common before matches, but off-season few ventured on. Exchanges were all in the spirit of the game, but if visiting fans turned to verbal violence they'd be given short shrift and thrown overboard. Football, however, seemed a distant memory. Try as they might, tykes could not escape the pull of the whale. Well, all but one, who seemed to have a few drops of berserker blood in his veins.

Can anyone remember an attacking midfielder called Mike Lester? Scored a cracking goal at Middlesboro' in a cup game I seem to recall. Where did he go after his spell at the club?
Franco tyke

We got him from Grimsby. Did we return him to the sea? Soz I've got a whale obsession at the moment.
Big 'n' Daft

I bet he had a whale of a time there then. Latest rumour I had on the whale saga was that he came from Morecambe after one of the fairground carnivals went bust and they did a runner, leaving 'Moby' as the only tangible asset left. What with his knackered rebuilt bus empire, I bet it was odds on that Paul Sykes who had an idea to put a motor inside the whale and flog it on to Bangladesh or some such Third-World republic under the guise of the latest motoring accessory. Obviously the plan failed hence Moby outstaying his welcome and de-camping in the Court House.
Franco tyke

THIS BULLETIN BOARD IS CRAP. WHERE'S THE FOOTBALL? I thought this website was supposed to be football related (since it's connected to the BFC website), instead all we seem to get is half-wits or Nobby-no-mates spouting drivel. Every time I log on, I have to wade through a pile of nonsensical, irrelevant or inane shit until I find someone with a decent opinion or at least saying something worthwhile. Tip to all those using this board to chat to their mates – USE THE FU**ING PHONE!
P***ed off

P***ed off . . . I've been visiting this site for a number of years. It existed a long time before it became an official BFC site, which is a credit to Radders and Co. that developed it. You fail to understand that this part of the site still remains unofficial and therefore people are free to discuss whatever they want.

Most people on the site have more in common than just the club and use it not only for football but to get to know each other. A lot of friendships have been made through the banter and non-footy related postings and long may that go on. Many people who no longer have ties with Barnsley and Yorkshire other than the club continue to feel part of it through what they read. Rest assured, when there is something footy related to discuss it is done to death. The season is closed, Bassett has indicated no more signings for now and that doesn't leave much to talk about. If you want rumour, go to teamtalk, if you want fact go to the newspage. If you want a mixture of both along with some banter and a general laugh, come to the bulletin board, where most comments are welcomed.

Try visiting some other footy boards closed season, most are dead, the ones that live on are the same as this one. Long may it continue . . . ooops I've just fallen off my high horse.
Anon

HEY – about that whale. No more information today??? One of the most surreal topics on here for a very long time!
Knut

There's a Prince of Whales colliery in Ponty. Could it have been named after Jonah?
    ps put me down as an agnostic
Scarf

I'm glued to this thread. Anyone want to make a wish? If so see you at the top of the steps in Whitby.
Captain Cook

At last, a true sailor among our crew. Yorkshire isn't generally renowned for its great explorers or its contribution to seamanship. In fact, a few years ago the adventurer Sir Ranulph Fiennes was driven to state that he would never allow a Yorkshireman on another expedition.

'People from Yorkshire . . . are dour and nurse a grudge. One thing you can't put up with on expeditions are people who search for trouble then nurse it when they have found it.'

I don't know which of his little expeditions he was referring to or the Yorkshireman involved, but what Sir Ranulph just can't understand is that we set our sights on bigger stuff.

Captain James Cook might have been a farmer's son from Marton-in-Cleveland, but as a young apprentice watching the fishing 'cats' sailing out from Whitby's harbour he dreamt of boldly going where no man had been before. His dreams came true. When the *Endeavour* slipped her moorings under the shadow of St Hilda's ruined abbey, the great adventurer really was launching himself into the unknown. Cook set new standards in virtually every aspect of seamanship: navigation, cartography, care of his crew and relations with the people he discovered. And to top it all he found a new continent, Australia, plus a host of weird and wonderful creatures the West had never seen before. A bit more challenging than wandering around with a camera crew and a couple of tennis racquets strapped to your feet, wouldn't you agree, Sir Ranulph?

Today, Captain Cook's statue surveys the North Sea from a salt-blown vantage point high on Whitby's West Cliff. Alongside him stands a magnificent whalebone arch, a reminder that Whitby whalers once braved the grey North Sea, bound for blubber off Greenland. Could the weatherworn Whitby bones have something to do with Tarn Whale?

I could have done with the navigational skills of Captain Cook right then. The more I found out, the less I knew. The more I thought about it, the more confused I became. Only the *Chronicle* could save us and they'd still not rung back.

The phone rang.

I tried to hide the disappointment in my voice as I scribbled down what my girlfriend told me. Of course I'd told Caroline about the whale, but I wasn't quite sure if she believed me either. I'd even urged to call her parents to see if they knew anything about whales on lorries; I was pretty sure she hadn't. That morning she did have a new lead though: apparently in Barnsley's Cawthorne Park Museum there's a statue of the preacher John Wesley carved from . . . yes, you've guessed it . . . a whalebone. I tried to sound enthusiastic, but it seemed to be another snippet that led nowhere.

The crew continued to scratch around for anything even vaguely related to whales, but to tell the truth we were just going round and round in circles. If this puzzle were a 10,000-piece jigsaw, we'd so far managed to come up with a half-a-dozen well-chewed bits. We needed more, something bigger . . . like the lid of the box for a start. I couldn't wait any longer and hailed the *Chronicle*. Unbeknown to me, Big 'n' Daft's patience had snapped just minutes later.

> Phoned the *Chrony* abart that whale and they said some nutter had been on the phone earlier going on abart it. He reckons they've checked a few 1968 archives but couldn't find owt. I suggested checking a few years on from that but he says they're too busy. Probably writing a story on the Queens Hotel having a sea view as appeared in *The Sun* today. 'Barnsley, famous for Arthur Scargill, black puddings and Barnsley chops' blah blah blah blah.

I stared into *The Sun*. There it was: an article about a typographic error in some travel brochure that led to Barnsley's Queens Hotel being attributed with a sea view. Rather than waste time on an improbable whale, the *Chronicle* was busy feeding the old, old myths. As Big 'n' Daft knew only too well, the whole tarn and every tyke seemed destined to be caught in the whirlpool of 'Arthur Scargill, black puddings, Barnsley chops, whippets and flat caps' forever.

It was then I had my first vague suspicions. True, there had been hundreds of postings and whale fever remained strong, but we still didn't have a shred of evidence. Without that, we were in danger of simply amusing ourselves until boredom inevitably set in. And beyond the crew, I had the nagging feeling that no one was going to believe my story of a whale in tarn. Time to break free and set a new heading.

At Anchor

THE *CHRONICLE'S* LACK OF ENTHUSIASM WAS A MERE irritation, brushed aside like a troublesome gnat. Rather than deflating my sails, the news (or rather lack of it) filled them with a renewed detemination.

To be fair to Paul, he had given us a new lead. Why not try Barnsley Library? I hurriedly consulted my charts. Of course! And better still, my brother's wife worked there. It may have seemed an unusual quest, but I knew she'd understand . . .

'A whale . . . in Barnsley?'

OK, so Hazel didn't actually remember Jonah, but she had to admit that the possibility of her husband and brother-in-law going doolally at the exact same point of time was remote. She agreed. That weekend she would consult Maurice and dive into the murky vaults of tarn history.

If anyone knew anything it would be Maurice. Deep within the library's bowels, he was gatekeeper of all that was and ever had been Barnsley. Rumour had it he knew all that could ever be known about tarn. He didn't seem to need a computer; hundreds of years of history were stuffed into his head. One word would send him scuttling along shelves of books and documents to pick out exactly the right nugget.

Meanwhile, back on the board, Casper and Big 'n' Daft were readying themselves to spread the hunt further. Preparations were made for their ascent to Valhalla: Friday night in tarn.

> Johnny Bummer says you can kip at his ALL weekend seeing as he invited you to crash – we can use his drum then as whale HQ all weekend . . .

> This is marvellous news! All I need now is confirmation of the whale story and the weekend is set up nicely.

The plan was simple. Rendezvousing with Johnny Bummer and Boli, they would establish a 'Whale HQ' before coming ashore in tarn on Saturday. Ducking in and out of numerous steamy inns and taverns they would surely stumble across an old salt who'd seen Tarn Whale. Much ale would have to be drunk to extract the information: a dirty job but someone had to do it.

I outlined the dive into the library to the duo and wished them good luck. Big 'n' Daft's mind obviously continued to be troubled by fleeting images of incredible animals.

> On Monday I will tell you about the flea dressed as a Mexican. Yes, that's right . . . flea . . . dressed as a Mexican.

> Is that true? I haven't got a clue what is and what isn't any more.

> Neither have I. As far as I'm concerned it's true but I'm not going to delve into it too deeply in case it's not and I really am going crackers. There's enough going on with this whale business.

Mexican Fleas . . . hmmm. Big 'n' Daft had revealed the coordinates: just a few leagues due north, to a sleepy backwater. This was one myth I could verify with my own eyes. I checked out tattered notes from others who'd ventured into those waters. Ever seen the film *Deliverance*? That's what this place is like, everyone is somehow distantly related . . . 'A graveyard with lights . . .'

Weird. Surely this was worth a visit: a myth I could verify with my own eyes. I would not tell the crew, they had enough to think about.

Our whaler weighed anchor for the night: a time of quiet contemplation of this mythical beast in our midst. As darkness fell, I knew firefly barlights would be flickering on across Barnsley. Friday night: how many hesitant questions were, even now, being asked far and wide that evening?

For two whole days the whale swept virtually every other topic of discussion off the board: a huge mammal, rearing up from the depths of a collective subconscious. The burning belief of those who'd actually seen the whale now began to infect doubters and agnostics. As the evening wore on the glass screen flickered with confused whisperings as newcomers and returning old hands met in the darkness.

> A mate of mine John CONFIRMS the big whale in Barnsley. Apparently 1968. And they all got crocodiled down from school to look at it but it was brown by then!! His dad-in-law confirms . . . bugger me.
>
> What big bloody whale? What are you on about?
>
> Guy at work confirmed the story, so now I don't think you are totally insane.
>
> WHAT IS THE F.UCKNG WHALE?

It's like a big fish – but is actually a mammal that lives in the sea.

DON'T PISS ABOUT – LET ME IN ON IT.

I left the late-night crew to their squabbling and set out into the night. Time to make my own enquiries in the real world.

The Cow

SINCE TIME BEGAN, THE AREA WHERE I LIVE, AT THE BOTTOM of a sloping hill, was nothing but marshy swampland. Higher up, friars and monks eventually established vineyards and grazed their cattle in the marshes below. This was the little town's far-eastern edge, its boundary marked by the marsh gate. Then, about the time the good fishermen of Hartlepool were doing their bit for king and country, the marsh was drained and cattle moved on. All, that is, except for one: a prized red cow. And because she turned to stone she's survived right up to this day. Nestling below the Vineyard, opposite Marshgate House, stands The Red Cow public house. This was just the place to take the whale.

The Red Cow was where I went to do business – and I don't mean office business, I mean *real* business. Her regulars included brickies, computer analysts, electricians, writers, allotment dwellers, air traffic-control-system salesmen, cabbies, musicians, painters and decorators. Late into the night every tongue could be heard: northerners, southerners, Scots, Welsh, Irish, American, Polish, French, Russian, Japanese, South African, Australian. Men born in far-flung corners of the world righted the world's wrongs, or just chewed the cud with folk born right next door. All human, and some distinctly inhuman, life ebbed and flowed through the Cow. Even as a calf, her belly was said to have swirled with beggars, villains and ne'er-do-wells: a 'thieves' harbour' she was dubbed back then. Not much had changed. Tom, the landlord, likened it to the League of Nations, or the bar scene from *Star Wars*.

But the Cow was a place to get things done – your house repainted or a rose-fitting rewired. Here were men who could 'find' things, like a garden gate, a weather vane, even the 'big end' for a Granada 2.8. Here deals could be struck: a mixer tap soldered in exchange for a colour printer, a black pudding swapped for a horse brass, unspoken exchanges of carrier bags filled with bacon, bottles, CDs, home-baked bread and leeks. This was a place you could talk to anyone, or even yourself, and old women with walking frames could eat sandwiches out of their hats without anyone turning a hair. Yes, this was the place to launch my marine mammal on an unsuspecting world.

Yet the Cow had not survived for almost 200 years without becoming a wily old beast. That evening, as I pushed into the dim yellow light of her belly, there was none of the usual babble, just a few people I didn't know that well dotted around the wooden bar. A strange evening. I joined in by standing at a different side of the bar to my usual place, an outrageous act that on any other evening would have been commented on by other regulars who respected time-honoured ritual.

In truth, not much had ever changed in there. There had been a few movements of doors and walls over the years, perhaps, but the central bar with its warm, carved wood, inset with gold-and-green Victorian glass, still proclaims 'Jamaica Rum' and 'Superior Scotch', as it must have done when Victoria was a girl.

I remember feeling hesitant, fearing that even here I might be pushing the bounds of the bizarre just too far, but I watched the door and decided it would be a case of 'first come first whaled'.

'A whale . . . yeah? Like . . . a whale man . . . wow . . . that's really somethin' man.' Zak shook his dreadlocks. Having been in

Kenya at the time, he really couldn't say. Further along the bar, Tesco Dave looked a better bet. He'd told me once that his mother could remember Zeppelins over London. He gave the whale a moment's thought, then shook his head.

'Nah.'

Silence descended. A stranger quietly drinking his pint spoke up.

'You mean like the Kingston elephant?'

We looked at him.

'The Kingston elephant?'

'Yeah . . . the Kingston elephant. They say that once, a circus came to Kingston and one of the elephants died. So they buried it near the railway station. But the thing is . . .' he hesitated, eyes glazing into the middle distance, '. . . but the thing is . . . *nobody* . . . knows where . . .'

The stranger's mind seemed to be drifting out to nearby Kingston. I remembered Pablo's 'Manchester elephant' and norman's circus elephant that had run amok in Barnsley, but kept them to myself. I sensed Jonah had disturbed another buried memory; another tortured soul, searching for a half-remembered ghost. But Pablo's tale of the elephant that walked from Manchester's Belle Vue Zoo to Edinburgh was a timely reminder of how the memory of a real event can be passed on and twisted through time. He'd got the story right, but the wrong way round.

Most of us think the fact the circus rarely comes to town these days, and that many zoos are closing, is a good thing. Perhaps it is, but a few generations ago there was a far worse existence for animals such as 'Maharaja', the Manchester elephant. He was part of a menagerie. It's only over the last 100 years or so that people have moved around; before that most people lived and died in the towns or villages of their birth. So if you couldn't get to the entertainment, the entertainment had to come to you. There weren't any proper roads back then, just uneven, overgrown tracks, bone-shakingly dusty in summer and treacherously muddy in winter. Menageries crammed with strange animals regularly jolted from town to village to reveal mysteries that existed beyond the locals' small worlds.

Animals transported in such creaking beastwagons were kept in appalling conditions. Lions, panthers, hyenas, apes, even rhinos, had scarely enough room to turn round, and veterinary care was unheard of. For most of their miserable lives the animals were shuttered away from daylight. Menageries made good business: you had to pay to see anything. Howling screams and roars from terrified inmates raging against their confinement must have been horrifying. Perhaps mercifully, many died; others were driven insane. 'Chunee', a vast Indian elephant belonging to Polito's Royal Menagerie, no longer able to bear the pain of a rotten tusk, went berserk during a walk in the Strand. Hundreds of shots from hastily summoned troops failed to stop his rampage. In the end they brought him down with a harpoon. Others were more fortunate. Treacherous roads took their toll on their prisons' ramshackle security and many succeeded in their bids for freedom. It was one of these escapees that would eventually be immortalised in *The Baboon*.

When 'Wombwell's Royal Number One Menagerie' rumbled screaming into Edinburgh and the shutters went up, Maharaja and the rest must have thought it was just another show. In fact, it was the end of the road. The menagerie was being put up for sale and all the contents auctioned off in Waverley Market.

In the throng was one James Jennison, who'd travelled north with a shopping list. Jennison was a director of Belle Vue Zoo, whose landscaped gardens, in comparison to a menagerie, would seem like heaven on earth to the animals. As the last hammer fell, he ticked off his buys: one baboon, one African antelope, one lioness and one seven-year-old Asian elephant named Maharaja. Sorted.

All were booked on the 10:05 express direct to heaven from Waverley Station and loading went smoothly until it came to Maharaja. Once aboard, the elephant decided trains weren't really his thing and smashed his head through the front to let everyone know. In the ensuing confusion, he emphasised his point by backing up and destroying the other end of his wagon. Just as it seemed a rampaging elephant was going to cause mayhem, in strode the fearless Lorenzo Lawrence. Although he'd achieved fame as the menagerie's lion-tamer, he proved to be more than capable of calming the distraught Maharaja – in fact he seemed to be the only one who could. In a flash of inspiration the lion-tamer declared he would solve this pachyderm problem by walking Maharaja to Manchester. This was a real stroke of luck for Lawrence as, like the rest of the menagerie, he was redundant and no one had bid for him at the auction. And the strange thing was Maharaja was normally quite a placid animal . . . he'd never been known to fly into a rage . . . it was almost as if . . . The fact that Lawrence was so skilled he could control animals with 'no visible signs of command' probably had nothing at all to do with the elephant's outburst.

Whatever the truth, the great journey began with Lorenzo and Maharaja covering an average of twenty miles a day for eight days. Up over the Pennines they yomped on another bizarre Pennine journey; maybe St Cuthbert kept an eye over them as they traversed his old stamping ground. Pablo also mentioned the tollgate incident, immortalised in a painting, which shows the punch-up that ensued as Lawrence and the toll-keeeper argued over the right price for an elephant. It never happened though – probably that was another elephant. By day eight they were in Bolton and arrived at Belle Vue two days later to be greeted by rapturous crowds.

Lorenzo Lawrence and Maharaja worked happily together for many years and both lived to a grand old age. Maharaja enjoyed giving rides to visiting children, a tradition that would continue after the elephant's death when he succumbed to flu. Years later, Lawrence was forced to call it a day when he succumbed to a broken leg after being squashed between two other panicky pachyderms.

The would-be tamer of the Kingston elephant simply disappeared as the Cow filled up, so I never got to find out more. Perhaps, like me, he didn't know much more. I made a few more whale enquiries but drew a blank. As the night wore on, most simply put my gibbering down to another case of a regular being 'over-refreshed'. Tom, the landlord, just stared in disbelief. Understandable really. Over the years he must have heard so much rubbish from the other side of the bar I doubt he could separate fact from fiction.

'Mind you, there used to be a bloke come in here . . . little fella . . . old Joe . . . yeah, he used to come in here . . . used to stand over there he did . . . before your time . . . an' he used to say . . . he used to say . . . now what was it he used to say?'

As Tom sifted through the huge mass of gibberish all landlords absorb over time, I glanced through the open door. It was a very warm, very still night. Somehow I knew he was out there. As the last trains pulled into Kingston station and the last commuters dribbled home, he'd be there, a restless soul shuffling through the shadows, moonlight winking off his shovel . . .

'Old Joe . . . he used to say . . . *Oh yeah! That was it!* "Who hung the monkey? Who hung the monkey?" Mad he was.'

The Flying Elephant

NOW YOU MIGHT THINK THAT THESE ANIMAL STORIES ARE mildly amusing, but hardly big news – just little snippets of half-remembered history. Maybe, but one animal was so famous his name lives on to this day. You've most definitely used it on a few occasions. In his time he roused the passions of entire nations and caused controversy that involved governments and royalty; it seems strange that even his story has largely been forgotten.

A few years ago his memory was resurrected and his name

flashed around the world. In the opening days of the 1970s, a Pan-American airliner inbound from New York's JFK drifted over the Cow's rooftop and lowered her undercarriage on final approach. Five miles away at Heathrow Airport a murmur of excitement rippled through the assembled world press as telephoto lenses were trained on this graceful silver-and-white bird. Seconds later the airliner lifted her huge nose and settled onto the runway as the shutters clicked. It wasn't anyone on the passenger list that caused all the commotion – it was the plane itself.

Boeing's new 747-100 Series had just completed its inaugural commercial flight. This was an airliner the like of which the world had never seen. The airport had difficulty coping with the baggage from her 336 passengers, twice as many as her predecessor, the 707, could hold. Her wingspan was greater than the length of the Wright brothers' first plane and her distinctive humped back heralded a new era in air travel. There would be no dull manufacturer's number for this aircraft. Only one word could describe a creature of such stupendous size: 'Jumbo'!

When that first jumbo jet's wheels touched the runway, she'd completed a flight of some seven hours. But unknown to most, she'd also brought to a close a bizarre 100-year transatlantic return trip.

The story began about 150 years ago with the capture of a three-year-old African elephant in what is now the Sudan. He was taken first to Zanzibar and then sold to Le Jardin des Plantes in Paris. The zoo must have discovered it had an excess of elephants, as he was quickly traded for a rhinoceros in a deal with London Zoo.

At the time he must have looked like any other elephant, for had the French suspected what would happen to him they would never have let him go. He arrived at Regent's Park standing at an unremarkable 5 ft tall, but soon began to grow at an amazing rate and was christened Jumbo. (Funnily enough, 'jumbo' doesn't actually mean 'big'; it's derived from the Swahili '*jumbe*', or 'chief'.) Over the next 15 years Jumbo grew to be the pride not only of London Zoo but of the whole nation. Britannia ruled the waves, the sun never set on her empire and her children were carried aloft on the back of the mighty Jumbo. At 12 ft high and weighing in at 7 tons, the world's biggest elephant was a symbol of Victorian supremacy.

Then disaster struck. Someone tried to steal Jumbo, and not just anyone – the great American showman Phileas T. Barnum, always on the lookout for crowd-pulling curiosities, offered $10,000 for the elephant. Zoo officials rushed out hurried excuses about Jumbo 'becoming difficult to handle' as soon as they found they'd misjudged the public mood. They were too late. How dare Barnum and his upstart nation attempt to make off with the great Jumbo? A national outcry ensued, fuelled by every newspaper. Hats, banners, scarves and placards declaring 'Save our Jumbo!' were worn and waved on the streets. Even the great and learned were moved to put pen to paper: 'England is not in the habit of parting with her pets. If stone walls and chains are necessary to confine Jumbo, England has the stone and iron and need not go to America for them,' wrote an indignant Ruskin. The Prince of Wales hotfooted it to the zoo to make the directors see sense. Queen Victoria herself was most certainly not amused. She stated that Jumbo could not possibly leave with Barnum: 'Great Britain can pay him his damages,' she's reported to have said sniffily. Parliament attempted to declare the deal illegal and the transatlantic tug of war went on for weeks.

Jumbo, of course, knew nothing of this. Happy enough with his partner Alice and well looked after by devoted keeper Matthew Scott, he continued giving gleeful kiddy rides and munching his way through bales of hay. But on the day 20 horses and a sunken cage turned up, even he knew something was badly wrong.

Barnum had won. Jumbo was taken to the docks and loaded onto *The Assyrian Monarch*. The British government hounded

Barnum to the last: a bill was quickly passed, stating that no British subject could travel on the same deck as the elephant. This was a cunning move – Jumbo was so tall that a section of decking had to be cut away to accommodate him, so the bill meant that two whole decks would remain empty for the voyage. The shipowners demanded compensation to the tune of $30,000, three times the amount paid for Jumbo. Barnum didn't flinch; he coughed up and the freighter set sail for the new world.

Barnum revelled in the controversy he'd caused. It was all free publicity for his latest attraction, billed as 'The Greatest Living Quadruped on Earth'. Jumbo and his keeper Matthew Scott arrived in New York to great acclaim and, after knocking them out at Madison Square Garden, he toured the US and Canada for three and a half years in his own specially constructed rail carriage. All the while Barnum urged the public to see Jumbo at the earliest opportunity, as if he kept on growing he'd soon no longer fit through the railway tunnels – it's estimated that about 20 million people did.

Sad to say, it was the railway that would seal great Jumbo's fate. After a late evening performance of The Barnum and Bailey Circus near St Thomas, Ontario, Canada, Matthew Scott led Jumbo and his faithful companion Tom Thumb, a midget albino elephant, back to their rail carriages. There should have been no more trains passing through that night, but as the rails ticked and shuddered beneath their feet Scott sensed something was wrong. The driver of the oncoming train made out the huge animal ahead and slammed on the brakes, but on a downhill gradient they had little effect. The engine bore down on them. Trapped between a steep embankment and rail wagons, Scott urged the panicking, lumbering elephants on. They had no chance. Tom Thumb was thrown from the tracks and suffered a broken leg, but poor Jumbo took the full impact, being crushed between the braking engine and a stationary train.

It was a scene of utter chaos. The engine knocked from the tracks belched out swirling clouds of steam, carriages had become derailed and in the midst lay the mortally injured Jumbo. Scott rushed to his side and all stood back in silence as the elephant gently wound his trunk around his lifelong companion. And so, a few minutes later, the great Jumbo died; Scott broke down and was led weeping from the site. He never really recovered from his bereavement, consoling himself by caring for small animals in Barnum's troupe.

News of the death flashed across around America and crossed the Atlantic as two nations united in horror-struck headlines, public mourning and cheesy poetry.

> List to the tale of Jumbo
> A beast of high renown
> Who famed became the wide world through
> The pride of London town . . .
>
> Full many a triumph Jumbo met
> When landed on our shore
> Alas! His life is now cut short
> We ne'er shall see him more.
>
> The beast that conquered all our hearts
> An engine has laid low
> Ah! Why did keepers him permit
> Upon that track to go?

But hey, wipe away those tears because, like they say, the show must go on! The ultimate showman certainly lost no time in making the best of this tragic turn of events. With great care, poor Jumbo was subjected to the world's largest taxidermy job. His bones (weighing 3 tons) were loaded aboard a railcar that made a mournful journey back to New York; passers-by no doubt doffed hats and hung their heads in respect on sighting the inscription, 'In this car lie the mortal remains of the immortal Jumbo'. Jumbo's hide (weighing over 1,500 lb) was first preserved in a ton of salt at a local pork factory before following his bones.

Death turned out to be a mere blip in the career of this legend. Barnum had Jumbo's hide stretched over a wooden frame and stuffed; his huge attraction was back on the rails in no time. Jumbo toured the States for a further four years and thousands queued to pay their last respects. By the end of Jumbo's live/dead tour, it's estimated the elephant had raked in over $1,000,000 for the showman. Always anxious to cash in on a hit, Barnum found another large elephant, which he dubbed Jumbo II. Like all Hollywood blockbuster sequels, he wasn't a patch on the original.

Jumbo himself was to go on in more ways than one. The elephant's reassembled skeleton was donated to the Smithsonian Institute of Natural History, while the mighty stuffed hide was granted, along with other exhibits, to the Tufts University in Massachusetts which, in turn, established a Barnum Museum. Jumbo was, quite naturally, a great hit at the university and immediately became their mascot. Generations of students would respectfully place a penny in his trunk at exam time for good luck. Not much rubbed off on the hapless pachyderm, though, as tragedy struck once more. In 1975, the university's Barnum hall caught fire. There can be few more combustible things than a 90-year-old stuffed elephant and Jumbo was swiftly reduced to cinders. Yet all was not lost, for into the inferno plunged a hero. Phyllis Byrne, a university administrator, grabbed the first thing that came to hand and dashed toward the blazing elephant to scrape together a handful of ashes. These were solemnly presented to Rocco J. 'Rocky' Cozzo, the university's athletic director, who kept them safely under lock and key.

Spookily enough, on the *very same* October weekend in 1999 that the Hartlepool Monkey took to the pitch, a new ceremony was initiated at Tufts University. On Rocky's retirement, the safe was unlocked and the peanut-butter jar containing Jumbo's ashes ceremoniously passed to the new director. Even as we speak, if Tufts University athletes or footballers have an important game on today, they'll be rubbing the jar for luck.

Of course, the old elephant has also been immortalised in language. Yes, if anything's bigger than big – hot-dogs, washing powder, eggs, ice-cream cones (only yesterday I came across a 'jumbo' apple strudel) – it just has to be honoured with his name. Walt Disney also paid respect to his memory with the creation of 'Dumbo', the flying baby elephant with oversized ears.

But perhaps my favourite memorial to him is in the little town where he met his sad demise. In 1985, the centenary of Jumbo's death, the Jumbo Centennial Committee in St Thomas issued commemorative silver coins. Legal tender in the town, they sold in their thousands. But a bigger, more magnificent memorial had also been planned. That year Jumbo took to the rails once more on a Canada-bound train (in sections of course, so he'd fit under the bridges). In the town where he was disassembled, his life-size concrete statue was reassembled by the good citizens of St Thomas.

He's there to this day, standing tall, head thrust to the heavens with trunk thrown back in full trumpet, proudly gazing into the clear blue skies, where his silver children weave their web around the world.

Flea

'A GRAVEYARD WITH LIGHTS' MIGHT BE A BIT HARSH, BUT TRING in Hertfordshire certainly is a sleepy old place. There would be little whale activity over the weekend as we waited for the result of Hazel's visit to the library, so I set a course north to this leafy little backwater.

All I could find out about Tring was: it is home to half the referees in the Premiership and it has a high street chock-a-block with hairdressers. These two facts may be unconnected, but I made a mental note to check out the man in black's coiffure next time I watched a Premiership game. More importantly, as far as I was concerned, it is home to Big 'n' Daft's fleas dressed as Mexicans. I'd never see Jumbo or the original monkey-hanging incident, but I wasn't going to let this marvel pass me by.

The Walter Rothschild Zoological Musuem is a real time capsule. Passing over the threshold I become a time traveller, hurtling back 100 years: every crystal display case, every shining carved banister, is exactly as it was in Walter Rothschild's day. It's an imposing Victorian building, a bit over the top to house a flea collection perhaps, but it didn't start out like that. It all began so innocently . . .

The same year that Jumbo's tour of the US came to an end, the first Baron Rothschild was pondering his son's forthcoming 21st. What do you get for the young man who has everything? Then he hit on it. Walter had always nurtured a great interest in nature. He'd spend many a long hour poring over his insect and flea collection. Come the day, the Baron presented his son with a plot of land and the funds to build his own little museum. What harm could come of that? This harmless little pastime would keep him out of trouble.

Walter Rothschild and his taxidermist set to work with vigour and big ambitions. You see, fleas and then insects were only the start. Soon their minds turned to voles, field mice. After all, a vole's no bigger than a cockroach, so what's the difference? A big one actually, because then you're into mammals. Next it's hamsters, then the odd rabbit, and before you know it the whole thing is out of control.

His taxidermist's patience must have been wearing thin long before Walter sauntered by with a polar bear, an alligator and a couple of lions, slapped them down on the counter and asked, 'What can you do with these? Ready a week on Tuesday?'

The fearless Captain Cook had blazed a trail that opened up a world of mysterious creatures never before seen in Europe, and the colonising, collecting Victorians grabbed nets and traps to follow with enthusiasm. There was a whole wide world opening up to lords and lieutenant-majors with double-barrelled names and double-barrelled shotguns: they shot first and asked questions later, and dispatched some hitherto unseen animals back to Blighty.

Now, I know a lot of people aren't too keen on stuffed animals. I remember as a child staring into fusty bell jars in a gloomy room near Lincoln Cathedral and being pretty appalled. They all seemed fixed in anatomically impossible poses, faces frozen in terror as if their very last thought was *'Aaargh . . . I'm going to be stuffed and slammed in a jar!'* But the occupants of this Noah's Ark were in a different league altogether.

Walter had tracked down every living creature that runs, walks, hops, flies, swims or just squiggles around a bit. Striped, spotted, dappled, dowdy or multi-coloured, Walter Rothschild, the great-great grandfather of the Pokemon generation, just had to catch 'em all. And every animal, furred, feathered or scaled, was a perfectly preserved silent witness to one man's driving passion. Take Mick for example.

Mick the Miller could run like the wind in his day. Ears back, tongue lolling, he belted round the track like no greyhound had ever done before. Of the 48 races he took part in, he won 36, including four classics. Admittedly, by the time we came face-to-face in Tring he was quite a bit slower. In truth, he hadn't stirred in over 60 years, having passed away in 1938, but from the twinkle in his eye I could almost believe the legend was straining to hear trap doors spring open once more. Flashing across the finishing line in pursuit of yet another hare, did he have any premonition that he would ultimately suffer the same fate as his prey?

I said my goodbyes to old Mick and meandered through the hushed galleries of Noah's Ark, a thousand beady glass eyes following my every move. Padding around the upper gallery I became distracted by a suspended flying circus: sharks, dolphins, spear-snouted narwhals, the awesome Indian sawfish.

But I was here for one thing and one thing only, and they knew it.

'He's here for the fleas,' whispered the spoonbill.

'Who?' asked the hippo.

'Him . . . walking up and down, round and round, faster and faster.'

'Say, isn't that the guy who's lookin' for a whale?' queried the three-tooth puffer.

'Wha . . . hayyy!' chattered the ringtails. 'The guy can't find a whale . . . how the hell's he gonna find the fleas?'

I spun round. They all snapped back to their glassy stares, but I could have sworn the wobbegong was shaking a little. I knew that, deep inside, they were all laughing. Refusing to give them the pleasure of watching my panicky search, I approached a curator, who kindly guided me toward a cabinet. Carefully undoing the brass clasp, I was able to confirm Big 'n' Daft's memory: '. . . sure enough, there was an exhibit where if you looked through a microscope thingy you could see a flea and its missus both sort of dressed like Mexicans . . .'

He was not going crackers. White shirts, red waistcoats, black dress and sombrero: there they were, arms (legs?) outstretched, clad in traditional Mexican costume. Why, Mrs Flea even had a tortilla in her hand (foot?), although on this microscopic scale it could well have been a flake of dandruff.

In Mexico, fleas were dressed as curiosities – a skill first practised in convents by nuns who excelled at fashioning miniatures. Walter Rothschild snapped his pair up in 1905 from a middle-aged woman who'd dressed them during long nights, so as not to be disturbed by her children who'd spent long days auditioning local dogs and cats for Mr and Mrs Flea.

Mission accomplished. I'd got my result: I'd seen something that couldn't be seen with the naked eye and reaffirmed Big 'n'

Daft's sanity. Yet for all Walter Rothschild's endeavours, he hadn't netted a whale – a blue whale. Now that *would* have been his crowning achievement.

Pleased with my success and feeling safe among these experts on preserved animals, I started asking careless questions – a big mistake. I simply enquired of a friendly-looking curator what he knew about whales. Not a lot, he admitted, but he'd try and help. I asked what he knew about 'touring whales'. It took some moments for him to stammer out a reply.

'Were you . . . thinking of . . . er . . . caravanning . . . or . . . er . . . birdwatching?'

We stood face-to-face, eyes darting from side to side like desperadoes in a spaghetti western. Neither of us dared move lest we were felled by the raving madman before us.

Whales. Wales.

Shutters were drawn in hairdressers' windows as I made my way back along Tring High Street. It was very quiet: perhaps too quiet.

'Ever seen the film *Deliverance* . . . that's what this place is like . . .'

Fearing that behind the blinds scissors were being sharpened, and a bouffant turf-war about to break out, I made good my escape.

Becalmed

AS YOU'RE NOW PART OF THE CREW, I CAN ONLY ASSUME THAT you're starting to feel like the others did at this point. 'This is all very well . . . *but what about the whale?*' If it's any consolation, I was wondering that too. But it's worth remembering that the first souls to set sail in search of whales didn't just pop off on a day trip, bag a whale and get home in time for tea. It wouldn't be a matter of weeks or months either; whales are probably the most elusive creatures on earth. In the days of sail, a whaling expedition would commonly last some two or three years; they were epic voyages beset with many dangers and hazardous detours. Many a crew member set out with thoughts of high-spirited adventure only to end up broken and disillusioned. I can only hope you are made of sterner stuff – this whale hunt may be a little out of the ordinary, but it is a whale hunt nonetheless.

Checking the entries made over the weekend gave cause for concern. One tyke began to rave about football, but the sale of our star striker seemed now strangely irrelevant and Johnno cut him short.

> Higgy was one of the best players we have had at this club for years. Pace, heart, and wonderful technique, a joy to watch last season and will be missed now. Why do we give players like Morgan awards when his technique is nowhere near that of players such as Hignett – surely we have to look and wonder why?

> Let it lie, I am more intrigued by the whale than Higgy's future. If you keep on dwelling on it, it'll destroy you. Get over it!

In fact we'd drawn a blank all round. Big 'n' Daft's report from 'Whale HQ' made grim reading.

> A couple more confirmations in Tarn last neet. The only problem is, no one can give any explanations as to why it was there, where it came from etc. as it was so long ago and no one remembers. So the whale exists but why, when and where did it come from . . .

We were but four days out and already there were dark mutterings of discontent. Deaf tyke gave vent to his frustration.

> Come on now, let's have an end to the whale bit. It's
> doing my head in. I've just spent the last 20 mins
> looking for more whale reports.

With morale ebbing away, Yankee tyke tried to jolly things along
by showing the crew a picure of the 'Grand Rapids Whale'. It
was impressive – a ceiling-hung blue whale skeleton in her local
museum – but even Big 'n' Daft, a man usually up for any
novelty, was unimpressed.

> Grand Rapids Whale is shite I'm afraid . . . compared
> to the Tarn Whale.

Late into the weekend, I'd had no word from Hazel. I sensed
something was wrong, but couldn't get her on the phone. I had
to concede that even my own family had better things to do at
the weekend than pursue mythical whales at short notice. I
finally broadcast that the dive into the library had been delayed
and was horrified to witness mutiny break out.

> Nah then . . . I nivver said the Grand Rapids Whale
> was all that . . . just offered to share our pitiful
> finback. See? Thet's what I get fer bein' a good girl and
> sharing . . . slagged off by mi own mates *sniff*
> WWAAHHHHHH!

> I wasn't slagging . . . just pointing out that our whale
> was far superior. I'm starting to lose interest in this
> whale thing a bit now . . .

'Starting to lose interest . . . if I can be bothered . . .' these
words thumped around my head. Big 'n' Daft had been the
first to defend the whale; together we'd shared our enthusiasm
in the hunt. If Big 'n' Daft didn't stand by me, all would be
lost. Were we about to let Jonah dive once more into the

obscure depths of the past? Darkness descended.

> Looks like it's down to me then . . . to see the job
> through. Tarn spirit. Never say die.

> Nope. I'm still with you on this one Statis. The
> novelty has worn off a bit since Thursday but the
> whale will be cracked. Put it down to a Sunday
> hangover. I'm sure my enthusiasm will return at work
> tomorrow.

> I would hope so. There's no point crackin on about
> it with no further developments. We'll bide our
> time.

> The whale hunt will be seen through to the end. Just
> had mi mother on the blower about the whale but
> she doesn't remember. I'd like to see a photo of it. I
> might write to the *Chronicle* to see if I can stir it up a
> bit . . .

Yankee tyke sobbing and two believers at each other's throats –
only the coming day would tell if our whale hunt would go on.
And yet . . . and yet . . . there was one posting that night that
should have offered us a ray of hope.

> Can't help you on the whale debate as far as Barnsley
> is concerned, however in response to a question in
> the *Rotherham Advertiser* the other week a similar
> occurrence happened in Rotherham in the 1930s.
> The whale is described by an old bloke who wrote in
> as being 'displayed on a low loader' and people had to
> pay to go and look at it. It was billed as 'the biggest
> whale in captivity'.
> Another bloke wrote in and said he went to a

similar exhibition in Manchester around 50 years
ago: 'They cleaned the inside, cut a hole in it and
charged people five shillings to walk inside. You
could actually stand upright inside it.' Probably a
similar exhibition to Barnsley then? At least it
suggests that you lot that remember it in Barnsley
haven't gone mad. I don't remember it though, well
before my time.

The rest of the crew must have seen that posting too, but no
one had answered it and I knew why. It seemed that without
any real effort, someone had found out more than we had;
they'd even got witnesses from Rotherham and Manchester.
My next step should have been quite obvious. I should have
contacted the *Rotherham Advertiser* the very next morning.
But there was no way I was going to do that. If someone else
was out there looking for him as well, then *they'd* claim him.
We had to find him first. Rotherham whale? Manchester
whale? No way. We'd come too far. This was *our* hunt.

Jonah was Tarn Whale and no bugger else's.

Worldwide Whale

THE NEW WORKING WEEK AND NOTHING WAS HAPPENING WITH
a vengeance. I took time out from shovelling e-mails, unglued
my eyes and looked around. Everything looked . . . different
somehow, like someone had been fiddling with the colour
control on a TV. The office seemed paler, greyer, more lifeless
than usual. Row upon row of PCs dredging for data, overseen by
pale human operators. I started to lose my bearings. Slowly but
surely I felt myself fading from their dull reality.

Mid-morning, Dear Boy, trembling with excitement, shuffled

into the office. Taking me aside, he gestured at me to look into the heavy plastic bag he'd brought. He nodded in quiet satisfaction. It had been quite a journey into work. A lorry bound for New Covent Garden had overturned on the Nine Elms road. Apparently there had been many casualties.

'Mmmmm . . . terrible . . . dear boy . . . all over the road . . . mmm . . . thousands squashed.'

Dear Boy swiftly scooped up some survivors and made off. Peering inside the bag I estimated that neither of us would have to buy a lemon for years. He placed his bag on the teetering dam wall of London detritus he'd built between our desks. Dear Boy rarely liked to be away from the Thames, so he regularly dragged bits of the Thames back with him. Driftwood and worn bricks dried out quite nicely in the office. His scavenging wasn't confined to the river either. We could have opened a second-hand bookstore or antique shop with the stuff he'd accumulated over the months. In fact, if there's still a reward out on St Oswald's missing arm, I know just the man the authorities should talk to.

And then, quite unexpectedly, we were called to a meeting – or should I say a *very important* meeting, for there is no such thing as a mere 'meeting' in the corporate world. I surprised myself by turning up for the *very important* meeting only 15 minutes late. Unusually, there was one other deluded soul already there. I smiled.

'You're new here, aren't you?'

Over the next half-hour the room filled in dribs and drabs. The strange thing about corporate meetings, I'd noticed, was that even when people were present, there was absolutely *no one there*. This was because 'meeting etiquette' stated that on being seated everyone had to place a mobile on the table so we could immediately enjoy beeping renditions of everything from 'Greensleeves' to 'Ride of the Valkyries'. It wasn't long before everybody was busily jabbering into their phones in an electronic peacock-like display of importance. Everyone was far too important to be in the place they were; they simply *had* to move on to the next meeting, where they were urgently needed. My phone didn't ring: this made me pathetic. Dear Boy's phone didn't ring as he didn't own one: this made him a lunatic.

Gradually it emerged that some weren't supposed to be there, a few were under the impression this was another room, and the whole event wound up when the person running the meeting didn't turn up due to being in another meeting that was running 34 years late. But the room did have a river view. Dear Boy spotted a couple of crows vainly trying to dive-bomb a heron as she sailed on her stately flight beneath our window, so the morning wasn't a complete write-off.

We returned to our desks. Dear Boy's head quivered over the dam wall of rubbish, checking out Peterborough FC's website for the forthcoming season's fixture list. I logged onto Barnsley's site. Little was happening on the board, some tykes clearly having something to do of a Monday. I continued my trawl for information. Various ways of searching had yielded nothing. The tyke crew had reached a dead end, the Cow knew nothing, the *Chronicle* didn't seem interested and even tarn library was dragging its heels. But there had to be details on the whale somewhere. After all, some stories might have been forgotten, but if you look hard enough you'll still find out something. Now (and not for the first time) I employed the most powerful weapon known to man in the hunt for the whale: the Internet.

Anything can be found on the Internet, or so they say. Given a number of key words, a search engine will trawl millions of web sites, dragging out the ones that contain those words somewhere. But things rarely turn out to be as easy as they sound. Various combinations of Barnsley/whale/Yorkshire came up with nothing. The above combination was not only rare – it simply didn't exist. Lots on whales, lots on Yorkshire and quite a few on Barnsley, but put together 'Barnsley' and 'whale' and there was nothing at all. I was becoming increasingly frustrated at stumbling across people having 'a whale of a time' or 'lying around like a beached whale'.

Then, tapping into Alta Vista, something quite remarkable happened. The search engine scurried back with fantastic news. One such site did exist!

My heart pounded. There, among a listing of hundreds of sites on whale migration and history, was one that contained 'Barnsley' and 'whale'.

Not only that . . . it was in the Top Ten!

But on checking again, I couldn't believe my eyes. The site it recommended was www.barnsleyfc.co.uk. Our hundreds of whale-related postings had established Barnsley Football Club on the pages of sea mammal research. Tarn Whale was now 'www': a true worldwide whale. I'd heard of courier companies that promise to send a package to anywhere in the world in 24 hours. So what? The ripples from my pebble had spread over the horizon and now encompassed the globe. The crew had delivered a mythical whale to the whole world! I imagined that from Mombasa to Miami, Bristol to Bombay, wild-haired academics researching the minke or humpback were bewildered to find themselves caught up in heated debate concerning the sale of a First Division striker.

The Internet had brought me full circle, back to tarn. In setting sail to find a whale we'd ended up finding ourselves. We were moving too far, too fast. Perhaps it was time to go back to the very beginning. Back to that exact place we'd seen Tarn Whale.

I rewound the last two days. The ripples contracted and reformed on the pebble: a gaping mouth and a sad eye. Then back . . . further back still . . . to where the very pebble had been formed. Big 'n' Daft recalled a blue whale in the Court House car park – Casper at the level crossing, myself somewhere near Boots. All these places mark the boundary of norman's dream . . .

'I think it wor on show in t'old market place.'

Of course it was. Where else could it have been? But first I will stand aside and let norman take the helm.

The Horsemen

THERE WAS NOTHING A NORMAN LIKED MORE THAN THE thrill of the chase. One particular band of Norman barons would often go crashing through dense Yorkshire woodlands, pursuing deer on horseback for 50 miles to the edge of the Denby Moors. On returning to their imposing stone fortress of Conisburgh one evening, however, they must have been worried men. They were expecting fellow horsemen, galloping up from the south, who intended to stop over at Conisburgh, the control centre and HQ for the new conquerors of England.

If any of the locals thought they were in for a quiet life after the Vikings ran out of steam, they were wide of the mark. It had all looked so good after King Harold went head-to-head with the Nordic King Hardrada, the 'Thunderbolt of the North'. At an epic clash at Stamford Bridge in Yorkshire, King Harold won through. But scarcely had he slipped out of armour and got the beers in than another big fixture demanded his attention on the south coast. With no chance of postponing the match, it all proved too much: Harold fell to an arrow, and the country to the Normans.

When the northbound horsemen arrived at Conisburgh, there would be much feasting on roast venison. But perhaps the evening was a little more restrained than usual; the wine didn't flow quite so freely amid forced smiles and polite conversation, and with good reason. The visiting horsemen were men on a mission, and that was what troubled their hosts. The guests were of a breed not seen in Britain before, men who would one day come to be more feared than even the war axe-wielding berserkers.

Tax collectors!

In one important sense, the Normans differed from previous invaders. They intended to impose order on the country and would make sure the locals paid for it. A few years after the Conquest, accountants and tax collectors were tasked with making a detailed inventory of every single settlement in order that money could be squeezed out of the population. The hunters of Conisburgh weren't under investigation themselves, but they must have been glad to see the backs of their visitors. There was another reason for the barons' rampaging through the forests.

The Normans had much in common with the Vikings – their grandfathers had been rampaging northmen who'd pillaged France, 'norman' being derived from 'northman'. Stag hunting was only one of their pastimes, the other being to kill anyone who opposed Norman rule, looked like opposing Norman rule, or basically 'looked at them in a funny way'. And in Yorkshire many were only too willing to oblige them on all three counts. This would lead to a situation at odds with the basic rule of taxation: there's got to be someone to tax in the first place.

Riding north from the northern HQ, the tax collectors noted the fine wooden hall, still in the hands of its Saxon owners: 'Winterworth'. A few miles further they skirted a wooded valley and scribbled down the details of Wyrc's stronghold: 'Wircsberg'. Up over the north side of the valley they came across Beorn's clearing: 'Berneslai' was entered in the book. But these successes were few and far between, the further north they rode. Time after time they scarcely bothered dismounting before shaking their heads and entering one word into the book: 'Waste'. When their findings were compiled into the Domesday Book, Yorkshire wasn't in the top ten of taxable areas.

In lands north of the Humber, any hint of dissent or uprising met with a swift, brutal response from Norman law-enforcement agencies. You could be punished for chopping a branch or have your eyes gouged out for harming a deer. Saxon and Norse blood boiled at such vicious officialdom. The Norsemen, despite their savagery, had a strong sense of justice: the word 'law' and our '12 good men and true' are handed down from them. The Saxons too had a straightforward approach to justice that could not tolerate the overbearing invaders. Perhaps Kipling put it best in his penning of a dying Norman baron's words to his son:

> The Saxon is not like us Normans. His manners are not so polite. But he never means anything serious until he talks about justice and right. When he stands like an ox in the furrow with his sullen eyes set on your own, and grumbles, 'This isn't fair dealing,' my son leave the Saxon alone.

True or not, these wise words fell on deaf ears. Uprisings and repression were frequent. Five hundred Norman knights were massacred at Durham. In response, the countryside between York and Durham was put to the torch: not a house remained standing. In this Norman fury, even York and its minster were burned. Yorkshire amounted to little more than a wasteland. Tax returns from this part of England would be few and far between for generations to come. The fenlanders too put up a fight, under Hereward the Wake: I can well imagine Dear Boy's ancestors scuttling through the marshes on furtive missions to recover enemy armour.

Perhaps it was the fact that Berneslai was close to Consiburgh that saved it from the ravagings further north. An uprising would be difficult to get under way with the new conquerors' HQ on the doorstep and retribution instant. Perhaps local rule had been negotiated with the Saxons at Winterworth, who, most unusually, had been allowed to retain their lands. Or maybe the families huddled on the banks of Berneslai's River Dearne just decided to sit tight and see how things turned out – 'see all, hear all, say nowt', as we still say in tarn. (The fact that the area survived relatively unscathed probably accounts for the survival of words like 'laikin' and 'siling' as well.)

Whatever the reason, we tykes survived this latest and, as it turned out, last invasion. Life gradually settled down as the Normans managed to get everything organised and taxed: new 'castles' laid foundations for island defences and heavily armoured mobile fighting units – or knights in armour – provided strict law enforcement. Ties with their old country and language dissolved and soon they would become as 'English' as any Norseman.

Over the years, many, many more horsemen would ride into tarn, but even to this day we're just a bit wary of any coming up from the south. You can hardly blame us, can you?

T'old Marketplace

YOU DIDN'T HAVE TO COME TO TARN BY HORSE; YOU COULD take the train. In fact, let's take a look at a tarn-bound train ready to depart from Manchester. One of Pablo's ancestors was probably the driver, setting off to brave the 'backbone of England'. His clanking, snorting goods train was a little out of the ordinary though. Long before anyone had ever thought of steam power, traders had to depend on oat and hay power – pack mules in single file often formed trains up to 50 animals long. Departing Manchester for Barnsley they'd begin with a perilous ascent into swirling, unpredictable Pennine skies. Ahead lay 60 miles of slippery stone causeway snaking over barren peaks and bleak moor.

But on top of weather and terrain there were other dangers out there. Hit-and-run raiders lurked at every bend and bush, ready to pick off the unprotected or unwary. Only a madman or a leper would travel anywhere alone. As a result the wool- and malt-heavy train would welcome other travellers en route: perhaps button or liquorice sellers who, unable to run to a mule, had to leg it; the odd priest spreading the word; a few pilgrims en route to visit their favourite saint (or bits of him); a sword swallower or a chap with a monkey.

Even if it were a fine afternoon in Barnsley, by the time they finally trudged up through Barnsley's Westgate they were probably cold, wet and hungry: it siles down over the Peaks whatever the weather. Peering into the warm, glowing belly of The Old White Bear they probably fancied a sit-down and a bevvy or two, but there'd be no time. Tarn market would be in full swing and that was why they were all there. Passing The Old White Bear, the butchers' stalls or 'shambles' on top of Market Hill would be thudding under carcass, game and flashing cleavers; the butter and fish market would be in full cry as hand-carts and horses jostled with pin-sellers and piemen. Our train would soon disintegrate, absorbed by a babbling market, always hungry for more.

With most settlements numbering no more than a few dozen people, markets were a commercial and social necessity. They were places to buy and sell, to get things done and to sniff out local gossip and news from further afield.

Barnsley became the commercial and social heart for 50 square miles of scattered rural villages and farms, a small community of no more than 150 families. But its position on the crossroads of north–south and trans-Pennine routes turned it into a trading post for travellers from all over the country.

There'd been markets in Barnsley long before the Normans came along, but the Crown and Church demanded some sense of order, for tax-collecting purposes, no doubt. The holy men were of the opinion that trading should be carried out under the watchful eye of the Almighty and marked out existing market places by erecting elaborate carved stone crosses; Barnsley's rough wooden cross (nowt too fancy for us, like) was placed on top of Market Hill. Royal charters were handed out permitting markets and fairs on fixed dates. Barnsley was granted a market day on Wednesdays and a four-day St Michael's fair in October. Many more were to follow: the February fair, pig fairs, the May Horse fair. And when the fairs were on, tarn was *the* place to be!

People flocked from miles around. Roads and tracks were jammed with tailbacks of tarn-bound drovers of the famed longhorn cattle; local farmers herding sheep, swine and chickens; endless packhorse trains and wagons whinnying in. Horsemen fought their way through squawking chicken-jams and honking goose pile-ups to thunder into tarn from as far afield as York and Leeds. Gentlemen from London dispatched urgent envoys tasked with hunting down fine local cheeses and the prized Barnsley Goose Pie. Streets adjoining Market Hill became an explosion of squabbling livestock, bellowing hawkers, dolls, buttons, pins, rat poison, candles, packthread or eels – whatever you were after, Tarn Fair was the place to get it.

At the foot of the hill another kind of traveller was drawn into the revelry. May Day Green was where tykes rolled up for all the fun of the fair. They wanted a laugh, a game, a song, a punch-up or just the chance to gawp at weird and wonderful entertainers. Minstrels, musicians, men with monkeys, jugglers, contortionists, sword-swallowers, performing bears, fortune-tellers, freaks – you name it and tykes laughed at it, were wowed by it, sang along with it or, if the act wasn't up to scratch, thumped it.

This was the way of life in towns up and down the country for hundreds of years. Fairs and markets were the only real chance the man-in-the-field had to live it up a bit. Life may have settled down after the Conquest, but it was still a harsh, uncertain life. Struggling through childhood, avoiding disease, dreading failed harvests, the grim reaper always seemed just around the corner. Not surprisingly, this life-and-death struggle was represented in the sporting action of the day.

Some of the entertainment might seem a little on the harsh side. Queen Elizabeth I made a great impact on tarn when she granted a further fair, St Helen's, which took place on May Day Green. This promised to be the most spectacular of all, an event where tykes were introduced to the queen's favourite spectator sport. They took to it with a passion. If you're squeamish, turn away now.

As a little girl Elizabeth had been very fond of bears. But the cute 'n' cuddly teddy hadn't yet been invented, so the young Queen's enthusiasm lay in bear- and bull-baiting. The bear pits of London caught on all over the country and if it was good enough for the queen's court, it was good enough for tarn. May Day Green was often the site of grisly death. Tethered to an old tree stump, bulls or bears were hideously mutilated by trained dogs. Other gruesome spectacles, including cock fighting, bull-running and whipping donkeys, kept Elizabethan tykes well entertained.

Other affairs of kings and queens meant little to the average tyke, though. From time to time a horseman might come riding by with urgent news. Gathering locals around the hearth of The Old White Bear, he'd thrill them with stories of great deeds, sword-rattling tales of invasion threats, a new world discovered over the oceans – it all seemed as remote as news from the moon. But it wasn't so strange to one man. He wasn't like the rest of us – he was like no other tyke that's lived before or since.

Black Tom

ONE FINE MAY MORNING, AS MOST TYKES GOT READY TO ENJOY the fair, Thomas Wentworth stepped out to the roar of the biggest crowd in the country. London was in carnival mood; many of the 200,000 people there had been queueing for hours. It was rare that the man-in-the-street got to see a living legend such as Tom.

Anyone would admit the boy had done well for himself. The Wentworth family had always been a cut above the rest. Their old hall at Winterworth had witnessed many marriages between well-off lords and ladies, but by Tom's day it had been transformed. An example of cutting-edge modern architecture, Wentworth Woodhouse was now a Renaissance palace. Its landscaped grounds and estates would have turned old Henry VIII green with envy.

Thomas didn't spend as much time there as he'd have liked, for his appointment as Lord Lieutenant of Ireland had landed him with a very, very tricky job. At the King's request he'd reorganised the law courts and the army and navy, increased revenue and crushed any opposition to the rule of the Crown. In fact, if there was any trouble anywhere in the kingdom (and there usually was) Tom fixed it for Charles I. For all this he was handsomely rewarded with titles, estates in Ireland and incredible wealth.

Now there are the rich, the very rich, the unimaginably rich and beyond that there's a category reserved for Thomas Wentworth. His personal fortune, in today's money, stood at, wait for it . . . *six and a half billion pounds.* No, that's not a mistake . . . six and a half billion pounds. Aside from royalty, Thomas Wentworth was the second-wealthiest person ever to have lived in this country. (The wealthiest was the top Norman stag hunter from Conisburgh Castle – he controlled Winterworth and most of Yorkshire and came in at a cool 12 billion.)

The most powerful man in the country, Thomas Wentworth, Lord Lieutenant of Ireland, Baron Raby, Earl of Strafford, Newmarch and Oversley, walked through the riotous crowd with a quiet dignity, raising a hand to acknowledge the tear of an admirer or a hysterical figure snatching at his gown. Some likened him to a great general marching to victory. He walked up Tower Hill with his head held high, as well he might, for it would soon be separated from his body. Tom Wentworth was to be executed for treason. On reaching the platform the man with the axe knelt and begged forgiveness. Wentworth calmly looked him in the eye.

'I forgive you, and all the world.'

Beyond the platform his gaze fell on a sea of grubby pamphlets waved by the crowd, which told of 'Black Tom's' hideous crimes. Rampaging through city streets for days, the mob had threatened the King's wife and children if this filthy traitor were not beheaded. Here and there he picked out a few weeping friends. And no doubt his gaze fell on a few silent men who looked away. For it was they who'd printed the leaflets; they who'd inflamed the mob. These Members of Parliament knew full well Wentworth was innocent. Their real grudge was against the King, but it's difficult to accuse a king of a crime against himself. His right-hand man made an ideal target.

One wild night, months previously, Thomas Wentworth had ridden south from Wentworth Woodhouse with, in his own words, 'more danger beset, I believe, than ever a man went out of Yorkshire'. In the bear-pit of Parliament the hounds ripped and snarled at the great statesman's reputation for week after week. It was clear he had no charge to answer: Wentworth stood tall. In frustration they felled him with an obscure Act of Parliament which allowed them to prove he was guilty . . . simply because they said he was. With the mob trashing the city, there was little the King could do other than sign his best friend's death warrant.

Rather than admit guilt that final morning as his accusers hoped (usual practice before meeting your maker), Wentworth gave impassioned speeches proclaiming his innocence. He knelt in prayer, then brushed aside the blindfold.

'Nay, for I will see it done.'

The mob held its breath as the axe flashed through warm May sunshine. A cry went up and horsemen sped in all directions screaming out news of a traitor's death. Many must have felt a bit ripped off that Wentworth's head never appeared on a spike at Traitors' Gate for them to gawp at, the usual way to round off a good day out at a beheading. The silent men turned a blind eye as Wentworth's supporters spirited the great man's remains on a final journey north to Wentworth Woodhouse. Still, he'd been guilty, without a doubt. New pamphlets, hurriedly issued, told of Wentworth's clear admissions of guilt in his last speech.

Thomas Wentworth has disappeared from the history books. Perhaps silent men prefer some of their work to be erased. But the Wentworths were far from finished. New occupants of the great house and tykes in tarn were to be bound together for all time. Thomas Wentworth's last words to his audience on that final day would echo down the generations to an era of more dark, desperate deeds and horsemen riding north.

'I pray that history judge me by my actions.'

The Storm

> YESSSSSS . . . Bloody computer wouldn't start up
> again for half an hour. Right, let's have it.

BIG 'N' DAFT WAS FIRST, OF COURSE. THE CREW ASSEMBLED on the board in a riot of nervous tension. This was the breakthrough we'd been waiting for. With news of such importance, I sensed I'd have a large audience for my announcement.

All day long the board had been crackling with newcomers and new sightings. Traveltyke reported a rare 'parental sighting' while chronic stand sifted office rumour.

> Reight then. I have had a word with mon papa and he
> said he can remember the whale. He didn't see it 'cos
> he was working 12-hour shifts at the time but he
> remembers there was an advert for it. He seems to
> believe that it was definitely 1968 as my mum was

pregnant with my older sister. He said the skeleton was being taken around the UK so everyone could see it. It was covered in a black tarpaulin to protect it. My mum can't remember it as she was busy nesting! But my dad is a more reliable source for things like this. And it was a BLUE whale. Big buggers them!

What's all this then? Who's this whale we've signed, is he any good? I'll get the top aquatic experts onto it, Jack Custard the office snorkelling boffin reckons he remembers the whale possibly at the Queen's Ground, will quiz him more when he comes up for a breath.

McDog the foul-mouthed hound bounded aboard, full of barking cynicism, to be welcomed by devout whale-believer Knut.

Blue whale, bollax! I'd stop takkin them tablets if I were you. It was a blown-up plastic pike from Kendray! But then again it could have been Arthur Scargill in his youth.

Welcome back mate. What is your opinion on the whale matter?

Seems a little fishy to me mate. I was too young to remember a whale swimming from the Cut into Worbro Res and then swimming up a stream to Locke Park and down Race Common Road to Market Hill. But it did happen! How are you Knut?

Well I believe it! And the whole whale discussion is brilliant.

But as the midnight hour drew close we were to have more than discussion. I had proof. Could there have been a longer day in the whole history of Barnsley? Hours dragged by and still no word from Hazel. I was about to give up when the phone rang. From deep in tarn library, Hazel's words bubbled down the line and as they did so I hurriedly scribbled them down with a blunt pencil, ready to release them to the world. Unexpected news, but surely now this would be good enough to confirm Tarn Whale's existence, good enough for any doubter.

Way down in the depths she'd questioned Maurice. He knew nothing, but his quest for knowledge overcame any doubts. Making enquiries in tarn's deepest, darkest crevices he'd disappeared for days, hence the delay. Now he'd returned with his haul . . .

Beyond my screen the air fairly crackled with uncontainable excitement. I rearranged my hurried notes with anxious hands and prepared to address the crew.

> 'kin hell, Statis. Hurry up mate she's pesterin me to go to bed!

> Come on Statis spill all you know. I'm getting desperate, I've even thought about asking the dragon's mother, the Medusa.

Deaftyke, who by his own admission was now a man on the verge of madness, fell silent. I pressed the key to deliver tarn-shattering news.

Original investigations into back copies of the *Chronicle* that were archived in the library had been swiftly abandoned. Records only went back to '71 (when the new library had been built on the site of The Old White Bear).

Undeterred, Maurice swiftly spread the word far and wide, eventually suceeding in making contact with one Mr Fretwell, Barnsley Market Officer in the '60s and '70s. He confirmed that in the autumn of 1967, eight rows of stalls were removed near the second fish market, between The Old Market Inn and

Wellington Street – in preparation for the arrival of a 30–40-ft whale that was to be exhibited. Once in position, the whale was boarded on three sides and a turnstile erected for the paying public. More than that he could not say, but he did identify an old salt, Harry Brookes, who purported to be an expert on matters relating to Tarn Whale. And there was more.

Hazel also unearthed a fragment from a 1967 copy of *The Times* which told of 40 whales washed up on beaches in northern France (date unknown), some of which were quickly preserved and then exhibited in France and England. It seemed more than likely Tarn Whale was one of these.

I waited for a rousing cheer from the crew. It never came. I peered into a sea of silence. Suddenly there came a lightning strike of tormented postings.

> But Statis I saw it . . . and I wasn't born until August 1967 so it must have been later – is it a case of back to the drawing board or was there more than one whale in tarn?

> This is only what I've got to date. People's memories an' all that . . . me you an' Big 'n' all saw this thing . . .

I tried to reassure Casper but we were being swept up in a deluge of disappointment. There was no word from Big 'n' Daft either . . . why? Casper and I clung to the wreckage of our sanity.

Then it hit me like a thunderbolt – 1967! The year Fretwell identified had blown us apart. I gasped, half-drowning in a tidal wave of realisation.

> Maybe a letter to the letters page via e-mail so we can make this week's issue . . . maybe a multiple e-mail?

> Just did it but m e-mail f.ucked up.

BIG 'n' DAFT! . . . You and Casper were the only ones to back me up so YOU MUST HAVE SEEN IT. NO DOUBT. I AM 1,000 PER CENT WITH YOU ON IT. It couldn't have only been '67 . . .

It's a really early memory possibly the earliest I've got . . . but '67 was too early as I was born in May '66. Sumdi who reads *Chronny* will be able to answer this. I'll e-mail or snail mail tomorrow.

GO FOR IT TEAM! Direct action in the form of an e-mail bombardment to the *Chron* . . .

I just did that but . . .

As Casper tried to steer us back on course and Big 'n' Daft vainly attempted to fire off a message, that's when I knew the hunt would go to its bitter conclusion for I could hear the pain in those messages flashing across the screen. 'But Statis, I saw it . . .' 'It's a really early memory, possibly the earliest I've got . . .'

Any time in the '60s would have been fine by me. I was born in 1958 so it didn't really matter to me when Tarn Whale first appeared; I would have been able to recall it. But to Big 'n' Daft and Casper the date was absolutely crucial. My news of '67 had cost us dear. Even more devastating, if '68 were proved correct, we were dealing with the crew's very first memories: the whale, embedded deep in our subconscious, was part of our very souls. Deep in his torrid cybersea the whale exerted a force that could no longer be resisted. My resolve hardened as out from that dark realm boomed a fearful warning . . .

'We have crossed the shadowline my friend . . . no way back . . . not now . . . to the death Ahab . . . to the death . . .'

I had started this, and what I had started, I . . . *Ahab* . . . would finish.

Ahab

I BECAME BOLDER AS THE DAYS WENT BY; IT ONLY BLACKENED my state of mind. The question 'Do you remember ever seeing a whale on a lorry?' had a startling effect on people. They immediately became motionless. Eyes wide open. Looking above their eyes I could see right into their minds, where a desperate attempt to weld the words 'Barnsley' and 'whale' together would be taking place. Sparks would fly. It was a brief, intense struggle – they really tried. It always ended in failure.

Next the eyes would narrow and they'd examine me from different angles. Sometimes they'd ask for a repeat of the question, as if buying time, while backing away slightly, looking for a door. Then the accusations would start: madness, drinking, joking. It always ended in complete and utter disbelief. Persisting with this line of questioning meant I'd soon found myself alone for the evening, being regarded with wary eye. I could hardly explain further anyway . . .

'Oh, it's not only me, other people saw it as well.'

'Who?'

'Well, I don't know who they are . . . just people, well *names* really, that I talk to . . . well not talk . . . sort of *communicate* with really . . . in fact I don't even know if they're real or not . . .'

Worse, I feared I was messing with other people's sanity. Casper and Big 'n' Daft's torment at the mere thought of having suffered some kind of marine mammal delusion was quite disturbing. What's more, I was setting up my own family as a target for ridicule. While making a phone inquiry about a whale in Barnsley, Hazel met with cackling howls of laughter. Still, in the teeth of these gales of derision, she'd got us further than anyone else had managed.

In my desire to grab onto any lifeline as evidence, I was shipping my sanity overboard at an alarming rate. *The Times* article, if you looked a little closer, was hardly firm evidence. If the French whales were beached in autumn '67, how could they have ended up in tarn almost immediately after? And had we really got the date right? Ever since Franco tyke's early account of an exploding whale we'd become fixated with '68 . . . perhaps it was later . . . but it had to be, if Franco were to be believed . . . but that meant Casper was only around 12 months old when he saw Jonah . . . perhaps Franco had got the date wrong . . . Fretwell *must* have had the wrong date . . . was there more than one whale in tarn? Perhaps oversized sealife was so common in tarn back then that no one remarked on it even to this day – tailbacks of octopuses squiggling in from Manchester, shoals of sharks hanging around outside the Odeon . . . Bring on the men in white coats. I was becoming possessed by the madness of Ahab.

Captain Ahab, the most famous of all whale hunters, was consumed by a raging lust for revenge on the great white whale, a fearsome beast that had chewed his leg off during a previous encounter, leaving him hobbling around on a stump. Sailing out from Nantucket aboard the *Pequod*, he and his international crew circled the globe facing untold danger and adventure before their apocalyptic showdown with the enraged sperm whale. The whale gives its name to Herman Melville's classic story of the sea, *Moby Dick*. When talk turns to whales, it's Ahab's adversary that springs to most people's minds. Some of the crew had dubbed Tarn Whale 'Moby' – the name had crossed my mind too before R Kid harpooned his real name.

If truth be told, I was starting to feel quite a bit of empathy with old Ahab. Melville's narrator in the book, young Ishmael, accused Ahab of monomania: total obsession with one thing. That's a bit harsh, really – it's just a determination to see something through to the end, as I'd explained to Big 'n' Daft when he wavered. Anyway, I wasn't out to kill a whale: I wanted to bring Jonah back from the dead.

In *Moby Dick*, the fictional captain shouts from the *Pequod* at passing whaleships, 'Have ye seen the white whale?' Well, the funny thing is, if I'd shouted back, 'Have yer seen t'blue whale?' old Ahab would have thought it was me that was utterly and completely barking mad.

Leviathan

DURING A WEARISOME VOYAGE LONG, LONG AGO, A SHIP'S crew chanced upon the shores of a fair island, a lush Garden of Eden. Tumbling ashore, the sailors set about feasting, drinking and making merry until a terrible cry came from their captain.

'This is no island but a gigantic whale floating on the bosom of the sea, on whose back the sands have settled and trees have grown since the world was young! When you lit the fire it felt the heat and stirred. Make haste, I say, or soon the whale will plunge into the sea and you will all be lost!'

Since the beginning of time, mankind has held the whale in awe, the above episode from the Arabic *Voyages of Sinbad* being just one reference to living 'whale islands'. Few would actually have seen one though – the first mariners, of course, and holy men on their lonely island outposts. Taking time out from worrying about axe-wielding Norsemen, Abbot Theobaldus contemplated breathtaking shapes out in the swell:

> Greatest of all is the whale, of all the beasts which live
> in the waters. Monster indeed he appears, swimming
> on top of the waves. Looking at him one thinks that
> there in the sea is a mountain. Or an island has formed
> here in the midst of the sea.

At the time of the Abbot's musing the whale was still the subject of mythology and folklore in almost every culture. The ancient Chinese believed a huge dragon, Yu-kiang, to be ruler of the seas. When angered, he would rise to the surface, transform into a bird and whip up terrible storms. This fearsome creature had the hands and feet of a human being, but the body of a whale several thousand *li* long. Islamic texts tell of a whale that was believed to support the whole world. Icelandic tales speak of 'horse whales' and 'boar whales'. The male narwhal was widely believed by mariners to be the mythical unicorn. Inuit mythology, Canadian Tlingit Indian stories and African legend all contain revered references to the mighty fish.

It is from a biblical story that Tarn Whale took his name. It tells of the people of Nineveh, who were living it up by engaging in the kind of practices that would make a late-night reality porno series on cable nowadays. God was obviously a little concerned about this and instructed Jonah to warn them to get back on the straight and narrow. Jonah, fearing these Assyrian pervies, felt he wasn't up to the job and fled to Joppa to stow away on a boat bound for Tarhish. God rumbled him, of course, and sent down a terrific storm. The reluctant prophet knew his number was up and the crew gladly let Jonah throw himself overboard. With death at hand Jonah called to the Lord for mercy and God saved him by sending a great fish to swallow him whole. Three days in the whale's belly gave Jonah plenty of time to think about his attitude problem and on being vomited back on dry land, he followed the word of the Lord without question.

It's clear God also invested the whale with power to strike fear into the hearts and minds of mere mortals. The Scriptures tell of the stupendous Leviathan, created on the fifth day. This monstrous whale is the embodiment of unmitigated power, a symbol of the evil that's the focal point of all human fear, and a terrible warning to all mankind.

Standing on shores all over the world, men have looked on the whale and marvelled at unfortunate specimens that drifted onto beaches. But capturing them? The Basques were the first to have a bash. While St Cuthbert was still a boy, lookouts on stone towers peered out to sea for whales that were foundering near the coast. The lookouts then directed flimsy crafts packed with fanatics, eccentrics and dare-devils into the Bay of Biscay. These were epic struggles: if their harpoon didn't strike the right spot the whale was capable of smashing the boat with a swipe of its tail or dragging them to the depths to drown.

Whales weren't the only monsters out there. Stormtroopers in landing craft livened things up even as far south as Spain. The canny Basques (well, those that didn't end up with an axe in the head) appreciated the virtue of Norwegian technology and with stronger, faster boats later ventured further into the bay.

Melville leaves us with the best account of those who sailed in search of whales. Although Nantucket was only a tiny island off the coast of America, its whalemen were masters of their craft. While we tykes were still baiting bears, they'd exhausted the ready supply of marine mammals off their own shores. Further and further they sailed in pursuit of the prized sperm whale. A whaling trip could last up to three years and such voyages were perilous in the extreme. Launching rowing boats from three-masted ships, the Nantucketers may have been masters of the chase and kill, but a handful of men in an open boat could easily be disposed of with the flick of a tail.

Whalers set sail from ports all over the world, venturing into uncharted oceans. Some said farewell and never returned. William Scoresby, a Whitby captain, described the Arctic as 'a desolate inclement region where the sea was crowded with new and strange horrors'. After years at sea, battered by the elements and always aware of nameless shapes lurking beneath the hull, it's easy to see how sailors' fears were expressed in etchings of fantastical sea creatures. Not all the horror was imagined either. Melville's *Moby Dick* may be fiction, but it's based on a true incident.

The whaleboat *Essex* set sail from Nantucket and never

returned. Many months later a French whaler happened across an open boat; coming alongside they found the remnants of the *Essex*'s crew dementedly chewing on the bones of their dead companions. First mate Owen Chase and cabin-boy Thomas Nickerson later told how the *Essex* had been rammed and sunk by a furious sperm whale. Adrift in small boats, the survivors resorted to murder and cannibalism in order to survive.

Over the years, a vast pool of knowledge accumulated about the whale, with stories swapped and fact sifted from fiction. The great mammals were placed in categories. The 'right whale' gained its unfortunate name as it was considered the right whale to kill; the mighty sperm whale from the abundance of sperm oil that could be extracted from its body.

In *Moby Dick*, Ishmael gives an account of current cetological opinions. Curiously for the great 'Is it a fish or a mammal?' debate that raged for years, he states a firm conviction: 'I take the good old-fashioned ground that the whale is a fish, and call upon holy Jonah to back me.' Whether Melville himself took that view I'm not sure. Ishmael's words could well be a sly dig at pious Nantucket society. A God-fearing people, slaughtering such magnificent animals might not fit too well with their religious beliefs: if the whalers continued to believe the whale to be a fish, they could pray a little easier in church. Ishmael's classification includes names we'd recognise today: finback, humpback, sperm, narwhal and others too numerous to mention here. And he ends up with the whales that still swam on the fringes of a Nantucketer's wisdom, those glimpsed at a distance, where fact, fiction and a storm-battered imagination fused to give birth to mythological sea creatures.

> A rabble of uncertain, fugitive, half-fabulous whales, which, as an American whaleman, I know by reputation . . . the Bottle-Nose Whale, the Junk Whale,

the Pudding-Headed Whale, the Cape Whale, the
Scragg Whale, the Coppered Whale, the Elephant
Whale, the Iceberg Whale, the Quog Whale, the Blue
Whale.

Only 150 years ago, Ahab and his creator couldn't be sure if the
blue whale existed or not. I was beginning to know what that felt
like.

Big Blue

MELVILLE AND AHAB MAY WELL HAVE SEEN A BLUE WHALE
break the surface or witnessed its tremendous blow from afar, an
immense 30-ft column of thundering spray, the highest,
strongest blow of all whales. But if any Nantucketer had decided
to give chase, they wouldn't have got close enough as the blue
whale is simply too fast. But it's not speed that sets the blue
whale apart from all others.

Had Melville ever come close enough to observe one, he'd
marvel at it in the same way we do today. The blue whale is quite
simply the largest creature to have lived on this planet – ever.
Most people are fascinated by dinosaurs, but not even the largest
could match a blue whale for size. A fully grown male will
measure anything between 65 ft and 101 ft, while the larger
female has been recorded at 110 ft. Diplodocus might have
come close, but its snake-like tail and long neck accounted for
about half its length – nothing can match a blue whale for sheer
bulk. Barnum may have trumpeted the mighty Jumbo as 'the
largest living quadruped on earth', but in the size stakes, next to
a blue whale he'd come nowhere. A blue whale's tongue weighs
as much as an elephant; its heart is the size of a Mini Cooper.

A newborn blue measures almost 20 ft and is already as heavy as an Indian elephant. It grows at an amazing rate, doubling its weight in just four weeks, something a human baby takes 17 weeks to do. Hardly surprising, as it packs away 50 gallons of milk a day (that's the equivalent of a whole milk float!) to put on 200 lb in weight each day. That's a staggering 8 lb every hour! When fully weaned at eight months, our calf is close to 50 ft long and weighs in at 50,000 lb. Now feasting on krill (creatures no larger than your little finger), it will swallow 4 tons of these shrimp-like creatures daily.

But other than comparisons of size, even today there's very little about the blue whale of which even the wisest, longest-bearded academics can be sure. It's believed that like other whales it circumnavigates the globe from polar feeding grounds to tropical breeding waters. Recent reseach into its underwater calling suggests that individual blues can communicate over hundreds of miles and that different pods, say in Antarctic or Pacific waters, have different regional 'accents'.

It's an elusive creature, to say the least. In fact, apart from appreciating the size of the blue, we're little better off than those old Nantucketers, for not even the experts are sure exactly what the whale looks like. No one's got close enough to make accurate drawings or models. The 110-ft model hanging in the Natural History Museum in London is utterly awe-inspiring due to its size and well worth a look, but it's a crude representation that dates back to the 1930s. The Smithsonian Institute has another model blue whale towering over the diminutive Jumbo: that's also pooh-poohed by the experts.

But I knew I'd come close to a blue whale once upon a time, and besides Big 'n' Daft, Casper and norman, there must have been others. The only problem was finding them.

Now I am no man of the sea. I doubt the River Dearne in tarn has supported anything more than a stickleback for many years. And although I can claim to have captained a ship, I hardly think a pedalo on Cleethorpes' seafront promenade, with only R Kid as my bawling crew, qualifies me for a task of this size. I needed to find some *real* men of the sea. And I knew just where to look. I'd heard tell of a terrible battle there, deep in the belly of a White Elephant, and whisperings of many strange creatures from oceans dark. Surely these men would know something?

I set sail south to an English Channel shining calm as a millpond. Shielding my eyes from the sun, a small boat glinted on the shore. I hailed her and drew alongside the *Sussex Maid*.

Catcher in the Sea

GROANING BUCKET IN HAND, THE LITTLE BOY RAN A BREATHLESS, pattering path along a crowded promenade. As the bucket became heavier and heavier, water slopped and slapped a zigzag trail in his wake. It was a long way from the East Pier, but he had to make it; he just *had* to. He had to reach The White Elephant just beyond the West Pier. It was feeding time and The White Elephant had an insatiable appetite. Marine delicacies were its favourite, the weirder and more bizarre the better. What's more, it paid handsomely for such tit-bits.

As the fisherman's young son tottered towards the pier, his load grew too much for his trembling grip. The occupant of the bucket, none too impressed with his jolting prison and reluctant to end his days in The Elephant's belly, sensed his chance. Slithering onto the pavement he determined to make a break for it.

A sea monster!

The cry went up and the crowd scattered before this slimy, wriggling horror bounding along the promenade.

Sam chuckled at the memory.

'It was only an octopus. I just picked him up by the head . . . 'cause that's the only place you can pick 'em up . . . and plopped 'im back in the bucket. You got a lot of money for an octopus, 2/6.'

We stared out to the milky band where sea shaded into sky. Diver Sam, Paul, John and me, sitting under the *Sussex Maid*'s varnished hull, drinking tea, eating custard creams and telling tales of the sea. Sam cast his memory wide out into the Channel once more, filtering 70 years of life at sea for any clue. Back to days when mackerel and herring fleets sailed, manned by bowler-hatted fishermen in long leather boots.

Ah, the fruits of the sea. One minute they're swimming around as extras in a deep-sea documentary, then before you know it they're oiling themselves up in vinaigrette or donning filo pastry jackets while cuddling up to Delia Smith and Ainsley Harriot as star fish in some cookery challenge or other.

'See your little nipper's done well fir 'imself.'

'Ooohh yes . . . Rosti crab cake! Looked lovely on telly 'e did . . . flat-leaf parsley an' toasted sweetcorn salsa . . .'

But, like young Sam's octopus, they're not really that keen to get caught. The old fisherman rolled up his greasy blue sleeve to show the scars – among the shiny herring hauled aboard are those who fight back at every opportunity. A spider crab can grow to the size of a dinner plate – and that's just the body, remember. The legs and claws flail far beyond that. Caught in a net (that a man can't tear apart with his bare hands), this crustacean will make short work of slashing it to pieces in minutes. And then there's the feisty French crab. On finding himself hauled aboard a boat, he generally vents his fury on the nearest crew member. Quite what Diver Sam makes of celeb chefs enthusing about 'wiggling the tongue delightfully in a crab claw' I don't know.

Then, no sooner have you caught one thing than something else comes by and decides to eat it. Full lobster pots are handy drift-through restaurants for a lucky octopus. A lobster might seem armour-plated against all kinds of attack, but an octopus can literally tear their shells apart with incredibly powerful suckers. I really can't see myself picking one up by the head and plopping it back in a bucket.

Next there are sharks, which can get caught up in a net and cause all kinds of problems – like sinking the boat and drowning everyone. Now they really can fight back. Diver Sam recalled one he tangled with. He couldn't identify what type of shark it was, but he reckoned it was about 30 ft long and, as that was also the length of his boat, it was all he needed to know at the time. The huge fish thrashed against the hull in a frenzy. The crew had to be quick: a shark's razor-sharp tail can inflict fatal injuries. It was kill or be killed. Somehow they managed to secure a rope around its tail and haul it backwards. With waterlogged gills it eventually drowned.

Yes, out on the frontline-shoreline it takes more than a sabatier and hollandaise sauce to deal with sealife. I reckon someone ought to invite Sam onto one of those celeb chef challenges.

'So what have you brought for us, Sam? A French crab? Snappy little fellow, isn't he? A lobster, *very* fresh . . . and in the bucket . . . is that . . . is that . . . an *octopus?*'

It would certainly liven things up a bit, although you'd probably need *Animal Hospital* and a crack medical team on standby to treat any survivors.

When we turned to whales, Sam shook his head. Shoals of dolphins and marauding sharks, yes, but there'd never been whales in these waters, or on land. Even the great battle in The White Elephant he knew nothing about.

Perhaps it was time to take a look myself. Retracing young Sam's steps along the promenade I chanced upon some sealife of my own. The cod offered little resistance, having already taken a severe battering, so I finished it off with chips and mushy peas before striding straight into The White Elephant.

Big Skate on a Truck

CONSTABLE HATED THE PLACE. TURNER DIDN'T SEEM TO MIND it though, whipping off a few sketches for his *Picturesque Sea Views of the South Coast*. But this small coastal town on the south coast just didn't do it for the hero of *The Haywain*. It was a fishing community like no other. The weather-beaten Hartlepool fisherman would certainly have been amazed at Constable's contemptuous description: 'Piccadilly by the sea, or worse . . . ladies dressed, undressed; gentlemen in morning gowns and slippers.'

The playboy Prince Regent George IV led the way with his onion-domed, candy-coated Royal Pavilion. Suddenly Brighton was the place to be. Courtiers, flunkies and high society fled London and decamped to the coast. For the next 100 years poor fishermen and parading fops lived cheek by jowl.

By the middle of the century bowler-hatted fishermen had to navigate their passage through a living reef of 150 pleasure boats packed with revellers, booming brass bands and orchestras. Brighton's seafront became a fusion of fishing and festivity. Fishermen became boatmen themselves, showmen of the sea, and the water a funfair. Fred Collins became the most celebrated of these skippers. His boat, the *Skylark*, was given rave reviews in the fashionable London press. As the cry of 'All aboard the *Skylark!*' went up, candy-striped blazers and giggling parasols pushed and jostled to do just that. Like Barnum, Collins knew when he was onto a moneyspinner, so he swiftly launched *Skylarks II, III, IV, V* and *VI*.

The visitors found strange creatures from the sea truly fascinating as well, though one creature choosing to drop another from a bucket at one's feet was simply going too far. By Queen Victoria's time a far more civilised way of becoming acquainted with the ocean depths had been devised. As land creatures were taking to the sea, so sea creatures were invited to up sticks and take up residence ashore.

Anybody who was anybody turned up for the opening ceremony. The band of the 19th Hussars played as the Lord Mayor of London, Sheriff of London, Lord Mayor of Brighton and Burmese ambassadors headed a procession of several hundred. Napoleon III, having by now given up on trying to conquer Europe, was welcomed with open arms. Nothing like this had ever been seen before. All agreed it was truly the wonder of Europe, an embodiment of the Victorian thirst for novelty, knowledge and exploration. Walter Rothschild may have been taking care of the internal exploration of new animals, but the experience always left them a tad on the immobile side. No such problem in Brighton: a quick nudge out of the sea into a tank and everyone could examine dwellers of the deep in their natural habitat.

The dignitaries wandered through another world, with wide subterranean promenades lined by columns carved with ornate shells, fish and birds and decked with flowers, ferns and shrubs. Silver starlights twinkled above their heads. And the tanks! At 60 ft long, the largest held 110,000 gallons. All around them sea monsters swirled, snapped, pulsated and gaped. It was as if the very seas had parted. They meandered along the ocean bed, spellbound submariners in great Neptune's fairyland.

Octopuses, dogfish, lobsters, sharks and rays obviously enjoyed their new home, as they carried on in much the same way as they had in their natural habitat, by devouring each other at frequent intervals. The original octopus, suspecting all might not be well, built itself a fortress of living oysters, but in an unguarded moment wandered out and was snapped up by a spotted dogfish. Another suffered the indignity of being attacked by its own food: visitors were enthralled by a gruesome tug of war as 20 hermit crabs took hold of the unfortunate cuttlefish's legs and ripped him to shreds.

The weird specimens tangled up in Channel fishermen's nets meant there was no shortage of attractions to marvel at. An 8-ft royal sturgeon sailed majestically in, far from its native Russian waters. The gruesome, slob-like fiddle fish slouched ashore, intent on eating anybody he was housed with. Sometimes crowds along the seafront heralded a new arrival. 'Venus', a 6-ft giant skate transported on a handcart, was queen of a great procession as she made her way to the largest tank.

At first fashionable loungers took delight in the Palm Court, skating rink and string quartets. It had a grand atmosphere, 'redolent of fishes, flirtation and ices', one eminent visitor commented. In the end it wasn't enough; dandies soon tired as the novelty wore off. The aquarium simply couldn't survive on the patronage of piscatorial enthusiasts such as Mr W.F. Booth, who spent much time pondering why mackerel only swam around their rock in a clockwise direction. Instead of attracting worldwide acclaim, Brighton soon found itself lumbered with an expensive and increasingly shabby white elephant.

As the twentieth century went on, the railways made it possible for greater numbers of people to journey to the coast. The old white elephant refused to die and conjured up increasingly bizarre attractions to tempt newcomers. Giants and midgets were paraded for amusement. Zulu chieftains waved spears, chanting fearsome war cries; Japanese temple dancers bowed and curtsied. Animals became more exotic: alligators, sea lions, the endangered manatee, birds and chimps who were, of course, encouraged to attend tea parties. Who knows, perhaps the Wakefield Dolphins first leapt from the old Elephant's Dolphinarium in the '70s?

Now, as I stood in his belly beneath stone-carved fish, he'd come full circle: an aquarium where you can walk on the sea bed through monsters of the deep. And there's still a reminder of the Battle of Brighton that, incredibly, Sam knew nothing about.

Never in the field of crustacean conflict was so much death

wrought on so many, to be witnessed by so few. In 1930, two armies of sand crabs faced each other like warlords of old – 1,300 armoured Norman knights claw to claw. The fighting was brief but terrible. When it ceased, the battlefield was strewn with broken bodies, dismembered legs and claws: 400 warriors of the sea lay dead. No one knows why the fighting suddenly stopped and everyone settled to a more peaceful life, but then no one knows how big the respective armies were. It may well have been a massacre, with 900 outnumbering a valiant 400 who fought to the last crab. Just another unsolved mystery of the sea, I suppose.

By late afternoon the boat came in: two fishermen lugged wicker baskets of angry, snapping crabs under the arches and handed Paul a battered, but eagerly received, copy of *Heroes of the Goodwin Sands*.

All in all, a pleasant afternoon. I bade Sam, Paul and John farewell and they promised to put the word out along the coast for any sightings of the whale. I must have looked a little disappointed that I'd found nothing. John tried to cheer me up with a final custard cream and confided that he was pretty sure that somewhere he'd got a manual giving precise details of how (if I had a naval tanker) I could refuel a NATO battlefleet while at sea. Would that be of any use?

I kicked along the pebbly beach where the *Skylark* once swooped beside the *Sussex Maid*. Lilting barrel organs rolled out from the pier as fairy lights flickered on. A carousel of gaily painted, snorting horses galloped in rolling circles above the sparkling sea. The Pavilion's onion-domes glowed creamy pink in early dusk. This was the borderland: a place that is neither land nor sea. Where creatures of the land took to the sea, sea-creatures took to land, fishermen became entertainers, and a prince baked a 'Hindu-Chinese-Gothic' wedding cake with exotic ingredients from the Empire.

That was a time of strange fusions. Up in Hartlepool fishermen would welcome shipbuilders; in tarn, billionaires would work alongside men wearing flowers in their hair.

Style Challenge

ALL FRILLY CUFFS, BLACK FLOWING MANE AND MINCING WALK, there he went, hand on hip, squealing in delight over a bit of chintz. No, not Lawrence Llewellyn Bowen, but very, very close. This was Horace Walpole and even their mothers wouldn't have noticed the difference.

Horace was a regular visitor to Wentworth Woodhouse. As the self-appointed style guru of his day, he simply *had* to be there, darling. If your fine estate or grand house received twittering praise from Horace and his Committee of Taste, you were in with the in-crowd. If he looked down his nose, forget it. And it was a tough job too: he whined in a letter that he'd been invited to one fine house at Gunnersbury twice a week for ten years; each time he had to pick a brand-new outfit. The strain must have been intolerable.

Horace visited the Wentworths many times, as passing judgement there was a big job, mainly due to events after old Tom's death. His son unfortunately died without an heir, so the title and lands passed to men from two separate branches of the family. Both of them were named 'Thomas Wentworth'. What followed is still a source of confusion around tarn to this day, so please pay attention.

The lands, house and money passed to Thomas Watson-Wentworth, the title Lord Raby to the other Thomas Wentworth. A nice title, but understandably the latter Wentworth was more than a bit cheesed off at not receiving the billions. He wasn't short of a bob or two though, and came up with a cunning plan. He purchased the equally extensive estate of Stainborough. All well and good, except Stainborough, on the south side of the Worborough valley, was slap bang next door to the Wentworth Woodhouse estate. The 'new' Lord Raby decided that here he would build a house far superior to Wentworth Woodhouse, only six miles away. The new Stainborough house was renamed 'Wentworth Castle' despite the fact that it wasn't in Wentworth and wasn't a castle. To cap it all (and confuse locals for generations) he did build Stainborough Castle just over the hill. Although this looked like a castle, it was actually a folly; a crazed attempt to persuade everyone the family had lived there for hundreds of years.

The Watson-Wentworths, after taking some time to figure out this whirlwind of renaming, took up the challenge and so began almost 100 years of intense rivalry. Each family undertook a furious 'estate makeover'. Besides grand houses, landscaped gardens and rolling wood and parklands, each erected countless hillside follies to produce two of the most spectacular estates in the land. In addition, each family sought new and ever-more impressive titles in an attempt to outdo each other.

But who would win? By the time of judging there was no dispute on the title front. Charles Wentworth, at Wentworth Woodhouse, had many titles and honours, but the clincher was 'Marquis of Rockingham'. This put him way ahead of William Wentworth, who came second with 'Lord Strafford'. All well and good, but only Horace could decide on the crucial style challenge.

Horace flounced along the façade of Wentworth Woodhouse, making notes . . .

'Great hall with noble pillars of yellow Scagliola *but . . .*'

A good start, but Horace was a teensy bit upset by the nasty workmen around. The Marquis always seemed to have the builders in. When he stepped inside things just got worse.

'. . . not yet finished, nor any part of the great apartment; nor is there any taste in the house . . .'

His sensibilities offended by all the banging and hammering, Horace brushed dust from his frilly cuffs and gave the house a thumbs-down. Could the parklands turn the voting around?

'A nine-pin bowling alley,' he sneered bitchily at a vista dotted with obelisks and follies, then pranced off to the Worborough valley. Would Lord Strafford fare any better? Horace was obviously a hard man to please.

'Wentworth Castle in Yorkshire! I had been there before, but had not seen the new front . . . nothing ever came up to the beauty of it. The grace, proportion, lightness and magnificence of it are exquisite. Nobody has better taste than this lord.'

You can almost hear Horace squealing in delight. Outside he fairly gambolled through herds of picturesque deer.

'. . . such a variety of ground, of wood and water; and almost all executed and disposed with so much taste by the present Earl.'

No contest.

Far be it from me to question a man of such impeccable taste as Horace Walpole, but it all sounds a bit dodgy. Lord Strafford had many other properties, one of them in Twickenham, which meant he was Walpole's next-door neighbour. Lord Strafford, a committed Tory (like Walpole) also found himself on the backbenches of Parliament as the Whigs became more prominent. The Marquis – surprise, surprise – was a leading Whig, rising to the office of Prime Minister on two occasions.

Horace also sniffily observed that the Marquis seemed far more interested in his horses, concentrating mainly on the completion of his stables, rather than on finer points of interior design. It's true that Wentworth Woodhouse took a long time to complete, but there was a reason for that, though Horace never mentioned it. The Marquis oversaw the completion of the biggest private house Britain has ever seen. Forget Winston Churchill's Blenheim Palace, or the brooding Castle Howard where *Brideshead Revisited* was filmed – at 606 ft Wentworth Woodhouse has the longest façade in the land. The Marquis's stable block alone is beyond compare. Designed to incorporate a riding school, it housed almost 100 of his beloved horses.

Horace must have been well pleased with his work, though both great houses, he may have reflected, were a little dated. Neither represented the very latest fashion, a style he, of course, was pioneering. His Committee of Taste raved about their experimental Gothic style, which basically comprised of ripping medieval illustrations out of old books and copying them. His ideas for the future found favour with fashionable society well into the Victorian age; even as he passed judgement in Yorkshire, plans were being drawn up for the Hindu-Chinese-Gothic palace in Brighton. Had he lived to see it finished he would have fainted with delight.

As the style challenge came to an end, the snubbed Marquis sensed that change was coming. Horace's twitterings would become an irrelevance. Rockingham's rough mental sketches were the first plans for a new landscape that would emerge in only a few years' time. Admiring idyllic park and woodland, the style guru failed to notice one feature that had already been noted by the country's first travel writer. Daniel Defoe wrote *A Tour through the Whole Island of Britain* after doing just that. Heading through the Worsborough valley towards Barnsley, his keen eye noted that the rising moorland to the south and west of tarn had 'a black hue or colour'. Horace turned back to ponder façades and pilasters, little guessing that the future lay beneath his feet.

The Grapevine

IF YOU'RE GOING TO PLAY A FOOTBALL MATCH YOU'RE NOT going to do it on a hill, are you? Not when a market's in full swing anyway. Only a tyke would be mad enough to try that.

Long before anybody had even dreamt of a football league – let alone a bulletin board – the forefathers of Big 'n' Daft, Casper and norman joined a throng of tykes leathering a ball up and down Barnsley's Market Hill. Undeterred by cries from the butter market and fish stalls on Broadgate, countless footballers rampaged from the Market Hill at the top before tumbling into Sough Dyke.

Irate traders had no option but to shut up shop as crowds flooded down onto May Day Green. Here other stallholders were bellowing for attention among performing bears, monkeys and an improvised wrestling match which was going on around the maypole, organised by a team of lads dressed all in white with buttercup and daisy chains wrapped around their heads.

In fact things were kicking off all over tarn as Horace finished his deliberations just over the valley at Wentworth. The inns seemed more crowded than ever, despite the fact a new one seemed to open every other day. The packhorse trains and wagons rumbled in as they'd always done, but one particular traveller on a tarn stopover at the Royal Hotel, en route to York, must have prised locals away from the hearth.

Stagecoaches weren't uncommon in those days, but his vehicle drew admiring whistles. Now this lad could *really* move; talk about horsepower! The coachman claimed that if they really got their hooves down, they literally *flew* between London and Manchester in a blistering four days rather than the usual seven and a half. Budding tarn engineers bent down for a closer look as the coachman pointed out the high-tech 'hoof-injection' system: state-of-the-art spring suspension smoothing out all those ruts, you see.

It seemed unbelievable, yet so much of the talk around tarn these days was. Someone had heard from a Midlands mule-train driver that somewhere down there, a bloke called Telford had built the strongest bridge in the whole world, not of wood or stone, but iron. Surely that would be too heavy . . . why didn't it fall down? Then up north, a man called Stephenson was experimenting with this new-fangled steam power in an attempt to . . . get this . . . make a machine pull people around on rails!

All this change wasn't remote; there was a definite buzz about Barnsley. Word went round the market and inns – on very good authority – that soon there would be a new way of getting in and out of tarn. A new system of canals widening the Dove and Dearne was to be built, south through the Wentworth estate and north as far as Wakefield. What could that mean? In the future, would there be no more packhorses or coaches or roads? Would everyone travel by water? Could the canals be linked to the new ironworks his lordship was rumoured to be considering? Seemed obvious really. If this 'iron bridge thing' caught on and there was iron under Tankersley Deer Park, then his lordship would be straight on the case, make a bob or two out of that . . . as if he needed to. Mind you, these canals could be used for other stuff. There'd been a rumour in t'owld White Bear only last week . . . mind you, it was late and they'd had a few . . . that it were all part of a plan for all England. They'd met a bloke who said his brother overheard that t'Frenchies were getting all stirred up with some mad bloke, Neapolitan or summat, and he was going to take over the whole world. Defence it was . . . these new canals were to transport the militia darn sarth reight quick if the Frenchies looked like invading . . . Ah, yes, well up at t'big house they'd know all about that.

Then again, in peacetime, canals would get more stuff to markets further away and cheaper an' all. Some said that wire-making over at Thurgoland was really going to take off because of it and the nail-mekkin' and glass-mekkin' too, coal an' all, though most knew that won't come to much – sinking these new shafts is a bad job, some of t'lads say pumpin' engines aren't up to it. Fills wi' water next day. Nivver mek it pay . . . that's why most have gid it up as a bad job . . . muck but no brass. Best to just keep tekkin' it from the top, up on tarn moor, way they've allus done.

Most likely it would be all t'newcomers from t'new cottages on south edge of tarn that would be using the canals, weavers flogging off their fancy linen. Aye, there's a bob or two to be made in that.

Mind you, most agreed the waterways could only be a good thing, what with the state of the roads these days. Shocking! Packed solid wi' trains and not just on fair days either. Sed took best part of a morning driving his geese in from Hay Green last week.

The taproom buzz of progress: rumour, speculation and half-heard fact. Things were changing, that much was certain, but the only things anyone could be sure of were the things they could actually see. Some said there were over 3,000 people in tarn now, and you could believe that – the evidence was in front of your eyes. The fact that there were enough tykes to organise a footy match was a sign of how Barnsley had grown and was still growing. Market Hill was now so packed on market days that you literally couldn't move. Some stallholders were forced to spill over Sough Dyke, decamping on May Day Green in order to ease the crush.

Out on May Day Green the wrestling match was over. Brawny men in white lounged around, repairing torn primrose and lilac garlands while wolf-whistling at and generally bothering the milkmaids. Strange men these, kept themselves to themselves. Try talking to them and all you got was weird stories: whistling birds of doom, lucky flowering beans, shining fairies and, above all, terrifying demons they fought against in some new world that one day they'd be masters of. Aye lad, aye – whatever you say.

Funny lads them miners, not that they'd ever come to owt.

Oh Ye of Little Faith

There's a great northern town they call Barnsley
That's noted for fresh air and fun
Where Mr and Mrs George Ramsden
Went with Airtyke their son.

A fine little lad was young Airtyke
All dressed in his best, quite a swell
With a stick wi' a Toby Tyke handle
The finest that Woolies could sell.

They dint think much to the market
Stalls were all fiddlin' an' small
There were no bargains an' nubdi being hung
In fact nothin' to laugh at at all.

So seeking for further amusement
They wandered up May Day Green
And there on the fish stall were a bloody great whale
The biggest that Barnsley had seen.

The old whale went by the name 'Findus'
He was old, full of blubber and flab
He lay in a somnolent posture
With the side of his face on the slab.

Now Airtyke had heard all abart whales
Of how they's ferocious and wild
And to see Findus lyin' so peaceful
Well it dint seem right to the child.

~ The Whale Hunt ~

So straight way the brave little fella
Not showing a morsel of fear
Took his stick wi' its Toby Tyke handle
And stuffed it up Findus's rear.

Now Findus jumped up in surprise like
And giving a kind of a roll
He opened his mouth as wide as owt
And swallowed the little chap whole.

Mr Ramsden had seen the occurrence
And not knowing what to do next
Said 'MOTHER! Yon whale's just et Airtyke'
And Ma said 'Eeeee well I'm vexed.'

The stallholder Mitchell was sent for
He came and he said 'What's t'do?'
Said Mother 'Yon whale's just et Airtyke!
'And him in his Sunday best too!!'

Mitchell pondered a bit 'fore he spoke like
And called it a simple mishap
'How d'you KNOW Findus scoffed Airtyke?'
'How do we know?' shouted Dad, 'There's his cap!'

The Mayor turned up next in regalia
And said with a whine and a moan
That Ma looked dead rieght 'an healthy like
And should get more sons of her own.

At that Ma got proper blazin'
'And thank you sir kindly' said she
'What and spend all our time raising children
'To feed bloody whales – NOT ME!'

Don't think for a minute that the whale hunt had fallen apart – that I'd deserted the crew on the cybersea, or that they'd drifted off to other matters. E.I. Addio's magnificent rendition of 'Airtyke and the Whale' proved that curiosity was far from spent. Even if he didn't know it, Addio's reworking of 'Albert and the Lion' (a monologue I remember from a dim and distant past) meant he was treading firmly in the footsteps of the great Ned Corvan. Could this poem signal we were on the brink of creating a legend that would rival the old monkey?

In fact, looking at the waves of new postings, the board was evolving into a virtual version of Barnsley on a market day. Jostling around the strolling minstrel Addio, new tykes were drawn into the babble of whale speculation, each trying to out-shout the rest in order to get their two'pennorth in. Above it all howled McDog. As barking as ever, he growled out a warning that all may not be as it seemed, although I was getting pretty used to that idea by now.

> Whale story is not true! I have contacted the *Chronicle* and they have no records of this happening. They do have a clip from 1968 of a big fat bloke lying totally naked on top of a trailer on Market Hill. Could that have been the fat whale?
>
> Remember how these stories start. Old man to young grandson: 'I was in town the other day when I saw a fat bloke as big as a whale totally naked.'
>
> Grandson to best mate's mother: 'Mi granddad and I woz in t'tarn when I saw this big fat naked whale that looked like a bloke on Wellington Street.'
>
> Mother to husband: 'Jim's granddad and his mother-in-law's great-auntie saw a big whale on Market Hill last week, must have been 4 metres long.'
>
> Husband at the pub: 'Missus says there was a massive whale on Market Hill yesterday, 15–20 metres long and it needed 3 lorries to carry it! There

> were crowds there and it really stank. It was still livin'
> when it got into the town centre but died from coal-
> dust poisoning shortly after.' Nuff said!!

After the storm, our fortunes had changed. Fresh recruits rolled in on a new wave of optimism and immediately picked up the hunt – hardly surprising as there was no other topic of debate on the board. Wind filled our sails; above us the red flag was flying high. Our vessel cut purposefully through a crystal-clear sea of certainty, dotted with islands of optimism. Exiled red proclaimed his faith and a mysterious tyke, revealing himself only as 'Jonah', gave further clues.

> I saw it. I reckon it was around '68–'69. It looked like
> the circus had arrived and it stood in the old market.
> It may have had a skeleton inside but it looked like it
> was real. It had some kind of a skin on it. I never saw
> it advertised but I passed it going into t'tarn having
> come off a bus from Wombwell. It was on a low
> loader. It was there.

> Oh ye of little faith . . . read on. It was there.
> Remember the days when the fair came to town and
> took over the site of the whole market? When a go
> on the Cocks and Hens was a tanner but you'd
> already promised your mum you wouldn't stand up
> so you had a go with the air rifles instead? That
> bloody Octopus thing that always made you feel
> sick? The whale was brought to advertise the fair
> coming one year. Could have been '68. That was the
> year the dodgems were constantly playing 'I Can
> Hear Music' by the Beach Boys. Find the year that
> was released and you have the year of the coming of
> the whale.

Brinner arrived next and, despite Scarf's shouted warning, stood shoulder to shoulder with the growing band of believers.

> Bugger off quick or StatisTYKE and B 'n' D will be asking you if you saw the whale.

> You know I think I did. It's one of those memories that's hazy and distant, like my memory of the fair (or t'feearst, I should say). Now I'm sure I saw it. God! This might sound really daft, but couldn't you get inside it? I'm sure kids were allowed to climb in its mouth!! I remember!

> That sounds like the best explanation so far. In fact the only explanation so far.

I had to agree with Big 'n' Daft that it was the only explanation so far. Although I've mentioned the growing number of fairs in our long-forgotten tarn, when later tykes talk of the fair, or as Brinner pronounced more accurately 't'feearst week', it meant only one thing: Barnsley Feast Week.

Once more onto the cybersea! I was no longer a greenhorn. Events may have been moving more quickly and I sensed we were drawing ever closer, but I knew well enough that Jonah wouldn't give himself up that easily. Tasking a few more search engines with the desperate combination of Barnsley/whales/fairground/circus I sat back and waited. Scuttling over distant horizons, their invisible eyes scanned the endless cybersea but reported back with little new.

Latching onto a site for the Bobby Roberts' Circus I circled its animated juggling tips and jolly clowns, scanning biographies of the Roberts family members. The history of their family circus stretched back to the nineteenth century. What's more, they'd travelled the length and breadth of the country with their show. If anyone would have knowledge of a travelling whale they would. I fired off an e-mail – we had to pursue every lead. In fact I fired off e-mails and telephone calls to anyone and everyone. Radio stations, magazines, libraries, haulage companies. *'Have ye seen the blue whale?'*

No one answered Ahab's cry.

I have no idea how many e-mails were sent in at that stage of the whale hunt. I do remember Brinner's posting late one afternoon though.

'FOOK ME . . . NEWSFLASH!'

This time it had nothing to do with whales, I knew that without looking at the message. Remarkably, it even caused a minor stir around the office. Overhead a graceful white bird lowered her long legs, drifted over the river and shrank to a dot between the chimneys of Lotts Road power station. We all watched. She was dead and yet alive.

The Day the Future Died

SO WHERE WERE YOU WHEN KENNEDY WAS SHOT? IF YOU'RE old enough I'll bet you can remember. Or when Elvis died, or Diana? Mrs Smith at Number 37 might pass away unnoticed (except by her nearest and dearest, if she's lucky); the famous will be noted and obituaries written. But legends are different: they are immortal. They cannot die. So when they do, death strikes home somewhere deep inside all of us, unlocking unsettling questions that are usually kept in check by the demands of day-to-day life.

That summer evening an aircraft crashed on take-off at Charles de Gaulle airport. As with any accident, it was a tragedy for everyone involved. Yet this was more widely felt. This wasn't just any aircraft; it was Concorde.

Concorde had crashed.

I recalled those childhood years of wonder. Was there a young boy alive in the '60s who didn't thrill to the beauty and power of Concorde? Excitement at Raymond Baxter's commentary as the prototype lifted off the Filton's runway, a graceful white dart soaring into the bright blue future. How many small hands up and down the country messily glued together their own elegant bird and examined her beauty from every angle? She was the shape of things to come. A perfect physical expression of mankind's technological dream, a symbol so potent that, although there were 14 of the aircraft in service at the time, no one ever referred to 'Concordes' – always *Concorde*. In a grim parallel, the next morning only one image blazed from every front page: a doomed aircraft burning skyward. The Great White Bird had fallen and a childhood dream had died.

In some way, this disaster affected everyone more than they cared to admit. The whale hunters were no exception. Short, sharp cries were replaced by a more reflective tone as weighty matters of the world were considered. Huddled in a cyber-version of a wake at The Old White Bear, tyke mourners assembled to give their opinion on the passing.

> Concorde! Why do people feel they have to grieve publicly about everything? First Diana, more recently Sarah Payne and now Concorde. It's a terrible accident, I know, but why do people ring travel agents for such things as passenger lists, photos of the deceased, how they would have died – would it have been painful and slow, or would they not have felt anything?
>
> These are not even media scumbags, they were ordinary British citizens ringing round the agents. When you ask them why they want pictures of these poor people they usually say that they want them to take them to church and pray for them. Can anybody explain this modern-day phenomenon? I've had about

> a dozen calls about it this morning! I even get some
> of them in tears sobbing their hearts out. I feel like a
> priest!

Strange indeed. Brinner attempted to explain it all via what he
termed the 'Diana effect'.

> I work at the bottom right-hand side of Hyde Park,
> and my bus to work takes me along Knightsbridge
> and past Kensington Palace. The week of her death
> and the funeral it was quicker to walk because of the
> traffic around the place. This meant having to walk
> through all the 'mourners' twice a day, as someone
> who thought her death was no more and no less sad
> than when any young mother gets tragically killed. So
> I had real first-hand experience of it.
>
> There was lots of stuff going on, lots of weird shit,
> and there was an unusual sense of freedom because
> it was genuinely spontaneous – it was something
> people did, which the media couldn't control, they
> could only report it – it wasn't their idea.
>
> But the main thing I felt was the huge degree of
> self-interest in most people who were there. Most of
> the time the atmosphere wasn't one of mourning, it
> was almost celebration – there was a real sense of
> excitement. People would be walking through the
> park and when they first caught sight of all the
> flowers they would break into huge grins and start
> running towards it. Later in the week the floral
> tribute was so huge that if you'd added your little
> bouquet to it it would have made no difference. So
> people started setting up new tributes, around the
> bases of trees and stuff, and started getting more
> creative with the stuff they left – playing cards, big
> placards, home-made cards, ornate candles, stuff like

that. The whole point of it was self-expression, not mourning. At the same time it was feeling like you're a part of something, but also expressing themselves, saying look at me, look I'm part of this, look how important I am. I would have been quite angry but they were all so pathetic I just found it funny.

But I reckon it's the same with all these things now and B&D is spot on – people have no lives, and they're so de-sensitised to their own emotions, an event like this seems to have such a big tragic impact that they somehow have to make themselves part of it.

Very, very sad in every meaning of the word. Who's going to be captain at the weekend then?

Well I think . . . yes, it's all very strange and all very sad. And I agree with what's been said here. But I think it goes deeper. The way our glorious information age is hurtling along, we seem to have lost any form of morality and humanity. There ain't no community any more. People feel isolated and in some strange way events like this are a release for the man in the street who finds him/herself disillusioned by and unable to relate to the heap of shite 'world' the media, TV and press present to them. Also in this case Concorde is different in that I think there was some huge emotional attachment to it. For many it was an icon of the future, a thing we believed in as a symbol of technological certainty – 'Even God could not bring her down.'

The *Titanic* was 'unsinkable' and they still bang on about that! Whatever technological breakthroughs are accomplished there will always be disasters because of man's willingness to strive for the almost impossible.

130

Spot on about the icon of Concorde making it a bit different. It is true as well that part of it, while I still think it's very sad, is that everything now is so marketed and polished – even our emotions, how we are supposed to react – that tragically, stuff like this seems more 'real' to us than our own lives. And it's wrong.

My dad died a year before Diana so when that came round I'd just learned all about grief first hand. There was some old trout on the news who I could have punched, arguing that Wills and Harry should be dragged down from Scotland and paraded in the open, so that we could all see they were grieving 'like the rest of us'. Of course they were fookin' grieving! That's why they weren't there!! Grief is a private thing. It's very sad that people think they are grieving when they're doing this. They are not. As you rightly say they're trying to form some community spirit, because society is atomised. It's exactly the same reason why each time the Olympics or World Cup come around it's bigger and more important. Ten years ago the only people who watched England were people who watched footie generally. Now your mum and yer dad and yer lass and yer gran all watch as well.

The whale slipped away as an irresistible undertow of sadness diverted us into a sea of contemplation, skirting the shores of distant childhood lands.

Just to brass you all off!! Was there all this gubbings going on when Elvis popped his clogs? I remember we came home from our family holiday early. We wont that bothered it wo only Scarborough!

I was with the parents in a caravan in Ilfracombe — heard the news, went running off to tell my sister and broke my arm en route. Bummer of a day all round really.

I was in Scarborough too when Elvis died, I remember it clearly, with my brother and grandma. I had a sore throat I remember that much. Do you remember seeing me around? I was a big fan of Corrigan's Amusement Arcade, used to have a tube of 50x1 penny pieces which I used to roll down the lines you got 2p or if you were mega lucky 5p . . . trouble was the winnings came skittling down the glass and used to go everywhere. When I ran out of money you could find me going round all the slot machines looking for lost money, best place was those penny pushes which occasionally dropped a load of pennies for no reason. When does the season start?

Eh bastard, that were my favourite machine!!! Loved it when the money came skidding down the glass. They've still got 'em, except it's tuppence. Allus remember a family holiday when we found this penny-slot that had jammed — you didn't have to put owt in, just keep pulling the handle and collecting if you won. Smart!

If the future had died, were we seeking refuge in the past? The trauma sucked our crew through a whirlpool to faraway havens on Yorkshire's east coast, packing bucket and spade for hot, sunshiny days by the sea. Scarborough, Skegness, Cleethorpes, Bridlington: tykes knew these resorts as well as they knew tarn market. Here we would be safe: meandering in and out of seafront amusement arcades with pocketfuls of pennies . . . fish

'n' chips in newspaper . . . fending off gulls with a wooden fork
. . . sand in yer sarnies . . . jumpers for goalposts . . . enduring,
memory, isn't it?

Yet even cocooned in the past the crew recalled tragedy that
crossed our path from time to time. Thankfully, it generally
happened in the cinema.

> Lassie. I always cried, always. Funny that seeing as I'm
> a hard lad and all that.
>
> What about Bambi? Where his mam gets shot –
> 'Mother . . .' Ahem, not me like, but I heard some
> wimps blubber a bit.
>
> Snow White. I roored me eyes art when Snow White
> died and she was in that glass coffin. Me mum had to
> tek me art on t'Odeon.

Kennedy. Texas. Grassy knoll. I was only a nipper. We'd just got
back from a family holiday in Skegness. Now let's see . . . Elvis
. . . I was part of an expedition. Tarn equivalent of the
Paris–Dakar rally at the time: a holiday in tropical Torquay. I
was first with news of the burger-eater's death, but nobody
believed me.

Hmmm . . . Elvis . . . whales . . . was there a pattern? Why do
legends seem to die when everyone's on holiday? The arcade
horse-racing game, ten runners and riders juddering along
grooves, then magically galloping backward at the end of every
race, now that was *my* favourite. I prepared to chuck my
childhood on deck with the rest, when suddenly . . . *bang!*

The future blew up in my face again.

Heretic

A BOMB OR A BULLET CAN END A LIFE, START A WAR OR change the course of history. A burning fuel tank can bring down a legend. But all that's nothing, compared to what a spade can do. A simple spade can cut humanity off from the future: game over. That's what happened to me. A workman's foot on a spade cut the office's Internet cable.

All around me, slow-blinking concern as the full gravity of the situation sank in. No workplace of the new millennium can function at all without the Internet or e-mail. The building snapped off like a light bulb, leaving everyone in the dark.

Reality alert! Reality alert! What to do? What to do? Dear Boy saw his chance and took it. He moved like a rat out of a trap, heading straight for the river. Scores of fingers jabbed mobile phones to escape social interaction. A few bleary souls dared to look up from glass screens then ducked back, horrified at making the first eye contact since God knows when. Others feverishly thumbed operating manuals to find out if there were any hints on 'making conversation'. I dared to tour the building and could almost smell mental fuses burning out.

I say 'dared' because other than Dear Boy and myself, very few others showed signs of mobility. Only if you were continually glued to the future could you be said to be working. Walking was at best a waste of time. At worst it could spawn a number of heretical practices: smiling – a sure sign you didn't take your work seriously; talking – why do that when you can use e-mail or snd a txt mssg?

I covered all floors in a few minutes, having a laugh and a joke with fellow heretics along the way. Stepping out of the lift I heard the building give a sigh of relief. The search engines ground into gear again and this close call with human contact was left safely behind. Out beyond Battersea Bridge a small figure zigzagged along the shoreline. I reinforced the crumbling dam wall with a tattered *Illustrated Guide to Minehead, Porlock, Exmoor and the Quantocks 1940*, and contemplated another Cup-a-Soup while looking through scribbled contact numbers I'd dredged up over the days. Waiting for the kettle to boil I picked up the phone and made yet another marine mammal enquiry.

The Kill

So be cheery my lads, let your heart never fail
While the bold harpooner is striking the whale!

Nantucket song

Direct Hit!

I knew you could do it!!! Can't wait to see the pics!!

Well done! My dad always asks about the whale now! He wants to know he got the year right!

Well harpooned there fella! Get some pictures, memorabilia, T-shirts, books and set yourself up on t'market. Nice bit of research there. I'm looking forward to finding out what this whale's all abart.

Tremendous . . . top one. I'm intrigued. Mail me the results. I'll look out fer the T-shirts whenever tykes are on the box next season. NE'ER MIND WHALES, WHADDAYA KNOW ABART ELEPHANTS?

Nice one Statis(Holmes)TYKE, but I've got an idea . . . how's about changing the ground's name to 'Oakwhale'. Deaftyke – a man nearly whaled out.

YANKEE TYKE, TRAVELTYKE, BIG 'N' DAFT, PABLO, THE exhausted Deaftyke and so many others raised a cheer that echoed across the cybersea, a victorious end to a traumatic day. But it was Ish, one of the very first to dismiss the ridiculous notion of a whale in tarn, who put a smile on my face so wide that I must have gone down in the corporate world's book as the most dangerous heretic on earth.

> To the world's greatest whale hunter! Well done
> statis . . . never in the field of whale hunting has so
> much been owed to one man by so many.

It had just been a phone call like all the others. I expected no reply, or to be treated with dark suspicion. It was a phone number from a site I'd come across the previous day: a site for the National Fairground Archive. Fascinating stuff. Based in the University of Sheffield library, it housed information on travelling fairs and show people spanning almost a century. Black-and-white photographs of traction engines, swirling Cocks and Hens, leather-clad bikers defying the Wall of Death – echoes of a long-lost people.

Unsurprisingly, the site refused to yield vital whale information and only succeeded in frustrating me further. To my disgust, the Yorkshire section made no mention of Barnsley Feast Week! But the Association was in Sheffield . . .

Now to most people a northern accent's a northern accent. But in south Yorkshire we can pick up the subtlest variation. There's always been a long-running rivalry between towns separated by no more than the width of a steel mill or mine. Naturally football brought this to the fore, even more so in the forthcoming season. Barnsley (the Tykes), Sheffield United (the Blades, or Blunts to us) and Sheffield Wednesday (the Owls, or Fowls) were in the same division, which meant four hard-fought Derby games. Could it be that out of regional spite the Blunts and Fowls had ignored the history of their neighbours?

The voice at the other end of the phone in Sheffield didn't seem fazed by my whale babbling at all. Quite matter-of-factly, she told me there had been a touring whale in the 1950s and '60s and they had some information. Not much, but I'd been shunned by everyone else and I wanted her to keep saying those words over and over again. I was quite literally stunned. I wanted to be in Sheffield that very minute. This was the proof we needed. I arranged to visit in about a week's time.

With nothing more to do I spent the next few days walking around, smiling and talking. The frowns didn't bother me: I was about to leave the company for good.

Ha! And about time too, you're thinking. Fired for idling. Now, given the amount of time I'd been engaged in the whale hunt, that might be a fair assumption. Not at all – I was being very well paid to sit around and amuse myself. So how could I afford the time to just sit around and pursue mouldy old sealife? What kind of business was I in? Not easy to tell, is it, as everyone now sits in front of the glassy future, and all businesses work the same way.

I'd passed a few words with Brinner and learned we were both old hands at the same game. We knew there had been great changes and sensed more to come. Brinner congratulated me in managing to escape 'the grubby paws of the industry' and told tales of his previous employer 'denying basic human rights'. Still not much of a clue, is it? Could be any office. Well, I didn't want to have to tell you, because you might not believe anything I've said so far. But I'll come clean now. It's bad news I'm afraid: I am a professional liar.

The Delusion

I'D BE PREPARED TO BET ANY AMOUNT OF MONEY THAT YOU don't work in advertising. How can I be so sure? Easy – you're reading a book. No one in the advertising industry reads anything at all, other than e-mails of course.

Call into any glass and polished-chrome reception first thing and you'll find all the daily newspapers beautifully arranged, crisp and pressed. Stay there all day (not to be recommended) and you'll notice they won't be touched; they hit the bin in the evening in exactly the same state. This is because no one has any time.

The majority roll up in the early hours and leave well into the night. A quick glance over an open-plan floor will show how the day is spent. At first glance all may seem tranquil enough, yet nothing could be further from the truth. Closer observation reveals row upon row of chicken-heads bobbing, hypnotised by their glass screens, feverishly pecking away at their dispensers to gorge themselves on precious data while crapping out e-mails. The really commited continue over weekends, making sure that any fourteen-hour-a-day, five-day-a-week slackers know all about it. This obviously leaves most with precious little free time to read, or do anything else for that matter. And they never ever come across anyone who doesn't work in advertising, although perhaps, by dawn's early light, they might glimpse a strange creature placing bottles on their doorstep.

The tiny minority who own the company put in equally long hours, mainly to ensure that the majority do likewise. They don't read either, devoting 100 per cent of their energy to the business. In fact a chairman or managing director recoils from an open book with a pale-faced horror usually associated with a vampire detecting daylight. 'I don't need to read . . . I know everything I need to know,' I recall one hissing as he shrank back into the darkness.

The only exception is the advertising industry's rag – he'll pore over that endlessly in search of any article he's contributed, especially if it's accompanied by a picture of him looking all heroic and purposeful next to a potted plant; he'll spend a lot of time looking at that. Such articles contain gems of wisdom all chairmen love to bestow on the rest of 'adland', as the business usually refers to itself. It's a fair enough description, although 'planet' might be more accurate – an advertising agency is a place as far removed from the rest of human life as it's possible to get.

And that's the thing that started to get to me: the building may have had a panoramic view but it could just as well have been built of brick. If you're going to advertise something, you have to try to understand the people to whom you're advertising.

You have to be able to grasp what life's like outside the advertising industry. All the information dispensed by the glass screens isn't much use: it's written by other industry people.

But does it really matter that they're so cut off? Probably just working hard on those cracking ads. Fat orange chaps slapping people's chops, or wrinkly men trying to swim faster than a pint of stout on the TV; posters plastered with big tits. As long as everyone knows where to buy the best fcuking clothing, surely it doesn't matter that they don't know what's happening outside? Fair enough, but it wasn't that stuff that bothered me. It was other stuff, like trains.

Early mornings I joined the majority pressing onto filthy platforms. I waited endlessly for trains that never came, or flung myself into the stinking air of an impossibly crowded carriage. Each stifling journey into the capital became a fight for survival, gasping for air as delay piled on delay. Tempers melted, shouting guards trading insults with angry commuters who jabbed at notice boards displaying great works of fiction. It seemed that fighting might break out at any moment; some mornings it did.

Settling down to my Cup-a-Soup I'd discovered that I'd been wrong. My journey had all been a delusion. The rail company I'd just travelled on wanted to tell everyone about how committed it was to 'customer satisfaction', to tell everyone about all the fantastic things they were doing. I found myself having to write about efficient railway companies, modern fleets of shiny trains, how staff in immaculate airline uniforms serving croissants and cappuccino would rather throw themselves under a train than see a customer failing to relax with a chilled Chablis in their well-appointed lounges. Rail travel was the closest thing to heaven anyone could get.

Anyone who had to travel by train, or even glanced at a news report, wouldn't believe that garbage. But no one around me seemed to feel we were manufacturing a complete lie. The chairmen and directors wouldn't *dream* of travelling by train – that would bring them into contact with the 'great unwashed' (advertising's label for anyone not in advertising), while the majority's only news was industry tittle-tattle. Most remarkably of all, the majority *did* travel by train and must have managed to separate grim reality from the fantasies they created. Deep down, most must have realised but kept quiet and got on with just doing their jobs.

By the kettle, or in quiet corners, a few whispered, though. Sure, the trains had been repainted and emblazoned with brave new logos while we spun candy-coated words, but it all amounted to the same thing: icing a turd. This strange situation didn't occupy our minds for much of the time though. We had more important things to do and, anyway, the real world was for losers. We were joining the pioneers of a brave new world.

The Shouting

I CAN REMEMBER WHEN, IF SOMEONE SAID, 'SEE THAT BLOKE over there? He's lost touch with reality you know,' it would be whispered in a sympathetic tone and probably accompanied by a sad shaking of the head and a tapping of forefinger on temple. If the poor unfortunate singled out was talking or shouting to himself then sadly you'd have to agree. In that first summer of a new millennium there were hundreds of such basketcases sitting around in advertising agency receptions. It was a natural stopover on a journey from the dull real world into the sparkling virtual world.

The barking men in shiny suits, crazy shades and trainers were architects of a new future: the dot com boys. The Internet would be the future for all time, a future of communication and speed. The sooner everyone linked up to the worldwide web, the better off everyone would be, simple as that.

Agency chairmen embraced these newcomers with

enthusiasm. They hadn't any grasp of what it was all about, of course. Nor had they any understanding of computers; you're more likely to see a baboon at the controls of a jumbo jet than an agency chairman at a computer. No, it was simply that the dot com boys had managed to get their hands on tens of millions of quid by shouting as loudly as they could to anyone who'd listen that they had a great idea for a business. This didn't actually exist, but that was a minor detail.

They rolled into agency receptions in search of the agency's expertise in promoting their invisible business. More importantly they came with huge piles of dosh, the one thing guaranteed to get an agency head's undivided attention. It was a marriage made in heaven. An agency chairman's true expertise is in siphoning off millions by duping the gullible into believing his agency knows exactly how to promote a product.

After a split-second's analysis of the dot com companies, it was concluded the virtual businesses would be tremendously successful. All it would take would be to persuade the entire population of the planet to spend their whole lives sitting on their bums tapping away at a glass screen, ordering everything over the Internet. This could be achieved by tomorrow at the latest (or sooner if we worked all night). That seemed to be the sum of current thinking. And the beauty of it was all you had to do to make it happen was talk or, even better, shout.

And so began the great shouting. If not glued to the glass screen you had to be shouting into a mobile while running to a meeting. While hopelessly waiting for a meeting to start you had to shout into your mobile because you had to be somewhere else. In the rare meeting that happened, everyone shouted at once – the louder you shouted the more important you were. 'The endless talking talk of the talky talk people,' as Dear Boy put it with a weary air.

In one memorable meeting, a rabid voice shrieked above the rest with such fervour that others fell away. Stalking the room with a crazed look in his eye, he banged the table with clenched fist to emphasise his tirade; he thumped it so hard that all the Nice biscuits jumped off the plate and Dear Boy woke up.

'Twenty-four hours a day! Seven days a week! A global network that will make business unstoppable . . . No barriers! No restrictions! Relentless . . . non-stop . . . Non-stop business in a world that never sleeps . . . whenever we want . . . 24–7 . . . we'll all be free . . . free to work!'

A rare passion exploded in the sterile room. I felt quite moved and had to stop myself from leaping up from my chair.

'Yes! Yes! Freedom! Freedom through work!'

I had to be careful, though. I was already under observation for heretical practices. My natural approach of 'see all, hear all, say nowt' was clearly at odds with the new mantra. The final straw came when I was accused of twin crimes. It was brought to my attention that I didn't talk enough in meetings. This led the minority to conclude I was wasting my time *thinking*. Guilty as charged, m'lud.

In this coming world, governed by speed, there was no time for all that thinking malarkey. I don't think thinking has always been an offence in advertising though – before the computer, I seem to remember lots of people thinking. Still, nice to have that onerous task off your mind I suppose.

And so this was the shape of things to come. The future might have been difficult to predict a couple of hundred years ago back in tarn, but what did people know back then anyway? There was no time for rumour that summer; the dot com boys and agencies were smart. They knew that, given enough shouting, the future would revolve around business on the Internet.

If you weren't blinded by money, you couldn't really say it would all pan out. I could never have dreamt that I'd find myself caught up in the hunt for a whale by using the new technology. That's the strange thing about new inventions: you can never be sure how they're going to be used. I'll bet the greatest tyke of all never dreamt what his passion would ignite.

The Navigator

JOSEPH LOCKE WAS FAMED THROUGHOUT THE LENGTH AND breadth of Europe. Tarn swelled with pride when the French nation awarded him the Cross of the Legion of Honour. In the presence of an approving Queen Victoria, Napoleon III (who always seemed to be on hand for grand ceremonies) beckoned Locke to step forward and receive the honour. Years later, the renowned Italian sculptor Baron Marochetti was commissioned to honour him with a magnificent bronze statue.

On his death, *The Times* mourned his passing and it seemed only fitting that the great man should be laid to rest in Westminster Abbey. So what exactly had this national hero, that everyone's now forgotten, actually done?

As a boy, Joe came to tarn with his father just as the great canal project was completed. Living not far from The Old White Bear on Shambles Street, Joe kicked around, not really knowing what to do with his life. All that changed when an old workmate of his father's dropped by. George Stephenson was really making a big name for himself in the new steam game. He reckoned Joe looked a bright lad, about the same age as his son Robert. All he needed was a break. Stephenson offered the 17-year-old Joe an apprenticeship. Joe accepted and travelled to Durham. He never looked back.

The boy became spellbound by Stephenson's great vision of steam power and railway engineering. George Stephenson, a self-taught engineer, was at the leading edge of this unheard-of science. Time and again, he fought to explain his dream to established engineers and public committees. Learned men struggled to understand his thick Northumbrian accent and feared for the sanity of this deluded northerner as he talked of huge machines pulling even huger loads through terrain that could never, ever be tamed. Yet of all the weird and wonderful ideas knocking around at the time, this was the one that would really take off. Locke, the Stephensons and Brunel were pioneers of a new technology that would transform the world forever.

Joseph Locke had found his true vocation and grew to be a visionary, a man whose inspiration and determination became the driving force behind the original 'worldwide web': fine steel strands that now encompass the globe. Remember that, at the time, few understood how to build what we'd call a proper road. It's almost impossible for us now to imagine the scale of the task faced by these first navigators. Little wonder that no one believed them.

Now I've laid a fair bit of track in my time, but it didn't weigh very much at all and it was arranged in a neat oval on a carpet. Out in the real world, hills, mountains, valleys, rivers, all had to be taken account of, not to mention the land itself: marsh, moor and layers of different rock. Next time you're out in the dales or fells, take a look around and ask yourself, how do I lay track through all this?

Over 150 years ago, out on harsh moors, Joseph Locke's unfailing eye weighed up vast swathes of land, his keen mind whirling through endless complex calculations. His teams of 'navigators' then set to work levelling ground, constructing viaducts, cutting embankments and boring tunnels.

To travel most inter-city lines in the land (and many in Europe) is to take a journey first mapped out in the great man's mind. Forbidding routes north, cutting through iron Pennine hills and on into Scotland; through the fenlands; south from London to the coast; Cherbourg; Le Havre to Paris and then on to Rouen, a route that incorporated the breathtaking Barentin viaduct, which surely qualifies as a miracle of engineering in any age.

Robert Stephenson, Isambard Kingdom Brunel, and Joseph

Locke had a friendship forged in the white heat of their technological revolution. They created more than steamships, engines and rail; they laid the very foundations of our world. Then, quite suddenly, they were gone. Stephenson, then Brunel and finally Locke died in the space of a year. None of them had reached the age of 56. *The Times* obituary salutes Locke as completing 'the triumvirate of the engineering world, now passed away'. Most are familiar with the cigar-chomping Brunel and his steamships, while George Stephenson and his 'Rocket' found their way onto the five-pound note, but Locke just vanished.

Well, he's not forgotten across the Channel. So proud were the residents of Barentin with their magnificent 27-arch viaduct, it was incorporated into their coat of arms. In 1951 they went further. Commissioning a cast from Baron Marochetti's statue, they erected their own memorial.

So why isn't he still remembered as one of the all-time greats in Britain? His career in Parliament probably has a lot to do with it. Both Stephenson and Locke took up seats in the House of Commons. Stephenson sized up the situation pretty quickly and went along with the time-honoured paper waving, a few shouts of 'hear hear!' and the odd snooze. But not Locke – his passion got the better of him.

Joe thought this would be the place to get things done and continually raised questions about government rail policy. The government didn't really have one, but naturally didn't want that pointing out. Anyway, the last thing a chap needs after a decent lunch at the club is some tyke banging on about railways, especially when one wants to slip off early for a rendezvous down in Brighton with that delightful filly from the music hall, eh? Perhaps they were even a little afraid of him. After all, look what he did to anyone who got in his way, like Huskisson . . . he'd *killed* old Huskisson.

Fair enough, so Locke did top an MP, but it wasn't really his fault. It happened at the opening of the Liverpool–Manchester line, the world's very first commercial rail link and one of the greatest days in world transport history. Both Stephensons and Locke drove engines coupled to the first passenger trains, all packed with dignitaries on a flag-waving first run. (At times they reached speeds we'd find incredible to this day – about 10 mph on some stretches.) On that day, one William Huskisson would have been better off staying in bed.

During a pause in that first rail journey Huskisson spotted a grand figure in military uniform among the VIPs: the Duke of Wellington. Recognising a perfect opportunity for a bit of brown nosing, Huskisson slipped from the train and made his way to the Duke's carriage. Bad move – he was out of his natural habitat. Unused to the outside world, Huskisson failed to notice a six-ton iron machine making a terrific noise and belching smoke and steam as it moved slowly towards him. The engine, driven by Locke, ran him down. A tragic accident and perhaps understandable: no one had ever seen anything like these engines before. Then again, there were thousands attending that day and no one else got run down. Proof, perhaps, that from day one MPs couldn't get to grips with the railways.

Back in the House of Commons, Joseph Locke just wouldn't let it lie. In one memorable clash he suggested that trains ought to be allowed to run on a Sunday, to a hushed silence from the house. A director of a Scottish railway company fairly exploded in fury.

'The man who would violate the Sabbath would have no difficulty in eloping with his host's wife . . . or stealing his spoons!'

Strong stuff. Yet after his death it was Locke's own wife who suffered the fallout from these exchanges. She'd never been keen on her husband being buried in Westminster Abbey, but felt it only right he should be honoured in some way. Brunel's statue stood in London's Embankment Gardens; Stephenson's at Euston, in honour of his London to Birmingham link. An application was made that Locke's statue be erected in St

Margaret's Garden, Westminster. After a long silence, the application was politely turned down. It was obviously not an appropriate spot for a suspected spoon-stealer.

Joseph Locke was eventually buried in Kensal Green cemetery, near his old friend Brunel, and a window in Westminster Abbey was granted to commemorate him. You won't find it there today, though. Some time early in the last century, it mysteriously went missing, a remarkable feat for a stained-glass window in Britain's greatest abbey. It came to light in 1952 and was handed over to tarn council, and now awaits restoration.

Perhaps the main reason Locke slipped away, though, was that his biography wasn't up to much. Stephenson's and Brunel's were the equivalent of award-winning drama documentaries of the Victorian age; Locke's write-up is a bit of a turkey. The book disappeared and took him with it. Which only goes to show, if you're not properly written up it's all too easy to slip the net of history, almost as if you never really existed at all. A lot like some marine mammals I could mention.

As time goes by, fewer and fewer tykes remember Locke's story either, which is a bit sad. For if any one man shaped Barnsley, and indeed the world, it was him. The year of his death, 1860, marked the beginning of a century that would be like none the tarn, or the world, had ever seen.

The '60s

DON JUAN WAS A SYMBOL FOR THE '60S. RISING TO SUCH A height that he could peer into second-storey windows, this magnificent beast could have created untold mayhem had he tired of his tarn tour. With hooves resting on a silken footstool, riding on a horse-drawn carriage and billed as 'The Educated

Bull', Don Juan's mighty bulk towered over an awe-struck crowd. Don Juan was without doubt the most fortunate of his kind: he got out of tarn alive. By the '60s, the days of bull- and bear-baiting were well and truly over. By the time of the coming of Don Juan, tarn was a very different place indeed. The quiet strength of this potent animal was a symbol of what lay ahead.

The market inn pundits had been wrong. Weavers came to tarn in their hundreds, miners in their thousands. Early miners were only scratching the surface, literally. The 'black hue' noted by Defoe was a sign of greater things deeper underground. While engineers like Locke and Stephenson worked on the surface, others carried out initial exploration of the underworld. The results were conclusive.

Yorkshire had an abundance of coal seams and all converged in one area to form the richest of all: the Barnsley Seam. For centuries, tykes had been standing on black gold. To the south, in Sheffield's Don Valley, more and more furnaces were glowing, all hungry for coal. To feed them, tarn's landscape and the Wentworths' estates were punctured time after time in order to feed from the seams and satisfy a never-ending demand.

Transport was no longer a problem. The canals now stretched north to Wakefield and south to Sheffield, and almost as soon as they were completed, Locke's railways arrived. It was the breakthrough that changed everything forever. Wherever a shaft was sunk, rails could be run straight up to a pithead. By the '60s this steel web soon covered the land. Tarn coal could be transported anywhere in the country, shafts were being sunk deeper than man had ever gone before.

Tarn's population stood at about 3,500 when tykes speculated about the canal network; now, only 70 years later, that figure had grown to 23,000. Barnsley pulled out all the stops throughout that decade. Though some punters may have rued the loss of horse racing in Barnsley, every tyke was right behind the use Joseph Locke's widow made of the old 'race common' after his death: Locke was to have a magnificent new park named in his honour. Once again, it was an event that turned many men to poetry.

> High Stile Field no more! This is now Locke Park,
> Where Barnsley's denizens may hear the lark,
> The luxury enjoy of shrub and tree
> And perfume breathing flower!

The opening day was declared a public holiday and the whole tarn turned out. A troop of the Yeoman Cavalry and Barnsley Rifle Corps band headed a procession some 5,000 strong in glorious June weather that was dutifully noted by tarn's first author-meteorologist. To be honest, I'm including this in an attempt to give my spell-check a nervous breakdown.

> T'sun shane I dubble breetness, nay, more then it hed
> ivver dun before; an t'claards hung rhaand i' snaw-
> white festoons, at a respecktfull distance, i' t'clear blue
> sky, an t'wind wafted nice an gently, just soa az ta mack
> ivvry boddy feel moderately cooil an cumfatubble.

Flags and bunting hung from windows and cannon-fire ripped the air in salute at the opening ceremony of new tarn's status symbol. Locke Park, with its bandstand, boating lake, gardens and, of course, Marochetti's statue of the engineer, was a glorious expression of hope for a prosperous future.

A state-of-the-art theatre was erected. Opera, theatre and the arts in general flourished. Sport really took off. A couple of months after Don Juan's regal appearance, a Barnsley 22 elected to bat first against an All-England 11 at Shaw Lane cricket ground. The tykes took a hammering, but a carnival crowd revelled in the opposition's silky skills. Walking to the crease, one visiting batsman may well have been greatly impressed by the warm reception. Perhaps he decided to settle in tarn, for one tyke described the match as: 'A rare treat when the celebrated opponents, Daft and Clark, displayed their skill with the bat.'

Market Hill and May Day Green remained the social centres they had been for centuries. Though the market itself could no longer be confined to the hill, stalls were still erected there and it remained the site for important gatherings.

The French attempt at 'world domination' speculated over in market inns became reality only a few years later. From Market Hill tykes saw the Pontefract then Woolley Edge beacons flare out the news. Tarn's signal! Gentry donned scarlet battledress and mustered excited militia onto the hill. Men who could have been expected to spend their entire lives in the villages of their birth set off for the great adventure. The seriousness of the French threat can be gauged by one John Gill's invitation to his comrades to drink all his ale lest the Frenchies get their hands on it. When the Hartlepool fishermen saved the day and they all marched back to their fields and looms, Gill must have returned a broken man.

May Day Green continued playing host to fairs, travelling shows and ever-more weird and wonderful creatures whose arrival spoke to tykes of other worlds far, far away. What fantabulous spectacles some of the animal performances were! Tarn witnessed untamed hordes of painted Red Indians on horseback whooping war cries as they faced the smoking pistols of the US cavalry. Wagons burned, arrows flew, scalps were scalped, men died with their boots on. For real!

Well, nearly real. In 1903 the Wild West met the Wild West Riding when the legendary Buffalo Bill rode his wagon train to tarn to re-enact the attack on the Deadwood Stage and Custer's mythical Last Stand.

There seemed to be no shortage of theatrical diversion. 'Pedro Pescador and his wonderful equilibristic double somersaulting dogs' packed them in at the Pavilion. The Cock Inn Music Hall tempted curious tykes into a highly improbable attraction, 'a full-grown calf with two heads, six legs, two tails, and a rather intriguing etc'. I'm 100 per cent certain that Big 'n' Daft's great-great-grandfather was first in the queue for that one.

Cavalry charges and gravity-defying dogs faded away: the whale hunters could never have witnessed such amazing spectacles, but the vibrant energy of tarn market lived on. In the 1960s Barnsley's heart still beat from May Day Green. Row upon row of sturdy green stalls stretched with ivory canvas spread out on solid cobbles from May Day Green and on to the railway station. Most tykes would recognise the description of C. Race, Town Clerk, as he recalled the market in the early years of the twentieth century: 'The cattle market held in the street, the naphtha lights on the stalls, the patter of the pitches, the colour and virility, the banter and good-humoured bargaining . . .'

Barnsley burst into babbling life every Wednesday and Saturday market come fair weather or foul. As a tiny tyke, I'd splash happily behind my mother past shining fish on the crushed ice of Mitchell's stall as we threaded through warm, steaming pitches that dripped rainwater down our necks. You could still find everything in t'market, or the scores of shops around it. Pablo would be relieved to know that if you wanted a 'five-legged green elephant with a glass eye' Charles Brammer in Regent Street would have it. If he didn't, he'd get it for you.

Bulls and cows continued to present unscheduled diversions. In any market town of the time, people were well acquainted with their roast dinners while they were still mobile. And of course some, like Sam's sea monster, weren't keen to end up on a plate as E.I. Addio recalled.

> Was there anybody abahrt when a bull escaped from t'abbatoir darn Pontefract Road and injured somebody outside the Wire Trellis boozer on Gas Nook? Apparently it ran amok through t'market and ended up gerrin shot on the waste ground between Kop end and up where Metrodome is now.

The cry of 'stop that cow' often went up, not that there was much chance of stopping a frenzied Aberdeen Angus – all ended up being shot. One cow-on-a-mission entered a house along Doncaster Road and demolished the kitchen walls in a last defiant act – one less family capable of cooking roast beef and Yorkshire pud that Sunday.

No one thought much about living cheek-by-jowl with the livestock. Cows herded from the railway wagons to Queen's Road cattle pens often barged shoppers out of the way, cramming into doorways around May Day Green in order to do a little window-shopping. Some even peered into prams to moo at new tyke arrivals.

One man was both horseman and entertainer. Astride his mount, sharply dressed in three-piece suit with cigar clenched between his teeth, Joe Edwards rode into tarn with a fistful of . . . well, dinner services actually. Everyone remembers him. E.I. Addio for one:

> Aye, Joe Edwards. Big f.uck-off stall, used to sell 5,300-piece dinner sets for 10/6.

It was indeed a huge stall, piled with bright crockery of every shape and size. But it was what he did with them that earned him a place in the tarn hall of fame. Hundreds of women, with tiny tykes in tow, crowded round Edwards' stall in hushed anticipation.

Joe's white-coated assistants plunged brawny arms into wicker baskets, plucking out tottering mountains of fragile china. Hypnotised by the master's staccato sales patter, tykes held their breath for what followed. Even McDog wagged his tail in anticipation:

> It was absolutely ace! I remember him dropping the lot when trying to top a teapot! Laugh? I nearly made tea!

Show time! Whole dinner services were hurled over our heads. Plates were magically stacked mid-flight, deft hands skilfully flipping, spinning, flashing crockery. Delighted squeals and gravy boats filled the air.

But for all the amazing shows on market stalls, none could compare with events that unfolded in late summer. There were probably many sheep and cattle fairs going on in tarn in the 1960s, but only one mattered to most tykes, especially us young ones – Good Queen Bess's St Helen's Fair. Through the centuries, that week remained a glittering jewel on tarn calendar: *Barnsley Feast Week!*

Everything shut down and everyone went to the fair, or 't'feearst' as Brinner correctly put it. Come the great day shop shutters were put up, and traders dismantled their stalls, swept the cobbles and left May Day Green silent and deserted by evening. Young tykes could barely contain their excitement; few slept. For through the veil of night, the magic men would come to tarn!

The next day the cobbles had disappeared, hidden by huge revolving striped canopies that blossomed from angular iron and wooden stems. We hopped aboard and were whisked away to another world.

The roaring, giddying switchbacks and waltzers weren't so much fairground rides as travelling art galleries, resplendent with carved gilt angels and heroic Atlantean figures. Fleeting minutes sailing through the air in majestic baroque gondolas, wrestling with the wheel of a sports car. Crowds pressed forward onto the Cocks and Hens and prancing barrel organ-powered stallions, reaching out to touch another world through those flashing circles of magic.

Barnsley Feast Week was the event of the year. In fact, for much of the twentieth century it was the only holiday of the year. Few people journeyed too far from their hometown and jobs. As rail travel gradually came within the reach of more families, holidaying further afield became more common, but

Barnsley Feast on May Day Green continued to mesmerise young tykes through the '60s and '70s. Big 'n' Daft, Brinner, Casper, Munich tyke, E.I. Addio, norman, StatisTYKE, Hazel, R Kid: without doubt all the whale hunters' paths unknowingly crossed somewhere in tarn market that magical week. Every year we rolled up laughing, ready for all the fun of the fair. And it was here, amidst the sparking dodgems, wailing sirens, candyfloss and clowns, that these magic men, it seemed, brought us our whale.

Don Juan's strength heralded the beginning of that tumultuous century in tarn, an era that was to amaze our great-grandfathers with invention and innovation that opened up so many different possibilities. Little could we have guessed that great Jonah appeared amongst us as a silent reminder that that era was about to end and that for our century of progess, there were those who had to pay a terrible price.

Sven

BRONZE-AGE MEN MUST HAVE BEEN GOBSMACKED TO COME across fish as big as a hill washed up on the beach, but there's evidence they put these finds to good use. Whalebone rafters have been found at some of their settlements. They probably ate the meat as well; the ancient Greeks, on finding beached whales, did. Pliny highly recommended whalemeat as an aid to dental hygiene.

But no one, no matter how mad they are, ventures out to sea to tangle with a 70-ton mammal if its only uses are as the odd steak, building materials and dental floss. The Basques looked on the whale as a valuable source of food and found an eager market for it in Europe; the tongue was particularly sought after, especially among the clergy and royalty. But the Basques also discovered that whale blubber could be melted into oil – the purest, cleanest-burning on earth.

By Melville's day the whale as food seems to have fallen out of favour, in the West at least. Aboard the *Pequod* Ishmael, musing on Stubb tucking into a whale steak by lamplight, tells us it seems too rich for any but an old whaleman's palate. However, he does ponder on his crewmate eating a creature by its own light, for the Nantucketers prized the whale as a source of fuel. The oil was also vital in the manufacture of many other things: soap, candles, detergent, paint, cooking fat and lubricants – perfect for keeping moving parts on marvellous new machines turning.

For the shipowners of Melville's Nantucket, whale oil was liquid gold. Nantucket – the richest island on earth? Embarking on their three-year voyages, the Nantucket whaleships had to be equipped with everything necessary for the cutting and boiling of whales into valuable oil. If the disposal of Jumbo was a huge task, imagine dealing with a 70-ton body on the open ocean. Hoisted alongside, the whale underwent the biggest butchery job in the world, blubber being stripped into sections or 'leaves' to be melted down in huge vats sunk into a bricked section of the ship's deck.

Tragic though this was for individual whales, the oceans are vast and such early whaling operations probably made no serious impression on the total whale population.

But as Herman Melville finished *Moby Dick*, he couldn't have guessed that he'd just penned an account of whaling from an age that had just come to an end. Joseph Locke was applying his mind to the new horizons technology might make possible. Over the North Sea, Sven Foyn, a Norwegian, tinkered away in an attempt to marry together other innovations.

Old Viking blood obviously ran through his veins. He succeeded, coming up with fast ocean vessels capable of lightning strikes and violent death. The kill was always the most difficult, dangerous part of any whale hunt. Both hunter and prey had an equal chance of meeting their maker. Skimming the waves in an open boat, the harpooner stood at the prow, balancing against the rolling sea, waiting for the right moment to strike. The harpoon didn't kill; it acted like an angler's hook. By attaching a line in this way the small boat was hauled closer to the whale until, exhausted, it could be stabbed to death.

When Sven chugged out into the fjords in a steam-powered boat patting his new harpoon, this struggle was tipped forever in man's favour. No longer would the whale be able to outrun the ship. The grenade harpoon, an explosive missile fitted with a time-delay fuse, could be launched from a safe distance to kill or mortally wound. The ships became bigger and faster and Sven updated his arsenal . . .

'. . . a darting gun? Excellent choice, Sir! All the accuracy of your traditional harpoon, coupled with the explosive capacity of the grenade. Ahhh . . . I see Sir is interested in the Cannon Harpoon . . . take note of how on impact the barbs extend to really grip into the flesh . . .'

Actually Sven didn't sell his secret initially. He got to work killing whales and establishing plants that processed whale oil into margarine, soap and a large fortune. Sven also turned his mind to other marine mammal matters. Killing a whale is one thing: butchering it, quite another. Among the characteristics that gave the unfortunate 'right whale' its name is its tendency to float when dead. Others weren't so obliging, so Sven devised a way of inflating corpses with air to make things a little easier.

Throughout the nineteenth century the steamships set sail and whales were killed in ever-increasing numbers as demand for their oil exploded. There were far more machines to be fed and, besides oil, a whale's body was useful in many other ways. Whalebone and baleen were the plastics of their day, being turned into ribs for corsets, shoehorns and hoops for all those enormous skirts. Blood was used in the manufacture of adhesives and fertilizer, skin fashioned into handbags and bootlaces, tendons stretched into string, gelatin boiled to make sweets. The list goes on and on; even teeth weren't wasted, being carved into snuffboxes and buttons.

Unfortunately for the whale, there was no alternative. When Foyn began tinkering with harpoons, synthetic oil and plastics just weren't around. That century may have been a whirlwind of inventions but they didn't come in a nice tidy order. The process of refining crude oil to the purity of a whale oil would begin but remain very, very expensive for some time. Anyway, to get at underground oil in the first place, drilling and pumping machines and engines had to be lubricated. Before they could be lubricated they had to be built in the first place. And such machines were far bigger than anything seen before. Forging and casting required huge furnaces, and furnaces needed fires that burnt at incredibly high temperatures. And those fires had to be fed: with coal.

The Big One

WEDNESDAY ONLY EVER MEANS ONE THING IN BARNSLEY: market day. One particular Wednesday, tykes were showing more than usual interest in Market Hill stalls laden with fat slabs of the famous goose that had honked into tarn for the last time. By midday inns were doing a brisk trade when someone noticed a distant thunder. Nothing unusual about that – but a storm in mid-winter? Christmas was only a couple of weeks away. The rumbling became louder. Market stalls creaked as the ground shook, from near and far dogs set up a fearful howling. Terrified tykes ran down Market Hill.

From the south edge of tarn came a flash as a roaring comet exploded from the earth. A volcano erupted and a thunderclap rolled out over the valley. Turning tarnward, shocked onlookers from miles around watched a column of liquid fire punch high into the sky. A boiling mushroom cloud spread over Barnsley and nearby villages; then it began to rain. Day turned to night as choking, hot ash softly blanketed tarn, creating a nightmare landscape bathed only in a red glow from the thundering jet of fire. Wrapped in this shroud tykes gathered to watch and wait. There was nothing else they could do. A few of the older men didn't follow those running to the Oaks. They shook their heads, remembering their father's horror stories of demons and spirits. Only a generation ago, no one in their wildest nightmares could have conjured up the hell of winter 1866.

Through the afternoon, huge crowds grew around the Oaks colliery No. 1 shaft. Some said this was what had happened at Lundhill – special trains were laid on, so people could come from miles around just to gawp. There was nothing to see; there hadn't been at Lundhill. Arguments broke out among tykes and out-of-tarners. Newspaper artists up from London jostled for a better view, furiously sketching the scene. Reporters scribbled away or shouted questions at anyone who might know anything. This was the big one. This was the biggest disaster ever to have hit the country, quite possibly the biggest to hit the world. 'Volcano!' would be the following morning's headline.

Men from nearby collieries were soon to be seen among ashen-faced women. News spread that an engineer was coming up from the Midlands and Parkin Jeffcock arrived by late afternoon. Initial assessments were grim. The column of fire had died, to be replaced by belching smoke. Cage and winding gear were smoking fragments welded to the tower. Another cage was hastily assembled and Jeffcock had no shortage of volunteers for a planned descent into the smoking shaft. They had no protective clothing as such, none that we'd recognise today anyway. The rescue party, clad in heavy, damp oilskins, goggles and rubber breathing tubes, entered the cage and disappeared immediately.

The demons so feared by the miners of old had been renamed, but that didn't lessen their ability to create unspeakable horror. Fire damp, invisible and odourless, slithered through tunnels undetected. But it was only one of many dangers facing engineers in this new world. Above ground, fire and water were a mine-engineer's allies, providing steampower to bore and pump. Below ground they were deadly enemies. Flooding was an ever-present danger. The only light source in the impenetrable blackness came from candles – the best thing to ignite a mixture of fire-damp and air. Ventilation and airflow were needed to breathe. Get it wrong, though, and the lethal mixture would poison the underground maze. Throw in the continual threat of sudden collapse and that these factors all had to be juggled at the same time and mining starts to look more like Russian roulette on a massive scale.

Night had fallen, not that anyone could tell. When the cage was hauled up, a murmur ran through the crowd. Smoking, coughing deep-earth divers surfaced from No. 1 shaft. At the front cries went up, a women screamed. Alive: a dozen. No one could be sure. They were carefully wrapped in damp blankets to be carried to the nearest inn. There was shouting. Someone threw a punch at a reporter. A woman stepped forward and bent to a charred half-corpse to pour brandy onto its lips. The cage was prepared once more.

All night it went on. The first descent could make no progess along the underground roadway. Beyond the few half-dead brought to the surface they could make out a wall of corpses. Fathers had shielded sons, but they'd died together, life snuffed out by searing heat or suffocation, eyes bulging, faces contorted in terror. Young tykes were burnt alive with their ponies.

More and more men poured into the shaft, venturing further into the labyrinth. Above ground the crowd kept up their vigil. Word went round that most brought up the previous day had died. By the thin light of Thursday's dawn many looked around and remembered the preacher's descriptions of hell. Just before 9.00 a.m. the cage came up more quickly. The mood had changed: there were arguments, shouting. Down the cage went again, and quickly up again. Men spilled onto the surface. There'd been a sudden change in the air current – their miners' sixth sense, refined through years underground, told them to get out. Parkin Jeffcock refused. If anyone was still alive he had to find them; with 26 others he ventured deeper into the mine. All he needed was a little more time.

At 9.00 a.m. the mine exploded. This time No. 2 shaft blew as well and it was clear an enormous fire was now raging underground. At 7.30 p.m. there was yet another huge underground explosion. In the early hours of Saturday, as crowds thinned, 14 further explosions were recorded. In terms of rescue, there was nothing more to be done. The shafts were sealed.

Headlines told of the greatest peacetime disaster in Britain since the Great Fire of London. Queen Victoria expressed her deep regret. At the time there was no accurate record of how many had entered the mine that Wednesday morning. Only much later was it determined that 334 men and boys perished. Add Parkin Jeffcock's rescue party and the final death toll was 361. There were only six survivors. The rescue of Samuel Brown was little short of a miracle. He was plucked from a flaming No. 1 shaft after the second explosion by two heroes, T.W. Embleton and J.E. Mammatt.

It was a year before the Oaks colliery shafts were reopened. Some bodies were recovered, many weren't. There were enquiries of course. Questioning, witnesses, recriminations and deliberations: it all took months.

While all that was going on, thousands more men were pouring underground into new, deeper mines. The rapidly growing labyrinth became so complex that sometimes tunnels met. You could go down a colliery shaft at one end of Barnsley, walk under tarn and pop up the other side at a different pit. Sometimes, when they were blasting new tunnels, older workings were breached. Near the Oaks colliery they'd often find bones.

The Holy Man

TO CONGREGATIONS FILING DOWN THE STEPS OF ST PETER'S church after Sunday service, the site of the Oaks colliery would have been easily visible. Black skeletal surface works across Doncaster Road were a constant reminder of how their world had changed, not that they had to rely on memories. Every week Barnsley's chapels and churches were filled with widows and orphans mouthing the miners' prayer as, day after day, more and more men left for their shift and never came back.

'Thy soul is a barque on the ocean of life, encountering its tempests, its trouble, its strife . . .'

The Oaks colliery disaster hadn't been the first: 189 died at Lundhill some years earlier. It wasn't the last either. In a 25-year period, 750 men and boys were killed in a ten-square-mile area of the Dearne Vally. It all made paper-selling headlines, but when the reporters drifted away tarn was left scarred and forgotten – until the next time, of course.

Standing on the steps of St Peter's, the curate must often have scanned the burnt earth and cast his eyes to heaven. What could he do? Wasn't he doing enough by his services and prayers: words of consolation, leading his flock through this dark time? It didn't feel like it. He wanted to do more, much more.

Was it a revelation? Was it divine intervention? Or was it the lads tearing across pit yards and waste ground belting a ball around that gave him the answer? Probably a bit of all three. The holy man saw the light. The curate became a man on a mission: he had a dream and no one would stand in the way of it. While explaining it to others, they'd no doubt nod and smile in agreement but wonder secretly if the good Reverend hadn't been at the communion wine. Tykes had tried it before and it never worked, or not for long. And was it really the sort of thing a holy man should be bothering himself with? Perhaps he knew what they thought. He didn't care, for this was no ordinary curate.

This was the Reverend Tiverton Preedy. Speak that name with awe.

Preedy was a determined man, and what he determined to do was establish a football team. Yes, there were teams around tarn, but they came and went: his would not. He would get together a team . . . 'Barnsley St Peter's' it would be called . . . and it would stay together!

So what was the good Reverend doing wasting his time with football? Well, walking around Barnsley, he could see the effects of constant upheaval and violent death and how tykes coped with it. He noticed how they took their minds off the horrors of the underworld. There were the fairs and entertainers of course, but these were passing amusements and he sensed a need for more.

Towns all over the country were undergoing transformations like Barnsley. As new technology cried out for new labour, huge movements away from the countryside towards urban areas were under way. First, people were drawn in from neighbouring villages, then from much further afield; towns became seething melting pots of different accents and attitudes. In tarn there were second-generation families of Irish, Kentish, and Lancashire backgrounds and many others separated from their birthplaces.

The sheer volume of this rapid, unchecked migration led to many problems throughout the country: housing and health were obvious concerns that few had the money, time or inclination to address. In Barnsley, Locke's new park offered a chance of fresh air and relaxation. John Staniforth Beckett's donation allowed the building of Beckett Hospital and dispensary; it was a welcome addition. Other notable tykes-about-tarn were sorting out clean water supplies for a still rapidly growing Barnsley.

Preedy didn't have the money for anything like that, but he'd recognised the need for something else. A need for an identity, a sense of belonging. Could it be that football – something everyone enjoyed – could become much more than just a game? Could it bring people together, offer a new sense of identity for the town, something to believe in, far away from the increasing day-to-day grind?

Football seemed to fit the bill on a lot of counts. It was very popular: men and women had played it for years. All over the country, countless makeshift footballs were being booted about by hundreds of rag-tag teams. The game needed no equipment, was easy to organise: two teams, one ball, jumpers for goalposts and off you go. Football offered a break from hard work, a chance for exercise and fresh air that could only be welcome.

Now I'm not saying that the Reverend Tiverton Preedy *invented* football or that Barnsley was the home of the game – that would be ridiculous. But football as we know it today was invented just down the road, among the furnaces of the Don Valley. The first official club was formed in Sheffield just before the 1860s began. It was a brave, visionary but ultimately foolish move, because if you're the very first club there's no one to play against. The 'dee-dahs' bluffed their way through early months, by arranging games of married men v. bachelors, then took on soldiers at the local barracks. When Sheffield announced it would form something called a 'football association', South Yorkshire became the birthplace of the modern game. Preedy and these early pioneers were right: the game took off almost overnight. Other associations and local leagues sprang up and were almost immediately followed by regional, then national, leagues.

Standing on the steps of St Peter's, the Reverend thought the wasteland across the road would be as good a place as any for a ground: Oakwell was born. Barnsley St Peter's joined the Sheffield and District league. A few years later they were in the Midlands league and had made a first appearance in the new Football Association Cup competition.

Preedy left Barnsley to take up a new post in London, but his football team did not fall by the wayside. Ten years after Reverend Tiverton Preedy had his dream, Barnsley ('St Peter's' had been dropped the previous year) entered the lower of the two national leagues, along with New Brighton and the mighty Glossop. We lost our first two games away at Lincoln and Port Vale. Our first win was at Oakwell against Luton. Barnsley's first away point was against Newton Heath. 'Heath' are still around today but they've changed their name to Manchester United.

Barnsley may have struggled up and down the Second Division, but they started to do well in the FA Cup. The 1910–11 season saw them go further than they'd ever gone before: the semi-finals. All tykes looked excitedly towards what the next year would bring.

The Glorious 12th

THERE WAS GREAT EXCITEMENT EVERYWHERE IN THAT TWELFTH year of the twentieth century. The furnaces were turning out machines that would have been unimaginable only a few years before. Some men's faith in the new technology was now absolute. There was no longer need of men like Preedy: the awesome vessel they'd built could defy God himself. Far away and over the seas, men were lighting celebratory cigars and ordering a little more ice in the Scotch.

More important things were happening around tarn. Barnsley stormed past the semis and faced West Bromwich at Crystal Palace: it ended all square at 0–0. Barnsley made sure football was coming home by choosing Sheffield's Bramall Lane as the venue for the FA Cup final replay.

Over at Wentworth Woodhouse there was an air of great

excitement. Maids, butlers, cooks and footmen swarmed over the great house furiously polishing, cooking and cleaning. It must have been a hell of a job: the house has 365 rooms and staff often got completely lost. Outside, gardeners pruned and chopped, all the while herding deer and buffalo into picturesque poses.

The Marquis of Rockingham was long gone by now and the house passed through the family to the 4th Earl Fitzwilliam. In a rare outbreak of continuity at Wentworth Woodhouse, by that FA Cup year it had passed on to the 7th Earl Fitzwilliam. By then the family were down to their last three and a half billion – in today's money – but still managing to get by.

As the 7th Earl waited for his visitors, there was great activity throughout the estate and beyond. Flags and bunting were dug out and festooned across every building; little children stood dutifully waving Union Jacks, not quite knowing why. But they'd remember that visit for the rest of their lives: it's not every day the King and Queen came to tarn.

George V and Queen Mary were entertained in the manner to which they were accustomed: grand banquets, balls, receptions etc. No doubt they admired the buffalo, the follies, the great house, but impressive as all that was, you could get it anywhere. The King was up for the main event: a spin round the Earl's estate to take a look at a vision of the future as it actually took shape.

The Fitzwilliams realised what the old Marquis of Rockingham could only dream of. To the canal network through their grounds they added railways to link mines and foundries dotted on the estate. It was an impressive set-up.

The occupants of Wentworth Woodhouse always felt the need to take care of the welfare of their workers. Villages on the great estate prospered: every detail of their stone cottages was considered, down to the fitting of garden gates so children didn't run into the road. They established and supported school libraries and technical institutions. Wentworth village itself was home to the growing number of people needed by both estate and house. The Rockinghams and Fitzwilliams were dream employers. This approach extended to new operations. In mining operations, safety was a prime consideration. A previous Fitzwilliam employed the Birams, a father-and-son team of mining engineers, to develop state-of-the-art safety technology in his mines. The Newcomen pumping engine at Elsecar required to keep the mine free of water was a worldbeater. Some years later it impressed Henry Ford so much that he attempted to buy it and ship it back to the States.

George V was suitably impressed as Fitzwilliam enthusiastically pointed out all the big moving bits; Queen Mary was enchanted by small children waving flags at their garden gates. If this was the future for their empire, it was looking like a damn fine show. It seemed that all the old problems surrounding mining had finally been overcome.

Mining was far from any tyke's mind that sweltering April afternoon of the 1912 FA Cup replay as Preedy led his team onto the pitch at Bramall Lane. Twenty-five years after the Reverend's dream took shape on wasteground opposite St Peter's church, the grandfathers of E.I. Addio, McDog, Airtyke, Brinner and the rest were probably screaming themselves hoarse, waving rattles and biting their nails through another stalemate at Bramall Lane. The deadlock remained unbroken at full time. Extra time saw little change.

A young miner, William Rushforth, watched the clock tick towards yet another replay. There were just two minutes of extra time to go as, wide-eyed in excitement, he watched Glendenning slide the ball through to Tufnall who raced unchecked into the West Bromwich box. As Tufnall steadied himself, time stood still. The Barnsley striker drew back his foot . . . and Bramall Lane exploded! One–nil. Tykes said it was the greatest moment in tarn history.

Far and away and across the seas, the cigars had already gone soggy when the Scotches got a little more ice than they could handle. The unsinkable *Titanic* settled at the bottom of the Atlantic, leaving those who had decided they could defy the Almighty an eternity to ponder their words.

King George V left Wentworth Woodhouse, congratulating Fitzwilliam on his work. What he couldn't really appreciate, though, was that in his kingdom men like Fitzwilliam were very few and far between. Most mining enthusiasts had different ideas – ideas that were already in operation.

With victory celebrations over, William Rushforth returned to work. After walking the two miles across the peaceful, wooded Worborough valley he entered a steel cage and disappeared below the earth's surface.

The Great Wave

SINCE CONFIRMATION OF THE WHALE'S EXISTENCE, THE grandchildren and great-grandchildren of the Bramall Lane crowd had been very, very busy. The whale was no longer a subject of doubt. Old quibbles between believer and non-believer were long forgotten. The board swirled with new arrivals and seasoned hands noisily preparing for the first sighting of our marine mammal. Wombella tyke sang her heart out.

> We'll follow the whale over land and sea,
> We'll follow the whale of Barnsley FC.
> We'll follow the whale over land and sea,
> Yes we'll follow our whale to victory.

> That's excellent. I believe it, don't know why but I do!

Loco the tyke's response means I should mention one aspect of the hunt that had changed. The very nature of the board meant that, besides not knowing who anyone else was, no one had a clue how old their shipmates were either. The general assumption (on my part at least) was everyone was the same age as me: this led to the terrible storm of disappointment of '68. Yet opening shots took place between believers and tykes who obviously were roughly the right age and could have seen Jonah.

No more tykes surfaced who'd seen the whale but, stranger than that, we now had a far younger crew aboard. Loco the tyke was only 17. The whale was long gone way before he was even born, yet he simply believed. Jonah was an article of faith, a faith so strong even the good Reverend would have been surprised.

The crew hauled on the ropes turning the whaler into the wind. Out on that sparkling sea of optimism, we crested a great wave of elation. There were songs, poems, film scripts . . .

> Free Willy 4! The whale gets stuck darn pit and needs rescuin'.

> I don't think he'd like it down Barnsley Main!! Way too dark and the coalface is too low for him to get to it! He'd probably knock all the support beams out anyway.

> How about, to the tune of 'Sex God' from Tom Jones
> . . .
> 'You may not believe it
> But we've got to say
> We caught a whale in tarn one day
> Not cod, not cod
> It wasn't a cod
> It was Barnsley folk that caught 'im
> And we used a rod!
> Not cod, not cod

It wasn't a cod
It was Barnsley folk that caught 'im
And we used a rod!'

Dun't you mean 'Sex Bomb'?

Freed from work, I could now devote myself to the final leg of our quest. Even so, I was dimly aware of someone else moving around the house. Doors opening, closing. Voices. Now I remembered: Caroline. I lived with her. So that was where the food kept coming from. She smiled and left me to my whale musing.

Pods of marine mammals leapt onto the board, posted to allow that most esteemed of all tarn cetologists, Big 'n' Daft, to cast an expert eye over them. As the first believer and an actual witness to Jonah, his learned opinion was awaited with bated breath. He'd already pronounced Yankee tyke's 'Minnesota Whale' to be 'shite': few others were to find favour, even a passable picture of a blue.

Pah! You could fit that on top of a transit. Tarn Whale was a wide-body long load.

Even our cats caught the mood. Ruby took to raiding a nearby pond, proudly delivering a procession of startled amphibians into the house. I'd noticed Millie drag a brass doorknocker under the sofa by means of some tangled string; the knocker was in the shape of a sea serpent. There was croaking coming from somewhere.

Whale story in the *Chronicle* . . . claim to fame. Well done Statis.

You're famous. Everyone's famous!

Yes, it was true! Izzy and Big 'n' Daft broadcast the news. So my persistence had finally paid off. Routinely ringing Paul over previous days, I'd finally worn him down, or maybe he feared for his safety if the whale nutter came up to tarn. Whatever, he'd done us proud and in the process punned his way into the *Chronicle* Hall of Fame. I even forgave the annoying reference to 'surfing' rather than 'hunting': 'Crate expectations as fans hunt the Prince of Whales. A whale of a story has been keeping Barnsley football fans talking on the Internet.'

Big 'n' Daft was right. We were famous: well, famous if you overlooked the fact that no one, including ourselves, had a clue who we really were. Still, it could only help the cause; someone, somewhere might have a photograph.

We would prove beyond doubt there had been a whale in tarn and it was clear from the crew's wild enthusiasm that our hunt was now at a magical conflux of currents. While I journeyed north to bring Jonah back from the dead, the crew were now determined he would live forever.

Inflatable

THE ANCIENT CHINESE WERE FAMILIAR WITH THE MYTHICAL whale-creature Yu-kiang. Their descendants didn't seem at all fazed by my request to create a new mythical whale.

The specifications were clear. Several thousand *li* might have been going a bit far, so I settled on 4 ft. The blue whale would, of course, be red. Down its flanks it was to carry a small dog named Toby and the legend 'Tarn Whale'. Plastic-skinned, it had to be capable of rapid inflation at the blast of a referee's whistle.

Deaftyke's suggestion of renaming the ground 'Oakwhale' was only one of the whale talismen carved out during our hunt.

Many long hours had been spent in deliberation and the weaving of this magical new myth. I can't be sure among the babble, but I think it was TV Tyke who first hit on the idea, very early on at the height of the storm.

> How's about . . . some inflatable whales for everyone to wave abart next season? That'd keep 'em guessing!

Before a friendly against the neighbouring 'Millers', hoylandtyke and Tattershall tyke quibbled about whether to take a blow-up whale to Rotherham or a blow-up Rotherham to Wales. Inevitably an argument broke out between Deaftyke and TV Tyke as to who would be responsible for inflating them . . .

> You can blow the buggers up!

> Worrabart thee, tha big puff!

> Oi, that's fisticuffs talk in Kendray! Good job I've flitted!

> . . . and frillicuffs talk in West Landern! Put 'em up . . . put 'em up!

We didn't invent the idea of 'inflatables'. They'd been around for a while. Our grandfathers' rattles and scarves were long gone and, what with worries about any object's potential to be an offensive weapon, plastic inflatables fitted the bill perfectly. Grimsby Town wielded blow-up haddocks at one point; Stoke City for some reason waved Pink Panthers. Up in Hartlepool air-filled bananas have been spotted.

The crew was determined Tarn Whale would be the greatest inflatable of all. It would not just be the one either – we wanted thousands. A friend contacted the Far East. The Chinese nodded in agreement: it would be possible. Longley tyke dreamed of 'a sea of whales' at away games. Deaftyke, the self-confessed 'man with a whale on the brain', displayed shrewd business acumen with an even grander vision . . .

> An idea . . . Why don't we petition the club to adopt the whale as a mascot, we could even charge away fans to walk through the hollowed-out creosoted carcass.

This ambitious plan in itself highlighted a problem: we already had a mascot. Back in the '60s Arthur Braithwaite, tarn dog breeder and friend of the club, had his favourite bulldog photographed with the players. On seeing Toby, the management decided to adopt him as mascot: Toby Tyke was born. He first made an appearance at the start of the 1967–68 season (spookily, the year of Jonah's visit) and has been our much-loved frontman ever since. As a pup, Toby was originally kennelled on letterheads, badges and scarves, but as he grew he sprang to life, joining the bizarre ranks of chickens, eagles, lions, dragons – and of course a monkey – that parade football grounds on matchdays.

It might look like harmless fun, but it's a job fraught with danger. H'Angus isn't the only one to get out of order at a match. Halifax's Freddie the Fox took a punch from Rochdale's Desmond the Dragon for cocking a leg on a goalpost and Swansea's Cyril the Swan is notoriously hot-tempered, having once been fined £1,000 for flapping onto the pitch. Then there's the crowd. Chesterfield fans became so excited on promotion that they ripped poor Chester the Mouse's head off; it was found later hanging from a pub sign. And please spare a thought for Southend's Sammy the Shrimp. At the annual Mascot Grand National he always comes in last. As he woefully admits, 'It's because I haven't got any legs.' Toby Tyke doesn't get involved in any of that stuff. He's famous for leading the singing, handing out prizes and trying to save nippers' half-time penalties, and we'd never dream of usurping him.

Some say these mascots are men in animal suits, which just goes to show some weirdos will believe anything these days. My nephew, Nicholas, assures me that Toby cuts his hair, though a barber's shop seems an unusual sideline for a 7-ft dog. Holding the scissors must be pretty tricky.

TV Tyke pondered the problem of two mascots . . .

> Maybe . . . Toby could get into a bit o' bother wi' whale afore kick-off, get swallered up, piss abart a bit inside its belly, then emerge, Pinocchio-like, wi' is dad and a load o' cod. It'd keep t'young 'uns amused.

. . . and Munich tyke cracked it . . .

> Top idea Toby is CLUB mascot. Findus the FANS' mascot!

Finally TV Tyke deduced the hand of fate in this appearance of our marine mammal . . .

> Was it a Big Thing?

Big Thing . . . of course! Just so nobody forgets the corporate world's hold on football, all clubs, stands, grounds (and probably individual blades of grass next) are sponsored, the team sponsor getting their name plastered across the players' shirts. During our Premiership season the Reds' sponsor was a mobile phone accessory company and now, in keeping with tarn's desire to be at the leading edge, we sported a name for the future: a dot com company. BigThing.com. A perfect fit in every sense.

> Idea for PR for BigThing.com. Give away inflatable whales/balloons in whale shape in corporate colours/logo. Free ads on news bulletins and

> exposure on Goals on Sunday guaranteed. Pre-Sky
> matches would also be an idea. The fans would take
> them in as they would be free whether they were in
> on this or not.

I don't know what Alityke does for a living, but the fact that she could come up with the above meant she didn't work in advertising. In fact, most of the stuff kicking off on the board would be beyond the ability of the slow-moving, data-chewing corporate dinosaurs: a heretical combination of clear thinking, open conversation and enthusiasm.

Forget three lions. Tykester was up for 'one whale on his shirt'.

> Nubdi really likes the new shirt with Big Thing on it
> so I think we should 'ave our own shirt with a whale
> on it. And we need a song.

Oldham Tyke jumped at the idea as Singer Tyke composed the song.

> By Jove I just bledy think he's got it. Class idea matey,
> when can I put an order in for three shirts?

> What abahrt to the tune of he's got the whole world
> in his hands . . . 'We've got a Big Thing on our shirts,
> We've got a Big Thing on our shirts, We've got a Big
> Thing on our shirts, Just like whale in tarn.'

'Pictures, memorabilia, T-shirts, books and set yourself up on t'market,' Big 'n' Daft had said. Out across the oceans our Chinese friends were ready to launch an armada of Tarn Whales to Oakwell. They wouldn't be ready for a few months, but a little detail like that never stands in the way of a resourceful tyke. A cry went out for help in assembling a temporary shoal of sealife.

'I got a blow-up crocodile if that's any good.'

A legend was being born before our very eyes. All that remained was to make sure I got my hands on real proof he'd been to tarn in the first place. With only a few days left to the start of the new season, no matter how strong the call of the whale, football would take priority, and why not? We couldn't do any more; all leads were exhausted. Sheffield was my only chance. If I succeeded, Jonah would live once more at Oakwell. If I failed, he would be consigned once more to the dustbin of history. This would be my finest hour.

Inland whale hunting

For Yankee Tyke, Munich tyke, Knut and all you exiles abroad — John Dennis on Talksport. www.talksport.net listen in 2 p.m. Susietyke

STORMS HUNG HEAVY OVER LONDON THAT SUMMER. THE MORNING of my departure dawned thick and yellow as the crew gathered on the board to say their farewells. Susietyke's posting about the interview of Barnsley chairman John Dennis didn't seem anything out of the ordinary, at least not at first.

Talksport Radio, as its name suggests, caters for sports fans. Every sport gets a shout at some time or another. *In the Boardroom* lets footy fans get inside their chairman's head by offering them the chance to question him live on air about transfers, managers, opposition, season ticket prices, pies or anything to do with their club. John Dennis, the Barnsley chairman, being interviewed by Brian Moore, was certainly not a programme any tyke would want to miss.

The station does have its limitations though. Its knowledge

of deep-sea mammals is non-existent, for example. Fishing yes; whales no. There's no reason to believe John Dennis expected anything trickier than irate questions about the sale of Craig Hignett or some nosy tyke trying to poke around in the club's finances. Certainly, neither he nor Brian Moore felt the need to brush up on current cetological thinking before appearing live on air.

A new cry went up as old Viking blood coursed through the crew. They would board and seize this prize to talk not only sport, but whales as well! They would ask Admiral Dennis for his view on Tarn Whale! Logic dictated that the chairman would know nothing about a whale in tarn. Logic, though, had been flung overboard long ago: the whale had now totally consumed its hunters.

Loco the tyke stepped forward to assume control with wide-eyed enthusiasm. I gave what advice I could as to a battle plan, but would not be taking part. At the appointed hour of attack – two o'clock the following day – I would be submerged deep in the National Fairground Archive.

I proposed using the weapon Casper invented one wild night long ago – the multiple e-mail. Deployed live on air, it could prove effective. Loco the tyke was enthused:

> So we need every song sent by a different e-mail address? Well I have two e-mail addresses so will do two, and who else will do 'em? You will do one so that leaves about four more! John Dennis won't know what's hit him!

I hastily prepared an explanatory e-mail. Taking careful aim across the cybersea, I fired at Talksport. This was vital to the plan: they would have 24 hours to apprise Admiral Dennis of the whale hunt and alert him to tykes closing in. The 'multiple e-mail' would blow a hole in the programme's defences as the show went out live, allowing the crew to storm on board. Loco the tyke set to work preparing the 'e' decks.

> Right I will get the e-mail address put it on the board,
> and me, westie/mcdog, and wombella tyke will e-mail
> the show with a song.

Munich Tyke, Yankee Tyke, even McDog were caught up in his
enthusiasm. A lightning strike of postings: a whale song, poem
or question, all to be fired in unison. Sensing the crew could
easily be ignored as nutters, optictyke set about designing a
'stealth' e-mail.

> E-mail a serious question and then attach a whale-
> related item. They'll have to mention it and then it'll
> be funny to see what JD has to say on the matter.

Understandably, the nerve of the less-experienced recruits was
tested to the full. Wombella tyke wavered but Loco the tyke and
Susietyke rallied round her.

> No sorry . . . I don't have the bottle, someone else
> mail the song I posted.

> WOMBELLA . . . PLEASE DO IT . . . I have sent one
> . . . I would send it but we need lots of different e-mail
> addresses otherwise they will think it's a windup
> when we are serious! DO IT FOR THE WHALE!

> I'll do it don't worry.

Outside my window, fat chameleon raindrops were kicking up
dust. In truth it all needed more thought, but the weather was
closing in rapidly. I had to leave them. I opened one last posting
from Ish.

Good luck in Bluntland. God speed StatisTYKE, the world's only inland whale hunter!

I returned the salute; it would be now or never. With Ish's words ringing through my head, I hoisted the red flag high, turning my vessel due north towards the gathering gloom of Bluntland. Plunging through mountains of spray, dull leviathans wallowed on my port bow – lorries . . . big lorries.

Octopus

DEEP IN SLUMBER, WE DRIFT ACROSS THE DATELINE INTO THAT fateful Friday . . . no hand tends the helm . . . no lookout keeps watch . . . our ship glides serene through the dark subconscious void . . . in only a few short hours we will . . .

Awake!

What fate has befallen us?

. . . we are off course that much is certain . . . too far north by the stars . . .

The ship trembles . . . listen . . . she tells us of our . . .

''Tis the valley! We are sucked into the valley!'

Her very timbers shudder in pain . . . we are being dragged down . . .

Strike not for the wheel! 'Twill be of no avail . . . we are powerless . . . this force . . . no man can control!

Black wave towers above . . .

Do you know of fear my friend? Fear that . . . *Steady yourself!* If you have a god, 'tis as well you ask his mercy this hour . . .

If once you did mock tales of the ancient mariners, you will mock no more! Chronicles deep-etched in horror . . . creatures bursting forth from subterranean lairs . . . proud vessels crashed to matchwood . . . lost souls dragged to foaming oblivion . . .

such things are not the product of fevered imagining or rum-laced yarn . . . *Such things live my friend!*

. . . surely now her keel will be torn asunder . . . we rise . . . he drags us to the crest . . .

DEAR GOD!

Whiplash strikes!

The beast!

Show not your terror to the cephalopod for he will feed on your fear!

By miracle we are spared.

Not so other tykes . . .

Behold them!

Gripped firm in iron tentacles they are hurled screaming into the void . . .

And there is more . . . far more . . . in this swirling vortex . . .

Ahead!

Snorting gilt and scarlet stallions, nostrils flared, teeth bared white . . . straining free from candy-twisted poles . . . proud-crested cockerels . . . frantic tykes astride hens the size of sheep . . . burning gold through cold night that is . . .

Hard a' starboard lest we tumble through the chasm of death!

Ask not of that place my friend. Many a sturdy tyke has ne'er spoken word in all his remaining days after entering there. 'Tis rumoured . . . in that wailing darkness . . . luminous bones dance a jig of death! From beyond the grave rise up spiders . . . witches . . . wolves . . . reaching out to claw the living . . .

Here!

Carved silver chests brimming with treasure beyond an emperor's imagining . . . *The bells! The bells!* . . . kings, queens, lemons, oranges, toffee-hardened apples . . . pastel clouds of fine spun sugar . . . bubbling rivers of corn . . .

Off the port bow!

What fantastical creatures are these? Fearsome armoured crustaceans! Iridescent metal shells sprouting fire-orange stingray tails. O'er polished lakes they charge, locking together in bone-crunching combat . . .

No, my friend!

Above booming thunder of mighty organ . . . siren call . . . *hear me!* Whirling steam mingles with glowing carved face . . . *hear me!*

This spell is powerful but our business is not here . . .

We must flee lest you lose your very soul in these giddy whirlpools of colour . . . fear . . . music . . . exhilaration . . . light . . . only the magic men can summon.

Aye . . . speak of what you have seen this night if you will, but be warned. Like sailors of old, you may be regarded with disbelieving ear. Chide them not. For only those who have witnessed the power of the magic men and surrendered to their spell . . . only they can say they have *truly* lived.

I must set a course due south and rest before the morrow. But stay awhile on deck, my friend. A last glance astern at star-studded tentacles fading in our wake: the octopus weaving his magic o'er a glittering tarn market long, long ago.

The Cyclist

THE NATIONAL FAIRGROUND ARCHIVE AT SHEFFIELD UNIVERSITY: a deep, windowless cavern no shaft of daylight can penetrate. It struck me as the very belly of the beast. Regimented steel-rib shelves, stacked high with countless manila boxes, each box carefully labelled. Walls lined in history, the air rich in paper and ink. Packed inside these broadsheet-sized boxes was every single edition of *The World's Fair*, the journal for travelling fairground people, a weekly publication stretching back over 100 years: 6,000 fading yellow newspapers. They would hold the secret of Tarn Whale.

But I needed a guide who knew their pages well. Allow me to introduce Mr Harold Wilkinson. I will describe him as he appeared to me that fateful morning in Bluntland. His face is grained by 50 years under Yorkshire skies, hair white and wild as moorland heather. Under rough-stubbled chin, a tight-knotted silk scarf. Standing a little over 6 ft, I judge him to be of wiry build, though I can't be completely sure as he's wrapped in onion layers of wind-cheating wool and corduroy, topped by a weathered khaki greatcoat, leather gauntlets stuffed into one pocket. A man of the land, then; but Harold is no farmer. Clutched in one hand were the tools of his trade: a wire-bound notepad and a well-chewed pencil. At his ankles thin strips of metal, bicycle clips . . . for Harold Wilkinson is none other than The Cyclist!

His mission: to record the movements of every travelling fair in 1960s West Yorkshire for *The World's Fair*. Frantically pedalling over hill and dale, greatcoat flapping in the wind, his eagle eye missed nothing. Every coming and going of steam engines and gallopers was dutifully committed to his notepad then rushed into print. Each article credited to this intrepid roving reporter bore only his mysterious nom de plume.

The guardian of the cave threw back her mermaid hair, explaining that meeting The Cyclist in person wouldn't be possible: Harold Wilkinson had passed away in the 1980s. Yet through his enthusiastic column in *The World's Fair*, he seemed real enough to me that day.

The learned Doctor went on to explain that there were no books, magazines or computer files on the whale. Jonah had slipped through the net of recorded history. Any evidence would lie somewhere in the pages of *The World's Fair*, dutifully recorded by The Cyclist. No computer could save me now. No clicks of a mouse would send me skipping across endless oceans of information. It would be just The Cyclist and myself in a race against time.

The Doctor retreated to find the manila boxes for 1967/68 fairground matters. Casting a glance in my direction, she regarded Ahab with wary eye. Did she detect signs of the madness? I drifted alongside racks of fairground books. Picking out first one, then another, my eyes, now finely tuned to detect the slightest mention of sealife, flicked over page after page.

It was the mention of Greenland harpooners and a whale that stopped me dead.

Giant

LET'S SAY YOU'RE GOING OUT WITH FRIENDS THIS EVENING FOR a few drinks. How much money would you take? You'll probably have a bite to eat as well and you don't want to be splitting the bill on credit cards after you've had a few, do you? So it had better be cash. You might want to go on to a late-night bar as well, or even a club. Then you've got the taxi fare to think of. How much?

I know a bloke who mulled this question over once: Charlie Byrne. In the end he decided to make sure he was well covered. Stuffing £800,000 in his back pocket he hit the town. You think I'm joking, don't you? Well, I'm not.

Charlie wasn't like you or me. He was a celebrity. He was big in London, but to be honest, he'd have been big wherever he was. For Charles Byrne ('the sight of him is more than the mind can conceive . . . that modern living Colossus') was (roll of drums) the Giant!

Anyone who was anyone wanted to say they were 'in' with Charlie, the man around town. Newspapers reported his every move. He'd have been on TV more often than Dale Winton, if TV had been around at the time. Charles Byrne, the feted 'Irish Giant', wowed society figures in the early 1780s.

'So you've seen the famous Maximillian Miller you say . . . and Daniel Cajaneus, the big Swedish lad? *Pah!* They're nothing! Mere *midgets* in comparison.'

Fame, celebrity and sensationalism weren't invented in the Internet age. The desire for constant novelty is a part of human nature and proved as insatiable back then as it does now. And back then, there was nothing that people clamoured for more than bizarre extremes from the human or animal worlds, 'freaks' as they came to be known.

Although billed as a staggering 8 ft 4 in. it seems more likely he stood around 7 ft 11 in. tall, but, hey, that's showbiz folks! No matter, everyone just had to see Charles Byrne: 'Take him, for all in all we shall scarce look on his like again.' An audience with Byrne didn't come cheap: 2/6 and 1/- for children and servants. Byrne was a spectacle reserved for the elite: some people wouldn't earn that in a year. The Giant and his manager were raking it in.

But the celebrity circuit was fraught with exactly the same problems we see today. Like boy bands now, once someone hit on a winning formula everyone jumped on the bandwagon. Pretty soon other 'giants' wanted a piece of the action. Byrne scarcely had time to bask in his fame when up popped the Knipe family with their 'Gigantic Twin Brothers'. They and big Patrick Cotter hailed from Ireland as well, Cotter even having the cheek to call himself the 'Irish Giant'.

The original and best giant was pretty cheesed off at others muscling in, but worse was to come. As the sea monsters of Brighton later found out, the fundamental rule of novelty is that it soon wears thin. Only a year after his arrival in London, giants were boring: been there, seen it, done it – yesterday's news. See ya.

Megastar falls on hard times! Shunned by his public. You can see it coming, can't you?

Charlie hit the bottle, big time. Only 22 and with little education, he'd never been the brightest bulb in the box. Even at the height of his brief fame, shows were cancelled due to him being 'unwell', vatloads of gin and whisky usually being the cause of his illness. Swiftly his health started to fail.

That was when he set out on his big **bender** around London with £770 (yes, that's the equivalent of about £800,000 in today's money). The money was in two notes, so I can only presume that his mates were paying for the drinks. Imagine getting a few lagers and a packet of cheese and onion in, then asking the barman if he's got change for a £400,000 note. All in all, it must have been a helluva party and his hangover could scarcely have improved when he woke to find his 'mates' had legged it with the money: his complete life savings. He continued drinking and sank further into oblivion. Surely death would be a merciful release for this now pathetic figure?

Well . . . no. It just kept getting worse.

While most people at the time lived wretched, miserable lives and met an anonymous fate, rich and poor alike were united by the same terrible fear while preparing to meet their maker. Celebrities were the most terrified of all. Charles Byrne, staggering drunkenly toward his deathbed, was petrified of shadows in the night . . . watching . . . waiting. He knew he was about to become the talk of the town once more.

Enquiring minds knew no bounds back then. Byrne knew full well that in his audiences were a few eminent gentlemen who were studying his massive frame a little too closely, all the while mentally sharpening their knives. London's medical men had an ever-increasing thirst for more anatomical knowledge and they didn't care how they came by it. They were particularly interested in freaks and went to any lengths to make sure they were first to get the scalpel in.

This wasn't a shady undercover business either. Byrne was tracked in the full glare of the media's spotlight. The OJ Simpson chase had nothing on this, a real celebrity manhunt! The public lapped it up. Even while Byrne was still alive, newspapers screamed: 'The whole tribe of surgeons put in a claim for the poor *departed* Irish Giant and surrounded his house just as Greenland harpooners would an enormous whale.'

Who would get him onto the dissecting table first? Hot

favourite was another big name, the aptly named John Hunter, Fellow of the Royal Society, London's leading surgeon and anatomist. In his time Hunter bagged over 14,000 specimens for examination, the freakier the better. He was first in line for a marvellous bouncy new creature from one of Captain Cook's voyages known as a kangaroo, and he'd been right on the scene when a Grampus whale was found in the Thames Estuary and brought up to Westminster on a barge. No way was Hunter going to allow a giant to escape him. He even employed a man called Howison to tail Byrne lest the Giant peg it unexpectedly.

Byrne knew all about Hunter, of course. The chase was continually on the front page and he was well aware the odds were stacked against him. Even after burial he was certain he wouldn't be allowed to rest in peace, for the surgeons were in league with notorious gangs of bodysnatchers continually sniffing graveyards for freshly buried corpses – they'd find him.

In the nick of time, as death loomed and the hunt reached its climax, the Giant devised a cunning plan. Scraping together the last of his money, he hit on a way to escape the ghoulish clutches of the medics. Charles Byrne decided burial at sea was the only way out. He found a group of trustworthy fishermen, paid them handsomely and swore them to secrecy. The instructions were clear: Byrne's body was to be sunk to a depth of 20 fathoms. Tell absolutely no one. The fishermen nodded. Sadly, Charlie had a terrible track record when choosing his mates, as the next day's papers made clear. Frenzied hacks even speculated on Hunter and Howison's next move.

' . . . determined to pursue their valuable prey even in the profoundest depth of the aquatic regions; and have therefore provided a pair of diving bells, with which they hope to weigh hulk gigantic from its watery grave.'

Hunter must have smiled as he read the article to Howison. They really didn't have to go to such tiresome lengths at all. Hunter sharpened his scalpel and stuffed banknotes into a medical bag before they disappeared into the night. They knew just the men to talk to . . . to settle this matter once and for all.

Predictably, Hunter and Howison caught up with the burial party. Plying them with drink, they proposed a deal – £500 for their enormous catch and no questions asked. With the equivalent of today's half a million dangling in front of you in exchange for a dead giant you just happen to have about your person, what would you do?

And so Hunter got his prize. Scurrying back to Hunter's place, the surgeon sharpened his knives while Howison got the kettle on, and a very, very big kettle it was too. And so ends the tall tale of poor old Charlie Byrne: cut up and boiled over the fire in Earl's Court.

The Giant may have been forgotten, but he's still around. Two hundred years after his death, Charles Byrne's still 'giving audiences in the West End'. His skeleton's displayed in the Hunterian Museum in Glasgow to this day, along with a boot, slipper and glove. Not that Hunter ever really admitted to acquiring the corpse at the time. Although he did mention in one lecture he'd come by the skeleton of 'a tall man'. Enough said.

Freaks

CHARLES BYRNE WAS BY NO MEANS THE ONLY HUMAN curiosity to live a tragic life and suffer a terrible fate. Funfairs are swirling circles of bright, glowing stars, fusions of giddying, exhilarating light. Perhaps that's what makes the shadows deeper . . . darker. There walk creatures our minds have cast out from the light and consigned to a dark, forgotten prison.

The Elephant Man, the Lion-faced Lady, the Human Ostrich, the Siamese Twins – there's no need to give descriptions of these people. But how could our grandparents have allowed such unfortunates to be paraded as freaks and sideshow novelties? How could they have allowed such human suffering to be exploited as spectacle? Well, things were very different back then.

The world was made up of only two groups of people. The very rich: royalty, nobility, clergy, military, medics, lawyers, wealthy merchants – a tiny minority. Then there were the very poor. These were the vast majority and among their number would be you and me. Only when the great movements of people began did the richer group expand a little to include those involved in commerce.

Byrne was an attraction for the rich. His manhunt blazed across their newspapers (most of us poor ones couldn't read at the time). And as for kiddies riding on Jumbo's back, they'd have been the offspring of the privileged few. The fishermen up in Hartlepool wouldn't have been able to even gawp at a travelling menagerie; they'd be too busy scratching out a living. If you did make a living you were lucky. Disease, injury and hunger meant dying was far easier.

But the unluckiest of all were those born with a deformity. This was an instant death sentence. Shunned by family who couldn't care for you anyway, and with no health service or social welfare, your number was well and truly up. All people wanted to do was gawp at you. So what would you do? Die in a gutter, wait for a call from the surgeons or leap into the hands of the bodysnatchers? Or would you turn your one 'asset' into a chance for some sort of life and a bit of money and companionship?

Not a great choice admittedly, but it was often the only one on offer. As the Giant found, it was a fleeting career (people soon wanted something a little different – like the odd dwarf), but it was better than death and there were plenty willing to make offers. Managers toured the country with their freaks, skilfully tapping into basic human nature. Most hoped to make it into the Premiership by stumbling across a human curiosity that really took off among the rich, like Byrne. But they understood that the desire for novelty runs through all of us:

even the poor could be persuaded to part with what little money they had if the attraction were 'freaky' enough.

Of course, we like to think we wouldn't have been dragged into anything like that. But be honest. Ask yourself – are you, even now, wondering what the Lion-faced Lady looked like? If you had the chance to see her, would you take it? Just so you could tell your mates not to go – nothing more of course. And anyway, whether you see her or not she's still going to be there; you're not doing her any harm, are you?

No? Well, what about the startling Rosina Bishop who hails from Southampton, or 'Mermaidia'. Now what kind of . . . come on, be honest. It's a chance to see a real mermaid!

Roll up! Roll up! Yes, you sir . . . you madam . . . step this way for the strangest tale of all.

The Prince of Humbug

ON A SULTRY INDONESIAN AFTERNOON WHILE ANCHORED OFF Java, an American captain heeded the cries of a Japanese fisherman who urged him to look upon a miracle he'd just landed in his nets. The sea captain was astounded. Marvelling at the fantastical creature, he knew this was his big break, that once-in-a-lifetime opportunity that has to be grabbed with both hands. Could it be that he, a humble sailor, had hit on something as big as the Spice Girls?

There was no time to lose. 'Borrowing' $6,000 of the ship's money to seal the deal, he sped to London. The creature caused a sensation. Over 300 people a day queued to see it in Piccadilly's Egyptian Hall. Quite probably some of the audience had seen the Irish Giant as children and now had the good fortune to witness another wonder of the world. Admittedly this was quite a bit smaller, but no less magical.

The captain explained the mermaid had been caught alive; it died shortly afterwards, but not before uttering a few prophetic words. It foretold that the good years were about to end and a terrible epidemic would strike the earth. The only way to avoid this would be to carry a picture of the prophet. Images of the mermaid sold like hot cakes and the catastrophe was averted. Oh wise mermaid!

After this brush with fame, the captain returned to America with his curiosity, where his luck ran out when he was summoned by his ship's owner and made to account for the missing funds. On his death the mermaid passed onto his son and seemed destined to fade into obscurity.

Some 20 years later a respected English academic, Dr J. Griffin of the Lyceum of Natural History in London, was seized by a panic attack while walking down Broadway in New York. A pity, as things had been going so well for him. The good doctor was travelling through America en route for London with a marvellous specimen he'd acquired: the sea captain's mermaid. Understandably, rumour spread from state to state of the doctor's find, the press taking up the story with enthusiasm. On reaching New York, Griffin felt it only right that, given the public interest – now verging on 'mermaid mania' – he should put the creature on display for a week or so before departing.

At Griffin's lectures in the Concert Hall on Broadway, the mermaid caused a greater sensation than it had done in London 20 years before. So popular was it that the tour had to be extended and relocated at a nearby musuem. In fact it caused more than a stir; the likelihood of a full-blown punch-up increased every day and on occasions only Dr Griffin's status as an academic saved him. The cause of all this bother? Well, there seemed to be a growing confusion in the minds of his audiences.

Everyone knows what a mermaid looks like. Old mariners' stories tell of seductive singing temptresses perched on rocks, combing long silken hair. But Dr Griffin's mermaid just didn't seem like the real thing, some protested. Little did they know, Dr Griffin wasn't the real thing either: *nothing* about the story was the real thing. The story behind the hysteria that gripped America was actually weirder than the creature itself.

'Dr Griffin' was actually a smooth-talking lawyer, Levi Lyman, working for a young entrepreneur who'd been offered the sea captain's creature, or the 'Feejee Mermaid' as he'd named it. He'd had the mermaid examined by a leading naturalist, who marvelled at its bone structure and said it looked anatomically genuine, although to any casual observer it looked for all the world like the top half of a monkey stitched to the bottom half of a fish. The 'mermaid' was a gruesome, shrivelled spectacle that appeared to have died in terrible agony.

Curiosities like these weren't really that rare: mythical animals cobbled together from various parts (like the two-headed calf in tarn) could be dragons, unicorns or whatever you fancied: Japanese fishermen had long turned out a profitable line in mermaids. What made this mermaid exhibition so spectacular was the entrepreneur who decided to exhibit it, for he was none other than our old friend, Phileas T. Barnum. This was long before his theft of the Empire's prized quadruped, but the Feejee Mermaid paved the way for what would come.

It was an elaborate plan: letters to newspapers relating to the eminent 'doctor' and his mermaid were all placed by Barnum himself. As mermaid madness took hold, Barnum kindly offered his own museum as a venue. And that was when Lyman suffered his panic attack. Standing on Broadway, the lawyer knew it couldn't go on. 'Come and See the Mermaid' blazed a banner stretched across the sidewalk, accompanied by a beautiful vision of woman/fishhood. The terrible fish/monkey monster looked nothing like that. No wonder the crowds were turning ugly.

Many were outraged by this obvious hoax; Barnum denied anything of the sort. 'Dr Griffin' never claimed the mermaid looked any other way than a shrivelled monkey fish. As for the advertising, Barnum just happened to use a well-known mermaid image. He never claimed the image was Griffin's *actual* mermaid. The Feejee Mermaid continued to pull them in and was equally successful on a following American tour.

All showmen used billboards and leaflets, but Barnum's outrageous approach to advertising – the trademark of his career – went far beyond that. His astute understanding of communication coupled with an ability to probe the deepest recesses of the human mind, enabled him to spread his message further and more effectively than anyone else had ever done.

His eye for a quick buck missed nothing. When a fossilised 10 ft 6 in. man, 'The Cardiff Giant', was unearthed by a farmer near New York, it was exposed as a stone-carved fake; but not before the farmer had started coining it in from thousands of gawpers. Never one to be upstaged, Barnum had a copy of the fake manufactured and placed on display. Thanks to his promotional skill it proved more popular than the real fake, leading either farmer or showman to coin the infamous quip that later would always be attributed to Barnum: 'There's a sucker born every minute.'

Some took a dim view of these antics. One investigator touring New York museums was shown the club that a native had wielded to finish off Captain Cook's career on a South Sea island. He then popped into Barnum's Museum and said he'd heard Barnum had the Captain Cook club. Barnum dug around and – surprise, surprise – he did!

Queen Victoria probably threw her weight behind the 'Save Jumbo' campaign in response to a previous Barnum stunt that didn't amuse her in the least. Tom Thumb, a tiny Yankee general, discovered by Barnum, thrilled the queen and her subjects until they discovered how Barnum had suckered them with a well-trained boy.

Not all his exhibits were fakes though: like John Hunter he paid fishermen handsomely to bring him giants. Live whales were caught and brought to New York; Barnum displayed them in huge seawater tanks on several occasions and people flocked to see them before, inevitably, they died.

Make what you will of this self-styled 'Prince of Humbug' but I'll end this short list of his hundreds of stunts with one he came up with in the 'Jumbo' years. When the great elephant was nothing more than a stretched skin over a wooden frame, he wasn't lonely on the second half of his American tour; hundreds of thousands turned up to see him after all. But he had one rather special guest. Barnum decided it would be a real crowd-puller if he were displayed alongside a live companion, and he knew just the one. Yes, Barnum brought Alice from London Zoo and displayed her next to her stuffed mate. Well, like they say, 'business is business'.

Over the years Phileas T. Barnum would amass and lose huge fortunes, be labelled showman, charlatan, con man, trickster or entertainer, and spark outrage or adoration in equal measure. Barnum's autobiography proved to be a bestseller. There were many who admired his astute understanding of human behaviour and naturally wanted to learn how to amass similar riches.

Thrown into the whirlpool of change that had been sparked in the '60s, many grabbed at Barnum's book as the way forward. Barnum was no engineer, and neither were they, but that didn't matter. Nobody knew the exact outcome of all these inventions and novelties that were being welded and stitched together anyway. But one thing was becoming clear: this period of great upheaval was the time to make a quick buck or two.

'There are only two kinds of people in the world: the outwitter and the outwitted.'

Many repeated his words over and over again in their dreams.

The Race

WAS JONAH REAL? A HOAX? WAS HE SOME CLEVER deception, made of wood and canvas perhaps? Half fish . . . half . . . God knows what?

No time to think about it. I had to concentrate on finding Tarn Whale, whatever he might turn out to be. The Doctor placed three manila boxes in front of me. I determined to deal with three years: 1967–69 inclusive. In itself this meant checking through just over 150 newspapers: an arduous but not impossible task. But I swiftly realised that the odds, like the manila boxes, were stacked against me.

A '60s publication is very different to a modern newspaper. Today's reader, well used to imagery exploding from every page, would be immediately struck by how few photographs there are. In a daily or weekly it was simply a matter of cost. There was a lead-article photograph for front-page news, then a meagre smattering of small ones throughout. In addition, readers brought up with spacious, airy layouts and large headlines would squint at the intense walls of text. Compressed lines of type cover every available surface (again a way of keeping costs down through fewer pages).

And remember, these were very old newspapers. Fading yellow and brittle with age, this would be no quick flick through *The Sun*. Each one had to be treated with the care and attention worthy of an historical document, which it was, of course.

Finally, take yourself well away from any natural daylight and turn the lights down really, really low. The cavern wasn't exactly brightly lit. In truth it could be described as positively gloomy. When I say *The World's Fair* was printed in small type I mean small – smaller than this, in fact. Try searching for a huge blue whale hiding in type that size, in bad light, for hours on end . . .

Only The Cyclist could save me. By scanning the rolling acres of type for his column I could cut out minutes of pointless, eye-straining searching and concentrate on the South Yorkshire region.

In front of me were 6 manila boxes and 150 newspapers. I knew there was no chance of escape to join in the attack on Talksport. Unknown to me, far above, hurried orders were being shouted on board the tyke whaler. Loco the tyke marshalled his crew and prepared for battle on the airwaves. What use would it be to broadcast Tarn Whale to the nation if I didn't find Jonah among this lot? I would though: I just had to. I took a deep breath and lifted the first box lid. The race was on.

The Boarding Party

Whale followers! What frequency is Talksport on and at what time? Please can you give us a brief on the whale story again. The details escape me once more. Ta. I will be here at lunchtime.

OVERHEAD, TENSE PREPARATIONS WERE TAKING PLACE. MID-morning passed in silence, punctuated only by the rustle of fragile newspapers. The Cyclist wasn't an easy chap to follow, as each week his article popped up in different places. Up to the summer of 1967 we were just getting to know each other really. I waited patiently as he dismounted and furiously scribbled down every last detail of show people attending fairs from Hull to Bradford. I soon recognised another regular entry that might be of use: weekly updates from tarn market traders. Nothing yet, but I wasn't concerned.

By midday, with only a couple of hours to go, Loco the Tyke took Susietyke aside.

Hey Susie, you know about the whale right?

> Not exactly . . . missed the start of the thread but
> basically a whale came to Barnsley in the '60s on the
> back of a lorry. Who set off the thread and why I
> don't know but it's been entertaining.

> You think it's been entertaining? I wasn't even born!

Loco the tyke was about to lead his young crew into battle armed
with sheer belief alone. My 'explanatory e-mail' would hopefully
have been analysed on board Talksport, for if Loco and the
others were questioned, what story could they give? Even the
woefully unprepared Eaststander was willing to give it a shot.

> I don't know much about it – all I can say is tell us
> about the whale!

I got to 1967, the year Fretwell had identified with such certainty
and still nothing: a first slight shiver of fear. We'd covered 50
editions. The Cyclist dismounted, stuffed the notebook back
into his pocket and paused for breath. His hawk-eye noted every
detail: Mrs Lily Burgess' toffee apples, Mrs Testa's 'Hupa-la',
Madam Petulengro's 'Stick Off', but no mention of a whale.
How the hell could he have missed a whale on a lorry? Surely he
must have wobbled onto the pavement somewhere on his travels
to avoid being run down by the monster!

What I had found was only disturbing. Barnsley's town clerk
may have recalled his childhood memories of 'the banter and
good-humoured bargaining, amid the steam engines when the
fair was in town', but there were darker references from
Alderman Barton of Hyde: 'Fairs and markets are a feature of
English life and should be allowed to continue . . .'

Ominous words. I rubbed my eyes and opened another box.

> I've e-mailed Brian Moore . . . I also e-mailed Mike
> Parry, Head of Sport as well.

> Well done mi'old! I just e-mailed Brian Moore and
> yesterday e-mailed that Parry twice from different
> addresses, so it is looking good I think!

> Talksport and the whale . . . will be e-mailing shortly!

The crew bore down on their prey with grim determination:
Loco the tyke, Susietyke, Eaststander, Optic tyke (with his
devious 'serious question with whale attachment'), Wombella
tyke, E.I. Addio, Yankee tyke, Munich tyke, McDog and who
knows how many other silent crew members.

In the cavern I floundered through 1968, fearful of reaching
August and Feast Week. My hands trembled with impatience. A
slight rip of paper! A sidelong glance from the Doctor; I shrank
back and refocused my eyes on the clock. Minutes were ticking
by. Almost time.

> *FIFTEEN MINS TILL JD MENTIONS WHALE!* Anyone
> not e-mailed the show yet, even if you don't know
> 'owt abart the whale still e-mail it!

It was Lindisfarne all over again. St Dennis must have thought
the airwaves safe; from this outpost he would spread a message
of football across the land. None could have had an inkling of
what lay over the horizon. Commanding a guided missile
packed to the gunwhales with berserker tykes, Loco raised the
red flag and wheeled her into the attack.

I made The Cyclist circle Barnsley Feast Week 1968 a couple
more times. Still nothing. My shoulders hunched forward . . . eyes
were aching . . . type swimming in shoals before my eyes . . .
nothing, nothing . . . *nothing*!

> *Come on you whale!* For those of us at work with no
> access to a radio any news of the whale yet?

The Cyclist pedals through the year once more . . . April '68: 'The number of sites lost to showland this year . . . quite alarming . . . many centrally situated markets have been lost . . . result of large number of cars . . . elsewhere ground has been lost to buildings.'

Sam Crow's jumping horses, John Murphy's Proud Peacock's . . . Joe Green's memories of . . . Unbelievable! Joe Green's memories of 'taking on' THE BOXING KANGAROO!

Out from the seething mass of his shipmates stepped hoylandtyke . . . He could wait no longer!

> Whale! . . . I'm going to try to get through and I'll ask him about the whale . . . I don't know much about it but I'll see if John does. My name will be Stuart on the radio.

> Go for it mate . . . just remember . . . It was a whale from the '60s and we want it as a mascot, there's loads of us on the internet arranging songs and inflatable whales to take to the ground! Give it your best shot!

The tykes struck home with all the force of an enraged sperm whale. Panic broke out on the *Talksport.*

> URGENT URGENT URGENT URGENT URGENT URGENT!!!!!
>
> I HAVE BEEN E-MAILED BY TALKSPORT ASKIN ME TO EXPLAIN THE WHALE STORY AND E-MAIL THEM SO OUTSIDERS CAN UNDERSTAND IT. QUICK ANYONE MUST KNOW THE STORY! SOMEONE!

> *The whale is on! The whale is on!*

> THE WHALE MENTIONED!

Somebody call Talksport. Who knows more about the whale . . . they want to know.

Sir Robert Fossett's Boxing Kangaroo is opposed in the regulation boxing ring by clown Frankie Fosse.

STUART YOU ARE THE MAN!!!!! WELL DONE MY SON!!!!

Following hoylandtyke's lead, the crew swarm aboard, rampaging over the *Talksport*'s decks in search of John Dennis. *Tarn Whale! Tarn Whale!* Panic breaks out, with defenders firing off urgent requests for assistance.

JD and Brian Moore baffled by the whale! They called the *Chron* after they started getting all the e-mails in!

NEED HELP WITH THE WHALE STORY!

Don't know the full story . . . certainly don't remember being only four at the time. The fans believe it would tie in well with the new sponsors BigThing . . .

The airwaves and e-mail lanes around the *Talksport* are thick with explosive messages as the huge vessel wallows in billowing clouds of confusion. Tykes press home the attack . . .

He thinks it's a joke! Statis would put him in his place!

Where is Statis and Big'n?

1969 . . . nothing . . . nothing . . . The Cyclist shrugs. Too dark, can't see . . .

EASTSTANDER AGAIN . . !

Bloody hell . . . there's nothing here! No photograph, not even a word. Very tired . . . can't read any more . . . nowhere else to go . . .

Whaaaay haaaaaaayyyy . . . National radio twice!

Whoops of joy as the crew clamber back aboard the whaler to leave the *Talksport* floundering in their wake.

Well done Loco. Statis will be pleased. I'm gutted my two e-mails didn't get a mention and one didn't even mention the whale.

Sniff . . . I got nowt . . . sniff.

He better offer to take me for a pint at the Norwich game . . . WHALE ON NATIONAL RADIO!

Do I get a pint an' all?

I think you should get five pints . . . yeah we were excellent, can't believe Brian Moore called it the 'TARN WHALE'.

Have a good day kiddo. Job well done!!

I was finished. I tried to stand. Legs convulsed in cramp. Back ached. After all this, after all the efforts of the crew in pursuit of their dream, I'd failed them. There was nothing.

Hoax! Deception! Illusion!

These words shot into me from all sides. I swear I could hear Barnum laughing. I was finished. *Finished!* How could I go back? How could I tell them? I forced a dejected smile at Doctor, drifting silently around her cave. Dipping her hand gently into a distant box, she turned toward me.

'Is this what you're looking for?'

The Time Tunnel

IT WASN'T MUCH: IN FACT IT WASN'T ANYTHING REALLY. AND yet it had a power beyond anything I'd seen before. Hazel told me R Kid spent quiet hours just staring at it – just staring. I took it onto tarn market, but tucked it safely under my arm. First I asked stallholders about a whale. I got the usual response: Sailor Sid said he'd never seen a whale; Mitchell's fish stall just laughed; George the Sockman, who looked old enough to have seen everything, and even Renee at her roundabout, didn't know anything; nor did Sid on Morris's Coats.

All a bit disappointing, but not completely surprising. Then I showed them it.

So it wasn't just R Kid and me! Sailor Sid didn't just look at it . . . no one just looked at it. It was some time before Sid spoke with hushed reverence, his gaze never leaving the photograph.

'Aye . . . oh aye . . . ah remember that . . . aye . . . ah remember t'whale.'

It was a black-and-white image and very indistinct, but that didn't matter: it was a photograph of a whale on a lorry. It wasn't in Barnsley, but that didn't matter either. Sailor Sid and Renee remembered. Sid on Morris's Coats recalled Jonah visiting Manchester's Piccadilly Gardens. Thousands turned out to see it apparently. He suggested Jonah could be renamed 'The Manchester Whale'. Hmmmm . . . I left, taking the photograph with me: no one would believe him.

I'm afraid that apart from a few fragments of fact found in that brief article in *The World's Fair* there's nothing more to tell.

204

The whale hunt had been a success. We did what we set out to do. We proved there had been a whale in Barnsley. There really was no hope of ever finding anything else.

There was much congratulation from the crew. Few were more excited than norman, who anxiously awaited my return from Sheffield.

> I can't wait for tomorrow mate. The Tarn Whale is one of my earliest memories and I'm looking forward to seeing the piccie and your report tomorrow. Like you I thought I'd dreamt it!

Andolio decided an award was in order. I was humbled. Not since Joseph Locke was honoured by the French nation has a tyke swelled with such pride. I wear it to this day.

> Tha deserves a medal for this lad! A medal as big as a dustbin lid!

Back in tarn, Hazel hoisted Jonah in the library, but little came of it. I did eventually speak to Anne, who remembered him; for years her children had regarded their mother as mad. During another visit to tarn market, I visited the council offices. On making my whale enquiry, the girl seemed surprised but quickly called her colleagues, who filed out – to laugh at me.

'Ev yer bin drinkin' lad?'

I continued to make other enquiries, but as the months slipped by they became less and less frequent: there's only so much humiliation one person can take. Out on the cybersea no reply came from all the e-mails I'd fired off. Many, many months had passed when, just for old time's sake, I fired off an enquiry at an old target: crazy Ahab's forlorn cry for the blue whale. Out from the black cybersea there came a lone voice.

'You're not mad . . . not unless I am too . . .'

Others followed. A trickle at first, then a flood, then a tidal wave carried me away.

'I have never told anyone about it before because it seemed so weird and unreal. I had come to think it was one of those recurrent dreams you have – but I have never forgotten it . . .'

'. . . for a while I used to wonder if I was the only one who ever saw it too . . .'

'. . . the occasional times I've mentioned it to people they haven't believed me . . .'

'I quizzed as many of my peers as possible; no one could remember the whale. I had begun to think it was a vision. How many friends have I lost as they listened to me out of the corner of their lifted eyebrows as I told them about the whale . . . it's an absolute relief to know it was not an hallucination at an early age . . .'

'The memory of it came back to me very vividly too. I was pressed by my curiosity to ask others . . . someone I asked said maybe it was a trivial thing, not worth remembering. I recoiled from that statement . . .'

'I was very small, maybe two or three years old . . . poor whale.'

'For years many have scoffed at me and gazed pityingly and bemusedly as I told them about the whale I saw when I was tiny.'

Not since I saw a big whale on a lorry have I been so awestruck. Across the world, Jonah sprang from the deep subconscious of hundreds of believers in cries of relief and joy.

I spent a lot of time looking at the photograph, a fuzzy image of a whale on a lorry. But that was only the surface, the entrance to a time tunnel. If you'd seen the whale you stepped into it and journeyed back through 30, 40, 50 years.

Who knows what lies buried inside us? Perhaps he's there deep inside you too. If you have even the vaguest dream of a whale, prepare to take that journey now.

It isn't much: but it's everything.

Photograph from The World's Fair. Reproduced by kind permission of Dr Vanessa Toulmin of the National Fairground Archive, Sheffield.

The Whale

The soul never thinks without a picture.

Aristotle

Awe

IF YOU NEVER SAW HIM BE WARNED: NO PHOTOGRAPH COULD ever do justice to Jonah. Even if this were the biggest book in existence, no image could capture the wonder of the whale.

Most were overwhelmed by his sheer size. To really understand the magic, take another look at the photograph and in particular look more closely at the bottom left-hand corner. Put yourself in the shoes of the little fella who's turned to the camera in sheer amazement. See Jonah the way we did. Big 'n' Daft and Casper believe Jonah to be their earliest memory. Big 'n' Daft spoke of being 'open-mouthed in wonder' and that's probably as close as it gets. Perhaps there are no words to really describe the whale to anyone who wasn't there.

It took me some time to totter alongside the whale, the vast brown, grey canvas of wrinkled leather skin, a mouth that seemed to yawn half the length of his body, from one end of the trailer to the other and then back again just to be sure. At perhaps seven or eight years old, I was old enough to rationalise his awesome size. Others, like Jill, were far, far younger.

'It had a great effect on me. I remember my father lifting me from my pushcair and carrying me up the metal steps . . .'

Before you could even walk, what impression must that bulk have made? Jonah was bigger than the very biggest thing I'd ever seen. He was longer than a row of houses . . . and . . . and . . . he was a living creature! Just like me! Jonah was quite clearly dead, but somehow that's not how it seemed. I think it was the eye; an unspeakable sorrow for his sad, closed eye. Barry saw Jonah in Farnham and said it was hard to imagine that the whale inspired anything other than awe in a young boy – but there was something else too: ' . . . a residual impression of sombre rest but I don't know if that is from my feeling reflected or from the whale'.

I knew what he meant. Though closed, this was a sleeping, warm, human eye – not at all cold, hard and fish-like. In tragic silence Jonah's eye spoke to me of distant realms, of a graceful, gentle strength beyond my imagination.

I'm sorry. I'll stop this reminiscing because if you didn't see Jonah, you don't have much to go on other than the photograph and my babbling won't help. In fact, as far as it goes with me there's not much more to tell. Other people remember other things. But first, let's get down to some hard facts.

The Lorry

IT WAS A YOUNG DUTCHMAN WHO TAMED THE BEAST. TWENTY-five-year-old Robert Hendriks must have been a man of remarkable skill and daring: his charge – the world's longest trailer. Most travelling attractions, no matter how big, are packed away in sections for transportation by road. That wasn't possible with a whale. Hendrik's fearsome ten-wheeled juggernaut was the only vehicle capable of carrying Jonah.

At 100 ft long, it may seem unremarkable by today's standards, but remember this was a time of corner shops, tiny delivery vans and 'bobbies on bicycles'. The motorways hadn't yet arrived and dual carriageways were rare. England was a network of leafy 'A' roads connecting hundreds of quiet 'Camberwick Greens' and market town 'Trumptons'. When a large truck seemed a snarling beast, what must Hendriks' monster have looked like when it loomed over the horizon? Try to imagine the space shuttle being driven through your High Street and you'll get an idea of the stir it must have caused.

Whenever Jonah took to the road (always accompanied by a police escort) special routes had to be planned in advance. Wherever possible, low bridges and awkward traffic islands were avoided. Even so, it wasn't uncommon for bollards and lampposts to be removed to allow the vehicle to squeeze through. Hendriks must have been an exceptional driver.

The Whale

PERHAPS I'VE LEFT IT A LITTLE LATE IN THE STORY, BUT JONAH was most definitely dead: stone-cold dead. I mention it here, because throughout the hunt I was amazed by the number of people who asked, 'Was it alive?' If I'd said I'd got a goldfish in a matchbox, I doubt whether anyone would have thought that was alive.

Perhaps most people associate 'whale' with the killer whale in *Free Willy* – a whale of course, but a mere tiddler in a comparison of size. Maybe we spend too much time seeing the world through glass screens. I could understand Big 'n' Daft rubbishing 'transit-size' whales posted on the board. As I said, no picture can do justice to the real thing. Jonah was a male 65-ft blue whale, weighing in at 70 tons. An average-sized blue, but certainly incapable of being transported alive.

Preservation and maintenance while touring was a monumental task: it wasn't a case of just slapping Jonah onto his 78-ft display bed and off you go. A young Anne obviously mulled over this one.

'Did anyone who remembers it wonder what its body cavity was filled with? This thought plagued me.'

Another whale watcher sussed that all was not as it should have been.

'I gruesomely remember that the whole whale wasn't visible:

about a quarter of it was shrouded in the lorry used to transport it. I assume this was to allow the internal application of preservative fluids, a process definitely best hidden from my inquisitive yet fragile infant mind.'

Initially his insides were removed, his lungs inflated with air, a refrigeration unit set up in his belly and 2,200 gallons of formalin preservative pumped into his body. It didn't stop there: a team of seven men were required to coat Jonah with formalin every day to keep him in peak condition.

Incredible? We haven't even started yet. Everything's ready: we've got the whale on the lorry; let's go on tour.

The Tour

THE DOCKYARD AT DAGENHAM, ESSEX, SERVING THE HUGE Ford plant, has witnessed the comings and goings of thousands of vessels and vehicles over the years. A Dutch coaster docking on 30 March 1954 after a short Channel crossing from Dunkirk probably caused little comment. Cranes swept over her as dock workers scrambled to secure the cargo with steel tendons. On the quayside, with unloading completed, final checks were made as Hendriks swung up into the cab and turned the ignition: a ten-wheeled monster roared into life. Towering over shoals of Anglias and Populars, Hendriks signalled to his police escort and ground the gearbox into first. So began a journey that would rival that of the great St Cuthbert.

Jonah was first displayed on London's South Bank, just by Waterloo Bridge. Significantly this exhibition started on 2 April: no doubt Charles King, the promoter, was wary of publicising his new attraction a day earlier for fear no one would turn up.

The following month, heralded by hoardings and advertising panels, Jonah resurfaced at the famous Nottingham Goose Fair.

From Friday, 21 May, for three days he wowed the crowds that flooded into this huge fair from miles around.

And from Nottingham – well, who knows? Apart from the few facts gleaned from *The World's Fair* and a *Times* article there's little to go on. Local papers must have sighted Jonah many times during his great journey; perhaps some of the advertising survives. At the end of the day, though, newspapers fade, old junk's chucked out and we move on. But that doesn't mean there's no more to tell. Because some things we all keep, in a secret, special place. And we keep them forever.

Memories

WHAT MAKES UP A MEMORY: A SIGHT, SOUND, SMELL, TASTE, OR a mixture of these? How deep are our earliest ones? Do we have memories that haven't yet surfaced? Do some sit on the borderline of fact and fantasy, never knowing which way to fall?

'I too have a strange memory of seeing a whale on a lorry and although I've never doubted it, I was not very old, and it all seems so surreal.'

A young Claire obviously remembered something back in '60s Lincoln. Susan started to think that a whale in Burnley 'was from some childhood foggy imagination'. Lindsey experienced something strange in Norwich . . .

'I began to think I had imagined the whole episode, which is rather disturbing.'

Anne and her younger sister were whale witnesses in West Bromwich:

'My younger sister was very scared of it, so we could never get too close. We were drawn to look at it with a morbid curiosity, standing a decent distance from it, acting in a not-interested way, but with this awful fascination and being drawn to look . . .'

Jonah inspired just about every human emotion: wonder, horror, awe, fear, sorrow, anger; many of these mixed together in the sudden rush of first sighting him. Jonah's assault on your senses was overwhelming and everyone that saw him has their own distinct, personal impressions of the visit. Some recall the sadness of the eye, and there were other aspects to the 'eye' story. Someone could not get the eye out of her mind for weeks after and with good reason.

'I also recall the whale's eyes, which were displayed in a jar of formaldehyde – or it could have been vodka.'

I never knew that. That's why his eye was closed; perhaps I blocked it from my mind. The mouth, too, was a source of fascination:

'It had big hairy teeth and gave me nightmares.'

Tina in Wolverhampton wasn't alone in trying to come to terms with Jonah's 'baleen', the fronded screen through which a blue whale filters krill from seawater. Someone else compared it to an enormous scrubbing brush.

Many were awed by Jonah's sheer size of course and grappled with comparisons as a way of explaining it to their nearest and dearest. Lesley listened:

'My husband saw the whale in Ashford Kent in the late '50s. According to him the size of the head was the size of our bedroom.'

Most viewed the whale from a platform that ran the length of his body. Others had a similar experience to Rod in Bristol:

'I remember walking through Jonah the whale when very young . . . we went up some wooden steps in his middle bit and walked through. I remember mostly the curved ribs inside. My brother and I could never decide whether it was a real whale or a model. It was so big and strange.'

Many could not believe Jonah was for real. David in Chester wrote:

'I had come to the conclusion that what I saw was a fibreglass model as I couldn't believe that anyone would be dragging a whale around Cheshire.'

There was another aspect to Jonah that I just don't remember, though many others do.

'The smell was awful. The residents of Cambridge were glad to see the back of it.'

Sailor Sid on tarn market and R Kid were among others who commented on the smell. Many stated quite simply that it stank – all that formalin, obviously.

I saw Jonah in daylight, but under different conditions he must have taken on a quite different nature. Judi and her sisters in Ripon:

'It smelt horrible . . . the whole thing was encased in tarpaulin curtains . . . when we went in it was getting dark and the whole thing was seen by the slightly eerie glow of sodium streetlights.'

Spooky. But as darkness fell, try to imagine Anne's experience in Bradford.

'It was raining and very, very dark . . . people were queuing up to get to see it. I remember holding my dad's hand. There was this huge, huge, dead whale there and it was the most horrendous thing I've ever seen. I too can remember the eye and the mouth, but I can also remember the fact it stank to high heaven and my mum said it made her feel sick and didn't go up to see it. I have never told anyone about this before because it all seemed so weird and unreal I had come to think it was one of those recurrent dreams you have – but I have never forgotten it . . .'

Despite the reluctance of Anne's mother, long queues appeared in many towns. The lorry was open only at one side and screened off with hoardings. Only when you'd paid your shilling did you get to see your whale. In the '50s this was a lot of money, but some had a lucky break, as Jill's diary entry for 19 May 1954 shows:

> After school Enid and I went to see Jonah, the largest whale in the world (it is dead of course) at an exhibition near the bus station. It cost a shilling to get in and we were just turning away because we didn't have enough money when a lady offered, in fact insisted, she should pay for us. We did not decline the offer but it wasn't worth a shilling – that great creosoted hulking bit of leather. Excuse the language but that is what it looked like. However I was amazed by the size of it.

Not everyone had to pay. I was among the lucky ones, as *The World's Fair* explains: ' . . . the proprietors extend a most generous invitation to the Education Authorities to send parties of scholars to see the whale free of charge.'

The need to keep Jonah firmly under wraps in order to maintain his mystery would explain the lack of photographs of the whale. It's doubtful that cameras would have been allowed at the display. They would have been of little use anyway. Back then there were no camcorders, digital cameras, wide-angle lenses or other sophisticated photographic stuff. Most families were equipped with the standard-issue 'Box Brownie'. This simple brown box was all well and good for snapping donkey rides on Cleethorpes beach in bright sunlight, but there's no way the trusty Brownie could have coped with a creature the size of Jonah. The shot you've seen was taken for *The World's Fair* on his entry into the country in 1954. This rare shot wasn't for the public, but for the select readership of showpeople only.

Despite freeloading schoolchildren, promoter Charles King must have earned a fair bit from his star attraction, since Jonah toured the whole of the UK until the end of the '60s and possibly even longer (we'll come to his demise later).

The tour wasn't without its problems, though. Apart from the smell and threats to lampposts and bridges, King was continually being presented with bills for damages due to the enormous weight of the trailer. *The World's Fair* noted that if Hendriks made a slip and ran onto a footpath 'the stones crush like eggshells'.

Time inevitably took its toll on poor Jonah. There was general disappointment among '60s whale watchers that the blue whale was no longer blue. In his natural habitat, his skin would have reflected the sea and sky, but years on a lorry and endless coats of formalin had transformed him into a dirty, brown/grey corpse. For tiny children of Ken's age, this was disturbing.

'It visited Hartlepool when I was a child . . . I remember it parked on its lorry under floodlights. It was very strange, even for Hartlepool. I was happy when it left to be honest, although I must have been all of three at the time.'

One father left his young son, John, woefully unprepared for Jonah's visit.

'Picture the scene: father tells five-year-old son (me) that we are going to see a whale. Son imagines a live whale in a tank. Father imagines tasteful exhibit of a stuffed whale. What appears, in Kilmarnock town centre, is a carcass on the back of a lorry, being stared at by horrified/fascinated townsfolk. Father's jaw drops. Son has mild hysterics and blots incident out of his mind for 30 years. Last week I saw a kid's exhibit of a large plastic whale and the whole thing came flooding back.'

Another John tells of his excited school trip from Derbyshire to Manchester's Belle Vue, a story that sums up the heavy air of melancholy that came to hang over this once-great animal.

'We disembarked into the drizzle and while everyone disappeared into various buildings I started to hunt down the whale. I was directed further and further away from the main concourse until I turned a dank corner to see this surreal non-event.

'I was hugely disappointed that it was so obviously dead. No one had told me it wasn't splashing about. I was also not happy about its colour: it was a morose grey and not blue at all. But I was quite impressed by its sheer size. It was truly the biggest living animal I've ever seen, before or since, alive or dead. It took my little legs some time to walk around it, which I did despite the rain thickening up.

'It did not improve. It was grey and wet and by now the water was streaming off its tarpaulin shroud and I decided to get out of the rain the same as everyone else. It is, however, the only animal I remember seeing that day and I'm strangely satisfied with that.'

Towards the end there were many complaints about Jonah's sad and sorry state from town authorities before he faded from view. There are many, many more memories I could add, but in an odd way perhaps I've told too much already.

I begin to feel uneasy with this celebration of a shared memory, all my talk of 'awe' and 'wonder' and 'spectacle'. We've turned away from such exhibitions of death: a whale exhibition would never be allowed today and no one would argue with that. Yet the memory of Jonah runs deep in all who saw him; those who never saw the whale will perhaps never quite understand. And there's one aspect of Jonah's story I haven't dealt with yet. To do that we'll have to turn the ship around and go back to the ocean.

But before we do, if you're feeling appalled about this ever happening or are sure you wouldn't have gone to his exhibition, ask yourself this question. If this book had no photograph of the whale, wouldn't you feel a bit disappointed?

Go on. Be honest.

The Great Slaughter

AFTER THOUSANDS OF YEARS SUBMERGED IN THE DEPTHS OF myth and legend, Sven Foyt's innovations turned the blue whale into reality overnight. The blue would become the greatest prize of all. A single adult could yield 120 barrels of precious oil. Pursued by steamships, speed was no longer its saviour; the fact that it sank when dead was no longer a problem. Toward the end of the century Foyt organised a whaling expedition into the last uncharted region, the Antarctic. There was nowhere left to run: the great slaughter was about to begin.

Sven took care of most preparations for the hunt, but things really took off when the tricky operation of processing a whale on the open seas was solved. With the introduction of ingenious 'stern slipway' whaleships, a corpse could be swallowed and cut up more easily. This made the operation so much faster. Some victims weren't even dead when dragged aboard, but what the hell? Time is money.

Concerns about the numbers being killed were raised but unfortunately that's as far as it went. The League of Nations huffed and puffed through the 1930s but with so many nations involved, each trying to out-slaughter the other, no one could ever seem to find a date in their diary when all could get round the table and talk. In 1931 alone it's estimated that 29,000 blue whales were killed.

The world's whale population had a lucky break when men took time out to slaughter each other on a grand scale. The Second World War was only a breather, though. The whalers returned with renewed vigour and the International Whaling Commission was set up to try and limit the killing. Everyone agreed: international treaties were set; men in suits made solemn promises and smiled for the cameras. Out on the oceans things went on much as they'd always done. In the 1950s, protests became louder and the blue whale was designated an endangered species, as estimated numbers were running perilously low. The hunting went on.

Suddenly everything changed. In 1966, only one blue was caught. Plenty of harpoons were searching, but this time even the whaling fleets got the message. There were virtually none left to catch; the blue whale was on the brink of extinction.

Estimates vary, but in that century of progress around 350,000 blue whales were slaughtered. To that toll can be added an estimated 1,000,000 sperm whales, 500,000 fin whales, 250,000 humpbacks and hundreds of thousands of others.

Two million whales were processed into dry statistics and bloody meat. One blue whale was not among that number though. For years he'd given harpoons the slip as he navigated the globe. In September 1952, attracted by huge concentrations of krill, he swam deep in cold Arctic waters. By now there were perhaps no more than 1,000 blues left in this rich feeding ground. This would be his final voyage too, but unlike so many others, he would come ashore intact.

Beached

WHALES HAVE BEEN SEEN ON LAND LONG BEFORE MEN stepped in to speed up the process. As is so often the case with these creatures, nobody's absolutely sure why. Death and illness account for some individual beachings. Disorientation, caused perhaps by an imbalance in their sonar, climate or food supply, can occur. In the case of mass strandings it's thought the bonding in a pod is so strong that many will founder while trying to stay close to or guide another out of trouble.

Beachings and strandings are more common than most think, with 30 or 40 cases around the British Isles every year. By and large these tend to be 'toothed' whales, such as the pilot. One hundred and forty-eight were found beached in Lothian, Scotland, during the '50s. The large number Hazel discovered in northern France were most likely toothed as well.

The blue whale is a 'baleen whale', feeding in deep oceans and rarely venturing near shore. Other baleens, such as sperms and humpbacks, are found in single strandings from time to time, but a blue is very rare.

When a whale does come ashore, for whatever reason, it's an instant crowd-puller. Back in 1910 a steamship captain off the Yorkshire coast reported seeing a huge object floating toward the shore. Next morning the inhabitants of Cloughton Wyke, near Scarborough, found a female fin whale washed up on the rocks. Crowds soon gathered to gawp in wonder. Not everyone was impressed, Scarborough councillors for example. A visiting whale is rarely welcomed by coastal authorities: it always outstays its welcome, and weighing in at 50 tons, the 50-ft Cloughton whale cost a small fortune to dispose of.

Imagine, then, the councillors' horror when, six months later, another fin whale popped up on the same beach – only this one was a 72-ft, 80-ton whopper. Smiling children posed for photographers alongside the dead mammal, postcards were printed and hurriedly distributed as far afield as Whitby. Thousands turned up to see it. The councillors were beside themselves: how many whales could one borough entertain? The piggy bank was empty and as days went by, the whale 'diffused an offensive odour in the district' according to one observer. Sales of pegs must have rocketed. One Mark Bennet, a horse slaughterer, stepped in and went about his grisly work. What he did with the whale I don't know, but its jawbones were erected to form an archway to his house on the Burniston coast road.

Across the Atlantic no one wants to know about dead whales either. In 1970, and after much buck-passing in Oregon, the task of disposal fell to the State Highway Patrol. They went in hard, lights flashing and sirens wailing. Naturally crowds had already gathered, so they decided on a spectacular. The whale was to be packed with explosives in the belief, as one officer explained to a camera crew, that 'the wind would blow the pieces out to sea'. In the resulting shower of blubber, several cars were severely damaged: the whale remained more or less intact.

The Prototypes

HUGE CETACEANS RARELY MAKE IT FURTHER THAN THE BEACHES in one piece, though it has happened. In 1865, a 70-ft fin whale was washed up at Pevensey Beach, Sussex. Somehow, it was hauled to Hastings cricket ground, where it is reputed to have pulled in crowds of 40,000. Later purchased by Cambridge University, its skeleton is now on view at the entrance to the university's Museum of Zoology. A 70-ft blue whale beached at Wexford, Ireland, just over 100 years ago is now suspended in skeletal form at the Natural History Museum, London, next to the model blue.

Still doubting the whale/football connection? This tale that surfaced during the hunt should convince you. At some time in the 1950s, Ipswich Town's hallowed Portman Road turf played host to a huge dead whale, the pitch being the only place able to accommodate it. It was by all accounts a long hot summer and after a few days cries of 'foul' went up from the crowd. The whale was shown the red card and reputedly sent off to a nearby village to be buried in gravel pits.

But the most significant beaching, as far as our tale is concerned, is that of the 'Whale of Man'. In May 1925, Bobby Shimmim took on one of his strangest jobs. A 50-ft Rudolph's Rorqual had swum into Horse Gullet on the southern tip of the Isle of Man. Unable to turn around, the unfortunate mammal died when the tide went out. On hearing about this, the Manx Museum in Douglas thought the whale's skeleton would make a fine exhibit, but it couldn't really be allowed to moulder on the beach. How to move it intact? Bobby, a threshing and haulage contractor, came up with a plan.

The whale was towed by boats to Derbyhaven, then rolled up the beach using winches attached to a couple of traction engines, and onto two trailers via a timber ramp. Onlookers lined the roads as the traction engine pulled its strange load to a knacker's yard where it was left to decompose. A policeman on a bicycle went on ahead to warn householders to close their windows as the mighty mammal was already beginning to hum. After a year buried in sand, the three-and-a-half-ton skeleton was taken to Douglas, where it remains to this day.

Renee on Barnsley market hinted at another strange overland journey. Renee's roundabout, tucked away in a corner, is famous throughout Yorkshire. The little carousel has spun thousands of tiny tykes in a little circle of magic for well over 50 years. As gurgling, pastel-wrapped tykes whirled round and round, she looked on Jonah and travelled the time tunnel. Oh yes, she remembered the whale. He was so big they couldn't get him off the lorry – not like the other one.

Eric

STAN UP IN TARN TOLD ME ALL ABOUT IT. AS A YOUNGSTER HE and a friend were standing at the bottom of Market Hill when they were surprised to be hailed by the most important man around: Joseph Jones, Mayor of Barnsley.

Jones had given his gold chain of office an extra polish that day and was in a very good mood, as well he might be. At his side stood the world-renowned American pianist and crooner Charlie Kunz. Throughout the '30s and '40s Kunz was massive. Mobbed wherever he went, he was a sensation bigger than Robbie Williams. This visiting star would usually have been enough excitement, but that day another American had come to tarn. Jones gestured to the canvas tent behind him.

'A tha gooin' in lads?'

The admission price was far too much for Stan and his mate. Jones reached into a pocket and pulled out two shiny sixpences, the Mayor obviously deciding this was an attraction no tyke should miss. Stepping inside the tent, the friends were confronted by the sight and smell of Eric.

Eric was a finback whale captured off Southern California and preserved in 3,500 gallons of formalin. After touring the States and Canada he was packed into a 73-ft box car and shipped across to the UK, the biggest single load ever to have sailed the Atlantic. Originally displayed at Southend Kursaal as 'an educational exhibit under the command of Captain H. Elmo LeBreque', he stayed for several seasons. Whale-watcher Chris tells a tale heard at his father's knee:

'While Eric was at the Kursaal he was one of a number of children invited to sit in Eric's mouth. Dad said that Eric smelt of paraffin. For his bravery Dad was given an "Eric the Whale" hat and a book telling the story of how Eric came to England.'

It seems more than likely that the mighty Eric was the same finback encountered by Gerald while holidaying in Great Yarmouth.

'The inside of the creature was hung with electric light bulbs and, for a fee, one was invited to walk through the body, entering by way of a sort of doorway cut just behind the head and leaving through goodness knows what orifice . . .'

It's now clear there's been far more whale activity throughout Britain than anyone has ever suspected. Jonah may well have been the biggest, but he was by no means the first whale on a lorry. Given these incidents, it would be nice to imagine that some travelling fair chanced upon a blue whale's body on a beach. Familiar with traction engines and pulling heavy things around, they hauled him off the beach and brought him to us. Unfortunately it didn't happen like that.

The Insanity

IT WAS IN SVEN FOYT'S HOME KILLING GROUND THAT OUR BLUE whale's luck ran out. Off the coast of Trondheim, Norway, he, like thousands of his brothers and sisters, plunged in terror, fleeing from the monster bearing down on them. There was no escape from the explosive harpoon, of course, and it was a contract killing. Jonah was intended for exhibition.

Prepared with Norwegian expertise, Jonah toured Europe for two years: Denmark, Holland, France, Switzerland, Germany. He created as big an impression there as he would in Britain. Hans remembers that in Denmark he was displayed with a dormouse in a glass case at his nose, as a comparison of the world's smallest and largest mammals.

So that's it then. All this 'wonder of the magic men' and their fairground excitement: in truth they're little more than heartless killers, anything for a fast buck – the sons of Barnum.

Not quite.

What I'm about to describe remains to this day beyond my belief. If you ever want an example of distorted logic, or outright stupidity, then please use this. Among the other things on display with Jonah were harpoons. According to one inland whale watcher, the one that killed him was there. In the early days of the exhibition there were Norwegian whalers aboard the lorry, who happily gave away autographs. Doesn't sound like the work of fairground people? Well, it wasn't.

The idea to kill a blue whale and send it on tour was the idea of a group of Norwegian businessmen. Their aim was to promote Norwegian industry; this, of course, was whaling. Let's just take a little time to think about that one.

Now, I've got nothing against Norway or the Norwegians, but as you may have gathered already I'm not too impressed with the advertising industry or the business world. It's a mentality that rises above national boundaries. In doing so it cuts itself off from the rest of us, understanding nothing of people outside its narrow confines.

A bit strong? Well, examples of stupidity from the corporate world abound, but the story of Jonah takes the biscuit: I've never come across one like it in my life. What did they think the effect of the exhibition was going to be? What did they hope to achieve by parading a dead whale in front of thousands of European children? Did they imagine that we'd all jump up and down and squeal in delight: 'Fantastic! Look at that great big dead whale that the men have killed with that big spear. When I grow up, I want to do the same thing! I want to kill lots and lots and lots of whales!'

Jonah was beyond an ad man's wildest dream. Millions were stunned by the most powerful advertisement the world has ever seen and they paid good money to see it. But like most great business ideas, it achieved precisely the opposite to what was intended.

Awe-inspiring Jonah most certainly was: I'll remember him for the rest of my life. But there cannot have been one person in the whole of Europe who came away from the whale with anything other than an unshakeable belief that whaling should not go on. If ever proof were needed, Jonah came among us as silent witness to man's cruelty. If this story brings him back to life and in any way contributes to the harpoons being put away for good then it will have been worth it.

The Haunting

JONAH NEVER REALLY DIED AT ALL – HE LIVES ON IN EVERYONE who saw him. And he's still hard at work. A child who gazed on him in France in the '50s gave up his job later in life, moved to Canada and became a marine biologist. Now he's furthering our understanding of the whale. Who knows how many more there are like him?

Spare a thought for French mice in the '50s too. Many met their maker after being pounced on by Jonah, a black cat, whose owner had seen the whale as a girl. The whale is still part of many family's lives, turning up in the most unlikely places, as Pat's story shows: 'Talking to my mother I realise this must have been quite an important occasion for us as we always referred to the steps nearby as "the Whale Steps".'

Why some of our parents can't remember Jonah remains a mystery. Even Anne's younger sister, who didn't dare go near him, seems to have blotted the visit from her mind. It all adds fuel to the debate among family, friends and complete strangers – Helen is probably still creating a stir in Loughborough: 'It was completely amazing. The man behind me in the corner shop remembered it as well . . .'

Then there are the sacred relics. Apart from posters and hoardings, postcards were printed showing Jonah on the front and the grisly message 'Greetings from Jonah the Giant Whale' on the reverse. I never got one, but another Anne (whose children didn't believe her in tarn) kindly lent me hers. I say 'lent'; these postcards are too precious to part with, being kept in safe places, as Carl in Lancashire notes.

'I had a black-and-white postcard of it on my crayon box for many years, which I will try and search out, as no one else seems to have any pictures or any physical proof of the whale's existence . . .'

Carl's comment also highlights that no place is truly safe. Squirrelled away safely in lofts, many were lost: this was little short of tragedy.

'I had a postcard and it's one of the greatest sadnesses of my life that I have it no longer. If there is any way of getting another image of this significant part of my young life I will be a happy man.'

Well, Fred in Carlisle, I hope all this has put your mind at rest.

Postcard or not, as I've said before, no one who saw Jonah will ever forget him. Come to that, even if you didn't see him, he'll still haunt you. This isn't a story you can just walk away from, not as long as there are people like this whale-watcher around: 'I have been in pursuit of the whale for ages! I recall it vividly! I bore everyone rigid talking about it.'

Wherever you go, whoever you meet, there's always the chance that you'll bump into someone like Anne, who saw Jonah in West Bromwich; she's determined to shake off life-long accusations of madness.

'I am so pleased that you have all seen this whale! When I have mentioned it over the years, everyone I have mentioned it to looks at me as if I am raving mad.'

Be careful out there.

The Wakefield Whale

BIZARRE THOUGH THE WHOLE THING SEEMS, I THINK WE WERE honoured: few ever get to see a blue whale, dead or alive. The closest most get is a fleeting glimpse before the great creature's gone. As far as I'm concerned Jonah's no different. His ultimate fate is still unclear and I'm quite happy with that.

There are aspects about the tour that are vague. Did he change ownership? It seems likely. What about details of the lorry? Well, if you're into that kind of thing, one watcher believes it was an Atkinson or Foden. In many ways I don't want to know much more: Jonah was the important thing. I don't need to find out what Hendriks had for breakfast. Then again, if you are reading this Robert, I'd love to meet you.

I've no reason to disbelieve Franco tyke's 'exploding whale of Wakefield' story. Perhaps he got the wrong year, as it seems likely from other sightings that Jonah swam into the early '70s. Franco tyke's whale could have been another. In fact, I've learnt not to disbelieve any story concerning inland whales or other strange animals.

Sightings from the '70s tell of other whales: these may or may not be related to Jonah, but that's not for me to say. Janet says the visit of a whale to Leeds was one of the formative experiences of her life, though she's adamant it was a killer. Ian reports the sighting of a 'normal-sized articulated lorry' carrying a whale that 'looked as if it had a regular coat of Dulux paint'. He thinks it was part of the 'Save the Whale' campaign. There's also word from the driver of a lorry that carted around a 40-ft whale which was the moneymaking operation of a couple of Swiss chaps. The driver maintains that this whale was often coated with diesel to keep up its shine.

There are sightings from as far afield as Domodossola in Italy in 1970: Enea saw a whale that stank and was a browny-grey on a lorry there. Sandra, also from Italy, often thinks about a 'very dry and sad-looking' whale that she and her mother saw in front of the town hall in Ventimiglia on the Italian Riviera in the '70s – Jonah? Well, if the travels of St Cuthbert are anything to go by, it's best not to discount anything at all.

So that's all I found out about the coming of Jonah the Blue Whale, but it's not the end of his story. Jonah obviously made a powerful impression on so many people – so how come I had so much trouble finding anything at all? Why did no one mention him for years? Why are there no books, or anything at all (that I've come across anyway) that record his story? And why, most mysteriously of all, should he rise up from the deep subconscious *now*?

So far we've dealt only with the *first* coming of the whale.

Second Coming

The past will not sleep, it works still, with every new fact
a ray of light shoots up from the long-buried years.

Ralph Waldo Emerson

Deflating

NOTHING EVER WORKS OUT QUITE THE WAY YOU THINK IT WILL.
Amid all the hysteria at finding Jonah, the whale hunters
overlooked a few practical problems. The first, as far as I was
concerned, was shelling out a small fortune for Chinese red/blue
whales.

> What are the odds of someone standing outside The
> Yorkshireman this season selling blow-up whales?

Hoylandtyke, obviously eager to identify himself at Oakwell as the
crew member who'd stormed the airwaves to confuse our
chairman, would find the odds were very long indeed. Besides the
issue of money, I didn't relish the prospect of bobbing around
tarn, surrounded by inflatable cetaceans, hunting down people I'd
never met: the weirdest attraction on May Day Green for years.

As whale hunters returned from the cybersea hunt to tie up at
the quayside of reality, fighting broke out. Now I hope I haven't
given the impression that we tykes are all the best of mates.
Every tyke holds unshakeable beliefs that he or she will defend
to the death. The bulletin board is strewn with rallying cries and
desperate last stands in defence of individual points of view. As
the fiery whale hunters came down to earth, they met a cold
front of new tykes, who had never been involved and knew
nothing about a whale.

> That bloody mammal! For Christ's sake let's harpoon
> this whale thing, I haven't heard such juvenile
> excitement since Geri left the Spice Girls . . .

> Totally agree. Never heard such shite. Get a grip guys?

Loco the tyke, Eaststander and the rest were hardly going to take this lying down. Fiery e-mails lit up the board and the battle raged on for days. Our Viking ancestors would have been proud.

> Who's FOR Tarn Whale? Answers please.
>
> I'm keen – humour, history and a bit off the wall. What do all the anti's want – rattles and scarves?
>
> If you want to take a whale take one but don't try to force it down the throats of others.
>
> I couldn't give a shit what mascot we have as long as we get promoted. Whale, dog, the Queens f.ucking corgis will do me as long as we do it on the pitch. That's my opinion anyway.
>
> I AM FOR THE WHALE, HARMLESS FUN!
>
> Well said kid, the real reds are behind you!
>
> PLEASE! NO MORE F.UCKING STUFF ABOUT THE DAMNED WHALE.
>
> F.uck off you nonce! You miserable shitehawk!

No one stood down: no tyke ever does. Come the great day, all that was forgotten though. The match against Norwich City on the glorious 12th of August generated all the excitement only the first game of a new season can. Oakwell was packed. Scanning the crowd I knew they'd all be there; perhaps there was a crew member sitting next to me.

A perfect day: bright blue sky, lush green pitch, blazing red shirts facing dazzling yellow canaries – the scene could have spilled out of a Subbuteo box. All eyes were on the man in black as he raised the silver whistle to his lips. A million hopes, fears and dreams crammed into those last few seconds: no points on the league tables, no fouls, no offsides, no goals, no saves, no near misses, no heroes, no villains. No inflatable whales either.

A blast on the whistle and the first kick of the season!

Come on you redzzzzzzz!!!!!

A close-run thing, but we won through in the end, 1–0: the perfect start.

But like I said, things don't always turn out the way you want them to. The pre-season Wembley euphoria evaporated in a nail-biting season that saw us drop perilously close to the relegation zone: a lurch strong enough to send our manager overboard. With a new hand on the tiller the ship righted herself and we lived to fight another day.

A disappointing season, but I saw the influence of cetaceans at work. I am now sure that the visitation to Portman Road of a huge whale in the '50s had something to do with Ipswich Town beating us in the play-off final. Not convinced? What about the home game against Queens Park Rangers then? R Kid reported a strange post-match incident. Filing away from the ground down Bala Street he noticed a tyke hurriedly punching something to the ground: a desperate attempt to deflate . . . that's right . . . an inflatable whale. We won that game 2–0. And . . . now get this . . . QPR were *relegated* that year. The power of the whale: case proven m'lud.

The whale lingered on the board too. I picked up vague proposals for the construction of a 50-ft papier mâché red/blue whale for the East Stand roof and recommendations that a blue whale be employed alongside two penguins in a new ball-boy policy. This is not as daft as it sounds: whales were employed by football clubs that year. Continual rain led to the introduction of a water-absorbing device – dubbed a 'whale' – at Charlton Athletic.

But why did our voyage happen at all? And why among a group of tykes who've never met to this day? Why was a chance question picked up with such enthusiasm by tykes who'd never seen the whale, or weren't even alive when he came to tarn? Is it because tykes have got nothing better to do? After all, we're all supposed to be unemployed miners, so we'd have plenty of time.

Does the answer lie in the bulletin board itself? The board continued to be as busy as ever: it's probably the most used board of its kind. Some I've visited muster no more than half a dozen postings a day. Our board, constructed by Radders and Co., will have hundreds; throughout the whale hunt there were thousands of postings relating to the whale debate. To answer this, I think we need to boldly go where few have ever been.

The Problem

ALTHOUGH NO ONE TALKS ABOUT IT MUCH ANY MORE, THERE used to be a time when all anyone ever seemed to discuss was mining. Open any paper or turn on the TV and there it was: endless opinions, discussion, facts and statistics about coal. It all seemed very confusing to a child born in a mining village. My father was always underground, yet continually on strike. Every miner seemed to spend his entire existence roaming the country, shouting abuse, waving banners and frightening old ladies and dogs. In the meantime, millions of tons of coal were still being hauled away from pit-heads to fuel the furnaces. Who was doing it? Did someone sort of press a few buttons and coal simply shot out of the ground of its own accord?

Yes, I've heard plenty of discussion and argument about coal. It was all around me and as a little tyke much of it went over my head. There were many, many experts around and inevitably that led to long and heated debates. The same words and phrases always cropped up: there was a 'problem' with miners; the unions were a 'problem'. In fact no discussion took place without being littered with 'problems'.

I always liked the ones that came to an abrupt stop: I sensed they highlighted the one and only problem. Like many miners, my father often absorbed a seemingly knowledgeable viewpoint in silence before offering a quiet invitation: 'Try goin' down a pit and see what you think then.'

This would be followed by an uncomfortable silence from the speaker. The loudest voices had never been near a pit, never mind down one. If you haven't been down, what do you know?

My only experience of underground was the London Underground with its broad, well-lit escalators, kiosks, broad platforms and arty murals. Other than that I've spent my entire life on the surface; I'm afraid that doesn't really qualify me to talk much about mining.

There was only one thing for it.

The Injection

APPROACHING THE CAGE, IT'S CLEAR THAT THIS IS GOING TO BE a far different underground journey – it is not an attraction Disneyworld would approve of. I sign a declaration stating that I accept full responsibility for whatever might happen next. Next I am stripped of my life-support systems: car keys, lighter, matches, coins, even my mobile phone; anything capable of generating a spark was left behind. I am handed a miner's lamp and helmet; remembering the piece of paper I've just signed, I make absolutely sure it fits firmly on my head. I'm given a small metal disk, then shown to the cage.

The cage is very small, with perhaps enough room for six people. I face the metal lattice door as the miner slams it shut and gives a signal to the winder. As the cage jolts and begins to drop, metallic grinding and groaning mixes with the gurgling of water streaming down hard rock six inches from my face. The cage drops further and further. I am being inserted into the earth. The cage seems to become smaller as it dawns on me that this isn't a lift. There are no bright floors skipping by beyond the lattice; on all sides I am surrounded by hundreds of miles of rock. The cage grinds on and on, dropping hundreds of feet below the surface. The miner tells me this is a slow descent. In a working mine the cage would have dropped much, much faster, over 70 mph. We keep on going. Every time that I think it must stop, it doesn't. Above me, daylight has disappeared long ago. We judder to a halt. Ahead of me is the total and utter blackness of a new world.

I inch forward into the blackness across an uneven, unseen floor and remember an old miner's words.

'Hundreds of yards of solid rock, bones of extinct beasts, fossils, flints, sub-soils, roots, green grass with cows grazing on it, the village you have just left – all suspended overhead and held back by a few wooden props as thick as the calf of your leg.'

I realise I'm crouching forward: is it because the jagged roof is too close or because I can feel the incalculable weight just inches above my head?

There is nothing like it on the suface; the darkest night does not come close. Little wonder that the first miners dressed all in white. For, like the astronauts venturing into deep space, this is without doubt another world. But even in space there's the sun. Here the blackness is total, impenetrable.

Bright light dazzles and here in this reverse world so does the blackness, so intense it claws at my eyes. The only thing capable of cutting it is my light and then in a very narrow weak beam. I throw the beam and pick out the walls of a tunnel. The light fades the further it flies and soon dies. The tunnel is plugged by a solid black void, a void that goes on for miles. And the void lives. I swing the beam back to illuminate the tunnel wall at my side and the void gladly rushes up to hover at my shoulder. Throwing the beam back, the void retreats to a point where you can still see it, watching, waiting to envelop you again.

And my light is strong; in the early days it would be candlelight, pinpricking the blackness, showing nothing but half-faces of men and animals. By yellow candlelight and with brute force of picks and shovels, men and women and children worked. Then came pit ponies, spending their entire lives in this underworld hauling tubs along rails. Things changed, and at the same time didn't change at all. Temperatures here could reach 90° F; men and women stripped to the waist. In a wet mine, the tunnels cascaded with water: I'd be splashing through black waist-deep pools. In a dry mine I'd be blinded by, and breathing, air thick with black dust. The coalface at Wentworth Pit left George Orwell with a vision 'like hell'.

'You cannot see very far because the fog of coal dust throws back the beam of your lamp . . . but you can see . . . the line of half-naked kneeling men . . . driving their shovels under the fallen coal and flinging it swiftly over their left shoulders . . . it is a dreadful job they do, an almost superhuman job . . . for they are not only shifting monstrous quantities of coal, they are also in a position that doubles or trebles the work . . . blackened to the eyes with their throats full of coal dust, driving their shovels forward with arms and belly muscles of steel.'

Further and further into the void the only thought is that the cage has been swallowed far behind me; stay close to the miner. My flashing light picks out snaking cables bundled together along the walls, feet skidding over metal trackways. Electricity and a jagged-edge snarl of cutting machines and explosives – all it would take is one spark.

It seems impossible to do anything down here other than stumble around. Yet millions of men and ponies were injected into the earth to scurry along a maze of black tunnels. This was where men dug out thousands of tons of coal and transported it to the surface in operations that went on around the clock:

miners were the first to experience the liberation of a 24x7 world. Men in a labyrinth of tunnels that ran for miles, who couldn't even see each other and had to set in place an operation and system of communication that had to cope with the threats of gas, fire, flood and collapse, all the while using the very tools that could spark disaster. It seemed impossible that it could ever have been done.

My walk was short. It could have gone on for two miles before the vein of coal was reached, but already I was too far from the cage. I realised I was clutching the metal disc very tightly. Every miner took one underground. It was the only way to make sure where everyone was, to check no one had been left behind at the end of a shift. If something went wrong it was the only way to tell how many had got out.

No, my father never really talked about life underground. There were things that could happen down there, things they'd seen that no man would speak of to his family. As the cage journeyed to the surface I realised that my father had said all he had to say about mining when he first set eyes on his newborn son.

'He's not going down there.'

For those words I will be eternally grateful.

Worlds

IF WILLIAM RUSHFORTH HAD ANYTHING IN COMMON WITH anyone as he went underground in that great FA Cup year, it was a man going for glory at the North Pole at round about the same time. Like Captain Scott, William and the others were venturing into a harsh alien world, never intended for man.

When we dropped from the trees, or whatever, it's clear we weren't really equipped to do a number of things. Open oceans weren't really for man, but we mastered them. Frozen wastes wouldn't support human life, but we got there. The air posed a problem, but we reached up and made it. We went further by landing on the moon. Cutting into the earth to work underground falls into the same category: it was a completely different world and new worlds need new ways of working. The seas might be different from outer space and space might be different from underground, but all these worlds did require one thing for men ever to have had a chance of conquering them.

I would like to have asked William about it all, but he's dead. Old miners don't tend to talk too much either. The miner who'd acted as my guide asked if I had any questions: I didn't. The mine spoke for itself. But one man understood the secret. He spent 31 years underground, from the age of 12.

Worth listening to, don't you think?

The VC

PARRY JONES PUT HIS THOUGHTS TO PAPER IN LONG WINTER evenings some 60 years after the Oaks disaster. The result was his book, *The Other Story of Coal.* He had spent over 30 years underground and survived a job where life and death were separated by the narrowest margins. He knew what was happening and, more importantly, why. Not much had changed in 60 years.

Imagine sitting round the breakfast table with your family before leaving for work. On the radio you hear a newsflash that goes something like this: 'In Britain yesterday, 600 men were injured, 140 of them seriously when . . .'

Even worse, these people do the very same job as you, the job you're about to leave your family to do. Imagine a similar news item had run yesterday and the day before, and that it would greet you tomorrow and the day after and the day after. Imagine these news items ran every single day of the year.

This was the life of a miner in Jones's day, although those figures never made the news. Let's face it, if it happened day after day it was hardly news, was it? The constant daily death toll never got reported at all. Three men crushed here, five burnt to death there, and a couple of drownings were hardly going to make the readers sit up and take notice. Very few were aware of what was really going on.

If the daily death toll didn't get mentioned, spectacular accidents did. Nothing small like a hundred or so dead, though – only the biggest made headlines. They were just the thing to keep readers gripped. Just a couple of years before Barnsley's FA Cup win, the Halton colliery across the Pennines blew up: one boy survived, 350 died and 1,000 children were left fatherless in a day. A few months after that match, a surface worker was decapitated at the Senenydd colliery in Wales. At least this time there was something to report from the surface: the explosion was heard 11 miles away in Cardiff. Speculation caused reporters to check through their 'disaster league table'. Yes, this would make the headlines! Underground, burning gas shot through the web of tunnels, suffocating or burning alive 418 men and boys. After 47 years the grim record no one wanted passed from the Oaks colliery to Sennenydd.

All agreed it was a terrible business, but Parry knew that newspaper tales of heroic rescues and appalling death meant nothing at all.

'After a frightful holocaust or the flooding of a mine the tales of heroism are recorded minutely, and the miner is praised sky-high . . . in short the miner is a gallant fellow but alas! Where is his VC?'

Jones knew only too well that outrage and sympathy soon fade. In parlours and drawing-rooms, morning headlines would be used to light tomorrow's fire. Cries for VCs were forgotten and reporters and sightseers drifted away; the coalfields were left to remember their dead. No one asked why this kept on happening, or even understood the fundamentals of mining.

The world wanted coal and it wanted it *now*. Demand seemed insatiable and Jones realised mining stood on the brink of a momentous challenge. During a lifetime in darkness he'd developed not only the sixth sense a miner needs to survive, but also a keen vision of the industry as a whole. Experience had taught him and other engineers how to combat the threats of the mine effectively, but he recognised that to work in that underworld required one thing above all else, greater than technical knowledge of steam and geology. Without it, absolutely nothing at all was possible.

Ever since men first ventured into this new world, its hazardous nature dictated only one way of working. Jones re-states this essential work ethic. After my descent into the earth, I can only agree.

> To isolate oneself is out of the question below ground . . . You cannot develop that insular individualism below ground as help is required from someone or other continually. The haulier requires the assistance of somebody to get his tram or tub back to the rails when off the track; the coal hewer requires the help of more than one in adjoining stalls, to raise the heavy collar onto the two arms of the set of timber he is placing to protect his own life and others. Under such circumstances comradeship is bound to exist, the growth of which is fostered by absolute necessity.

Teamwork is fundamental to working in and exploring the underground, outer space, oceans and frozen wastes. Only through teamwork can such complex operations be undertaken. On every shift those underground had to balance the needs of safety and production and, ultimately, place their lives in the hands of their workmates.

It could be done, as they proved, but it was a delicate balance. As Jones penned his desperate thoughts, the cry went up for 'coal now and from anywhere', and round-the-clock production was imposed on the mining industry: something had to give. Formidable though the underworld dangers were, they could be countered through experience and teamwork. But all the dangers of gas, fire, flood and explosion were as nothing compared to the greatest danger of all, and that lurked at the surface.

Black Gold

IF EVER MEN WHO WORKED UNDERGROUND COULD BE CALLED lucky, William Rushforth was among that number. The mine he entered in the year of the coming of the King bore the name of a long-gone marquis. Coal was mined at Rockingham colliery for just over 100 years and there is no record of any fatal accident there.

The approach to mining pioneered by men like Fitzwilliam was soon swept aside by a new breed of mine owners. Unlike early coal magnates, who lived and worked alongside their men, this new breed had never been near a coalfield and didn't have a clue how one worked, as Parry Jones ruefully noted: 'Of all the British industries it can be said that none is carried on by such numbers of people who know next to nothing about what they own and supervise.'

They did know one thing about coal, however: it could make them rich beyond the dreams of avarice. While men like Fitzwilliam could fund their own explorations, the entrepreneur had to raise a large amount of investment money from others who were offered shares in the operation: they wanted that money, and more, back very fast. Distant shareholders tasked their agents, 'the lords of life or death', to pursue the dream ruthlessly.

Of course there were regulations. When Jones began work as a boy, a mine owner had to be qualified – this was obviously ridiculous to the entrepreneur. Such experience took years to acquire, but relevant certificates were easy enough to come by. More important was the new battle cry: 'Those in the know are staggered by the illimitable powers granted to these men who are shouting perpetually about "incentive" and "initiative".'

Profit was to be the sole driving interest that crushed all in its path. At the time of the Oaks tragedy they showed their priorities were firmly in place. Shareholders expressed: ' . . . their cordial sympathies with the proprietors of the Oaks colliery, not simply for the great loss of property entailed, but the crushing sorrow endured by the terrible loss of life of their workmen and the bereavement of those connected with them.'

Safety measures that could have been employed weren't. Safety lamps were around when the Oaks colliery exploded, but they didn't give out enough light and slowed things down. Candlelight was faster. Men continually killing themselves caused a terrible loss of property and an annoying break in production, but no more. When newspapers broadcast tragedy, the mine owners knew full well it would be enough to shed a few crocodile tears and mouth 'tender and heartfelt sympathy on behalf of the directorate'. It would all soon pass over. And the enquiries would inevitably find blame in some miner having used a candle down the mine. Much tut-tutting around the boardroom table: would these men never learn?

Human life, like their words, was worth nothing at all.

> It is a notorious fact in the coal mines of this country that there exists a greater 'to do' when a horse is killed than a man . . . in the case of a horse a new one must be purchased: therefore there is no end of inquiries as to how the accident occurred, but there are plenty of men searching for daily work.

> . . . if any reader doubts the indictment regarding
> inefficiency, stupidity and the crass folly of modern coal
> chiefs, then irrefutable evidence is the glaring black
> monster at every pit-head – the rubbish tip. It's a
> colossal monument to the illiteracy of modern mining
> heads.
>
> Coal owners are very consistent in one respect – they
> are governed by an untiring hatred of anything that
> savours of collectivism . . . merciless to their own class, the
> workers and the community . . . their only goal is gain.

Recognised mining practice was thrown out of the window. Time was money. So a few more died, so the landscape was scarred – so what? Waste material, for example, used to be stored underground. The coal owners came up with a quicker, cheaper solution. Jones knew that as black is to white and night is to day, so is the upper world to the underworld. Below ground, cooperation born of necessity; above ground, savage competition for profit, crude survival of the fittest.

In the considered view of coal owners, the men of the underworld were beginning to make unacceptable demands. A living wage, for example. This, in their view, was madness. Holidays too were unheard of. A miner recalls slumping over evening meals gripped with a characteristic tiredness, 'the stupor of the miner'. But paying men who were not working was simply a ludicrous suggestion.

> In no other industry can so few be found taking that
> hard-won rest which is vital to every person that does
> useful service . . . the reason is obvious – the dread
> uncertainty regarding the miners' occupation,
> coupled with the insufficient he is generally in receipt
> of . . . Thousands of thrifty miners, in order to exist,
> eat up what they had stored for their children's
> education and provision for old age.

> The coal owners as an astute commercial body
> have realised long ago the power of the press as a
> medium to make an imprint on the mind of the
> people . . . hence a number who are interested in coal
> also control some of the principal newspapers of this
> country.

The public had already formed a very different impression and for a very good reason that Jones himself recognised. Entrepreneurs needed to manage public relations to their advantage and had absorbed Barnum's ideas completely, but in their burning desire to become the 'outwitters', they had no need to influence newspaper editors. They'd gone one better; the conman would have been greatly impressed.

Needless to say, stories of miners' fabulous wealth abounded. Suggestions that a man might take even two weeks' holiday were ridiculed. Surely this would turn them all into loafers and layabouts. Every single minute of working time, every penny, every day's holiday was hard fought for. The coal owners shrugged off any attempt at negotiation. Cries for safety measures and more efficient working procedures continued to fall on deaf ears. Any request that might slow the rush for profits was blocked by one stock phrase – 'business is business'. And for some it was a very, very good business to be in.

As Jones completed his work, another man who'd been working for 30 years passed away. Perhaps there's no better example than Lieutenant Colonel Sir Joseph Hewitt JP to demonstrate how different the worlds of the pit owners and miners were. When Parry Jones went underground at 12 years old, Hewitt was a 26-year-old solicitor. His lucky break came on easing his way into the managing directorship of a colliery: the lad did well, but no one knew until afterwards exactly how well. From Wharncliffe Woodmore colliery alone he'd been giving himself little 'incentives' in terms of pay rises. By the time of his death he was trousering bonuses of £5,000 a year and charging £25,000 for his legal work. A miner would be very lucky to earn £50 a year at the time. It was a battle that would rage for well over 100 years: teamwork and time versus greed and speed.

The Pressure Cooker

IT ALL STARTED ON MAY DAY GREEN, AS FAR AS I CAN MAKE out. A special officer stepped forward to a group of protesting miners and waved a sausage at them. He could afford to eat; they couldn't.

So began a century of trouble. It wasn't only the miners, of course. The whole world was expanding into a meaningless mass of confusion. Britannia ruling the waves and the sun never setting on the Empire was only half the story. The country was in a state of chaos. This was a time of invention, destruction, creation, confusion, fabulous wealth and horrific poverty.

What do people generally think of when anyone mentions the Industrial Revolution? My money's on a northern town with smoky mills, pits, matchstick men and matchstick cats and dogs. Oh yes, I can taste the Hovis and hear brass bands even now. It's a strong image and it certainly has a very good foundation. When a French aristocrat, Alex de Tocqueville, sat down and wrote 'what I saw on my holidays', things were certainly well out of control up north.

> A sort of black smoke covers the city. Under this half-daylight 300,000 human beings are ceaselessly at work. The homes of the poor are scattered haphazardly around the factories. In Manchester, civilised man is being turned back almost into a savage.

And the south? Well, surely it was all endless skylarked summer, fine carriages, decent chaps and crinolined ladies? Not really, and I lay the blame for our national forgetfulness firmly at the door of one man: Dick van Dyke. Yes, that happy-go-lucky 1960s popular entertainer has a lot to answer for in my book. I think you know what I'm talking about.

'Chim-chimeny, chim-chimeny, chim-chim cheroooo . . .'

What a luverly place London must have been back then. Chipper old Bert the Sweep enthralling those sugary little children with his mockney antics while Papa was at the City.

'Good luck will rub off when I shake hands with you . . .'

I doubt it very much, Mr Van Dyke. Admittedly, some things would have rubbed off: lice, fleas, tuberculosis perhaps. There'd be a good chance of your malnourished hand rubbing off itself if I grasped it too firmly. If you thought 'a sweep was as lucky as lucky could be' then clearly you'd been at the gin or got too close to the Thames.

My river scavengings with Dear Boy would have been quite different back then. There'd have been a lot more things to find: rotting carcasses were ten-a-farthing. Human bodies and excrement turned the Thames into an open sewer. In fact, our first beachcombing expedition would probably have been our last – a couple of minutes and we'd have keeled over to join the dead pigs and children floating past the House of Commons.

Hundreds of thousands were drawn to the capital believing its streets to be paved with gold as expanding docks bustled with trade from all over the Empire. Victorian London generated enormous wealth and empire, and squalor on a scale never seen before. People died in such numbers, of everything from typhoid to TB, that the dead could no longer be buried. Stories of corpses bursting from overstuffed graveyards competed with burnt miners for lurid headlines. Not for nothing did the small enclave of wealthy west London refer to the east-end sprawl as 'darkest London'.

New machines, new ways of working, masses of people

flooding in to sprawling towns where 'every advantage has been sacrificed to the getting of money', as one Dr Robertson pointed out in the Commons, but no one was listening. The country became a massive pressure cooker that threatened to blow throughout Queen Victoria's reign.

Everywhere, everything was breaking down in a mass of confusion. No one knew what was happening or where it would lead. A lucky few children rode around on big elephants; most dropped dead on the street. Four years after whupping Napoleon at Waterloo, the Duke of Wellington was ordering sabre-wielding cavalry into a crowd of starving Manchester weavers. After the 'Peterloo Massacre', regularly shooting people who kicked up a fuss was the only policy most governments came up with. The 4th Earl Fitzwilliam rode down from Wentworth Woodhouse to object in the strongest possible terms about Peterloo. He was told to shove it and dismissed as Lord Lieutenant of Ireland for good measure.

Streets were filled with people waving the French flag and demanding revolution, or at least clean water and toilets. The hedgerows were alive with rioting labourers trashing mechanised threshing machines. Earl Grey suggested to Wellington that something should be done; the Duke thought the existing rules 'perfect'. Shareholders trousered fortunes; mines blew up. Journalists attempting to report shootings were quickly locked away. Mobs smashed machines in farms and towns: they hated the railways. The Duke of Wellington hated the railways: he suspected they could be used for moving around the people who hated both him and the railways. More pits were opened around tarn. The Great Exhibition proudly displayed the glorious achievements, while over-stuffed east-end graveyards displayed rotting corpses.

People streamed into the streets waving red flags. More people got shot. Furnaces and shipyards churned out mighty dreadnoughts. The Duke of Wellington loved the railways when he got the hang of this 'buying shares' business. More mines blew up. Empires collapsed. The troops stopped shooting people on the street as they were needed to fill the trains to go to France to shoot Germans. We won! The country was fit for heroes at last. The heroes came home to no jobs. Troops started shooting the heroes.

Mr Van Dyke, if you'd been caught cavorting around a pretty west-end park with a dodgy bunch of cartoonish characters, it would have been seen as a clear incitement to riot and you'd be looking down the wrong end of a rifle. Perhaps that's what actually happened and 'they' edited it out. Well, you never know.

Spectemur Agendo

WHEN PARRY JONES PUT PEN TO PAPER HE KNEW THE pressure cooker was about to blow again. The whole country was on the verge of total strike. Surely no one in their right mind would think of cutting wages and increasing hours? Wages were cut and hours increased. The General Strike of 1926 followed. Decent chaps took time out from the club and rallied round to drive buses and trains. Hurrah! None went down the mines, though. And so it seemed this turmoil would go on and on forever.

Above ground there were many, many changes over the years. But the earth stays the same: life underground never changes. The guiding principle of going underground to mine anything at all will never alter. Whole communities were founded on the principles of teamwork. Mining communities were the first 'self-preservation societies' – they had to be. When the reporters drifted away, our grandfathers were left to get on with it; if they hadn't been reported on, of course. Cooperative societies of traders were started up in response to high shop prices. In some cases, workers in mills weren't paid money at all, but were given company 'tokens' that could only be spent in 'company shops' where prices were higher. Nice one.

Small wonder that every aspect of life revolved around communal activities: societies, clubs and teams. In the upper world a miner lived life to the full:

> . . . sport has a great fascination for him. Football takes the palm in the realm of recreation, which is followed with the same vim as 'working on the job' . . . religion, politics, cooperation, friendly societies, trade union organisations, literature, music and all the fine arts receive his patronage.

And, of course, miners kept pigeons. When you lived an underground life, what greater thing could there be than nurturing a creature that flew? While we're at it, there were black puddings around. High in fat, maybe, but try squeezing into an 18-inch seam underground to hack out coal with a lightly drizzled salad inside you. After eight hours breathing in coal dust, a skinny frappucino wouldn't do the job – you'd down a few pints as well.

The country needed coal, but hated the idea of paying anyone to get it. The miners may well have fuelled the Industrial Revolution, but mining communities really did become an easy target. Everything was so dirty and the men were all black; didn't they have baths?

Some things from these years were never, ever forgotten and fuelled this war of the worlds for years to come. Talk of VCs wasn't far off the mark, but I don't think any miner wanted a medal. Then again, they didn't want abuse either. William Rushforth always used to bang on about that FA Cup win to his little daughter. Unfortunately, she didn't take much notice. My mother remembered one other thing he'd often repeat: 'Earthworms.'

Thousands of miners never forgot the word Winston

Churchill spat at them. As with Wellington before him, a few inconvenient things have been dropped by the imagemakers. The great leader labelled the miners 'the enemy' and thought nothing of declaring war on thousands on the underground frontline. Perhaps he was a shareholder. His words were never forgotten and the battle raged on and on.

Undoubtedly miners' unions were the strongest and most committed of all, simply because of the very nature of the work. Parry Jones leaves little doubt as to what they were all fighting for back in '26: '. . . it is for us to see that those who are dependent on us should receive the standard of life that is due to them. We may barter ourselves, but our children cannot!'

He might as well have used a peashooter against a tank. The 'other story' was the one that became generally accepted: the media and a tangled web of share ownership and self-interest saw to that.

But Jones was a man who knew exactly what he was talking about. He knew the coal seams wouldn't last forever; he could see the damage to the countryside. Even back then he was suggesting research should be done into wind and waterpower. Until someone comes up with making money from shares in wind, we'll have to wait awhile for that to take off.

Jones's warning of black monsters of slag at pit-heads came true in another great cup year. England carried off the World Cup and, though a little tyke, I could feel the terror that filled our house. At Aberfan one October morning, a glaring black monster stirred to life deep in the Welsh valleys and brought down hell on earth: 116 children and 28 adults perished as the slagheap crushed a primary school. My mother, close to tears, held us tight as if to shield us from that terrible thing.

Nothing of the dangers was ever spoken of by our coal-dusted fathers, but as little tykes we knew well enough. As a child I knew that the men were rarely at the pit-heads. I had the strange sensation that wherever I was, at school, market, at play or sleeping, far beneath my feet men were toiling in cramped dark seams of coal.

Day and night the earth swallowed our fathers and we were well aware that, should it choose, the earth could hold them there forever. Few had phones, but we were attuned to other signals of life and death. How many families shared the end-of-shift ritual recalled by one young tyke, waiting for the click of the gate latch that signalled Dad had made it home again? The dread of our mothers at the sight of a dark-purple NCB ambulance, the shadow of death passing through fearful pit villages, somehow seeped into our young consciousness. All prayed it wouldn't stop at their door.

It couldn't go on forever, though; the coal seams would one day run out, but no one ever got the chance to find out when. The world was changing again at the time of the coming of the whale, although of course we didn't know it then. It was time to end the old conflict forever. A shopkeeper's daughter had a plan: what was needed were new ideas, for a New World Order. In future everything would rely on initiative and incentive! The time had come to sweep away the enemy within once and for all.

The Battle of Orgreave proved the last of the War of the Worlds. The Duke of Wellington would have approved of events. The year-long strike in response to plans to close 20 pits and put 20,000 out of work at a stroke, set brother against brother, father against son; it dealt a seemingly mortal blow to the community. As horsemen rode north once more, battle lines were drawn and South Yorkshire was turned into a police state.

The village of Orgreave and its coking plant stood on land once owned by the Wentworths. It was here that 4,000 miners gathered to establish a picket line and 4,000 police were assembled to keep order. This would be a trial by TV, with millions of witnesses. TV cameras recorded the ensuing violence. Many who saw those images sympathised with the miners, but this time the evidence was clear – the miners deserved what they got. The screens showed that, in response to a barrage of stones and bricks from the miners, mounted police launched a baton charge that cut down men and women as snatch squads apprehended 79. The only thing was, the cameras had recorded those scenes – none of the footage was live. Much later it emerged that incidents of stone-throwing had been shot from various angles and edited to make them appear far worse. Even stranger things had happened in the editing process. The sequence of events had been reversed. In reality the horsemen in body armour with batons and riot shields charged first, raining down blows on miners in T-shirts and trainers defending themselves with stones. Still, in an editing suite it's easy enough to cut together whatever 'reality' is needed. Afterwards 79 miners faced charges of riot. None of the charges were upheld in court and South Yorkshire Police were faced with damages of almost half a million pounds.

It was a trial and execution that Tom Wentworth himself would have recognised. Just as the pamphlets on Tower Hill were clear evidence of Wentworth's sins, TV screens around the world were clear evidence of the miners' guilt. Barnsley's coat-of-arms bears a miner along with a motto that echoes old Wentworth's last words, *spectemur agendo*: 'judge us by our actions'. Once again, silent men in the shadows made sure that would never be allowed to happen.

Mining is still a tricky thing to talk about for some, while others have very firm opinions. I'll gladly listen to what anyone says, but I am my father's son, so I'll always offer the same invitation.

Go down a pit, and then see what you think.

Barnsley Main

THE MINES MAY HAVE GONE, BUT THEIR LEGACY MOST certainly lived on at Oakwell. Now, we've never been a big club and I don't want to go banging on about 1912, but for a long time that tyketanic year really was the high point. Decades of shuffling around the lower division followed. In '68, the year of the whale, the Tykes were promoted to the old Third Division of the Football League. Was this the start of something big? Our optimism proved unfounded. Barnsley floundered, sinking back to the Fourth.

No matter: ahead lay the path of a true Reds supporter. Nail-biting wins piled on nail-biting losses that piled on nail-biting draws. We were never a big, glamorous club, but what did that matter? As long as the Reds went out and fought for it, that was all most wanted. Of course, promotion to the old First Division and winning the FA Cup again would have been a welcome bonus too. We carried on dreaming . . . one day . . . one day. Perhaps the very next win would set us on our way. Urging the lads on until my throat was hoarse, shuffling over a coal-dusted Ponty End, swinging from red-flaking barriers – that was the way things had always been for us tykes. At winter evening matches, beyond the floodlights, heavy coal trains shunted and clanked away from pit-heads as they had always done, as they always would.

Well, that wasn't to be, but the miners left something more than just their support.

Just as the pits started to wind down, things finally started looking up at Oakwell. Manager Allan Clarke, staring across from the West Stand towards Barnsley Main colliery, decided that if his team were to really learn teamwork, there was only one place for the lesson. Brush remembers it well.

> Yes! I saw it on the telly. The team got dressed up in miners' gear, orange boiler suits, cap, lamp etc. Clarkie wanted to show the lads how the locals earned their £2 to spend at Oakwell each week, it seemed to work.

It certainly did. In the late '70s and early '80s we clawed our way from the old Fourth to the Third to the Second Division in three short, glorious years. The foundations were laid for that amazing year when Barnsley would magically transform itself into Brazil!

Copacabarnsley

A HOLIDAY IN SOUTH AMERICA DOESN'T COME CHEAP, BUT IN 1997 thousands of holidaymakers eager to soak up that heady Latin atmosphere in Rio really did waste their money. If only they'd travelled north and turned off at Junction 36 of the M1 instead. Still, I suppose the travel agents just didn't have time to get Oakwell into their brochures.

That was the season like no other; tarn was the hottest spot north of Havana. The 1997–98 season was the club's hundredth in the League and the Premiership finally came within our grasp. Danny Wilson inspired the team to play football the like of which we'd never seen before.

Red shirts gave way to gold and green as a joyous carnival erupted on the terraces at every home game. Brazilian flags waved in summer skies, curly wigs, balloons, whistles, drums hammered out a Latin beat. Children were held aloft with painted faces. Tykes sambed through Copacabarnsley towards the promised land of the Premiership. There were even demands that Barnsley's away strip be changed to that of the Brazilian national team.

Where did all this Latin fever come from? Was it devised by some marketing team intent on trying to get rid of a shed-load of Brazilian memorabilia? There was enough of it around at the time. T-shirts, keyrings, mugs, banners, you name it. If it was the marketing men, they must have been fiendishly clever. How could they have persuaded tykes that watching the Reds, no matter how well they were playing, really was like watching legends like Pelé, Jairzinho and Rivaldo? What's more, a tyke cannot easily be prised away from his or her sacred red shirt, never mind fork out for another team's colours.

It didn't happen like that at all. Such passion can't really be generated or promoted from the sterile corridors of an advertising agency or manipulated by the media. No, it was all down to one tyke who must have been completely overcome during an away game at Bolton. I wasn't there but Almatyke recalled that for a 20-minute spell, the opposition never got so much as a sniff of the ball. The unlikely combination of 'Barnsley' and 'Brazil' rolling around this tyke's head suddenly found expression in a familiar old tune, 'Blue Moon': '*It's just like watching Brazil . . . it's just like watching Brazil!*'

This lone voice might well have been drowned by the roar of 'Come on you Reds'. But it wasn't. Another, then another, then more and more took up the chant and the whole thing spread through the terraces and tarn like wildfire. Over the weeks it snowballed as everyone rallied to this new flag that would signal a glorious new era.

'*It's just like watching Brazil . . .*'

And it was. It really was. Or at least that's how it felt. OK, so the Reds could never match the Brazilian national side; any tyke would admit that. But that wasn't the point. The crowd had created something they could call their own. Instinctively they matched steamy Latin passion with their own passion for tarn. As Brinner might have put it: '. . . there was an unusual sense of freedom because it was genuinely spontaneous – it was something people did, which the media couldn't control – they could only report it – it wasn't their idea . . .'

The season drew to a close and the crucial home fixture against Bradford City became the big one: one more victory and we were up. Bradford, trying to avoid relegation, would make sure there were no local favours that afternoon. A draw wouldn't be good enough either.

Oakwell was packed to the rafters with red-and-white, gold-and-green tykes banging drums and singing 'Brazil'; on the touchline a 7-ft bulldog wearing sunglasses cavorted and waved. I was there with R Kid and Alex. Up in East Stand, near the away end, cascading Bradford crimson.

Wilkinson headed in the first for the Reds at the Ponty End. I didn't get a good view but we all went mad. All knew it wasn't enough, though; we'd seen too many games where we were hit near the end. Eighty-seven minutes and the score was still 1–0. Would they pull it back and deflate us all or could we . . . two minutes to go . . . two minutes . . .

'*Redfearn . . . he's got absolutely no support, so he's going to have to . . .*'

They were there, I knew it. William Rushforth standin', shartin' . . .

'*. . . going to have to turn and feed it to Clint Marcelle . . .*'

The Reverend Preedy, praying . . . 100 years of dreaming . . .

'*. . . Clint Marcelle goes for glory!*'

Straight in front of me: a perfect view. The striker drew his leg back in slow motion. Marcelle's boot made contact with the ball. Time stood still as the awesome power of thousands of tyke minds focused on the ball/foot, foot/ball . . .

'*AND GETS IT!*'

No longer was there a game, a pitch, players, crowd, or me . . .

'*That surely is the goal that takes Barnsley into the Premiership for the first time in their league history!*'

. . . everything merged into one thing . . . *tarn!*

I was one drop of a tyke tidal wave pouring down to engulf the heroic 11. We staggered blindly through 'Danny Wilson's Wonderland', carried forward on a wave of sheer emotion, beaming, hugging, staring, crying, kissing goalposts. A tyke knelt and plucked a few blades of sacred turf, held them up to the sky . . . and ate them.

'. . . *like watching Brazil . . . it's just like watching Brazil . . .*'

Floating back through the emptying East Stand I noticed an elderly tyke standing alone and silent above the red, white, gold and green sea. As I passed he grabbed me urgently by the shoulder and shook me, demanding an answer. He had tears in his eyes.

'*Did tha iver think tha'd see it, lad! Did tha iver think tha'd see it in thi own lifetime?*'

Choked by my own damp eyes there was nothing I could say. Magic.

The Bison

I REALISE I'VE USED THE WORD 'MAGIC' QUITE A FEW TIMES. WE all use it I suppose, but that afternoon at Oakwell *really* was magic, in the true sense of the word.

I need to be very clear here, because we all think magic is to do with spells, potions and wizards and doesn't really exist in real life. Try and forget about all that: put it right out of your mind. What I'm about to say may well unlock the very secret of this story of a whale . . .

The word 'magic', as used by those who study human behaviour – anthropologists – has a very clear and definite meaning. To understand it, we have to travel back in time to when we were cavemen, right back to when we hadn't even thought of clothes and had no language. When caves have been discovered from that time, we've marvelled at paintings on the walls: buffalo, bison and deer. To know why these were painted is to know the meaning of 'magic'.

They weren't knocked up on rainy afternoons as men whiled away time waiting for PlayStations to be invented. Nor were they painted where everyone could have a good look. They're usually found in the deepest, darkest reaches of a cave, the most difficult place to do anything. The cavemen didn't just admire these animals; it's far deeper than that. Let's take a tribe who hunted the bison, for example. Early man had one overriding need: to eat. If the bison was their source of food, the bison was their entire world. No bison, no tribe, as simple as that. This tribe devoted its whole life to understanding that animal: how herds moved, where they were found and at what time of year. Of course, they also had to work out a way of killing the bison. Again, this was a team effort; no one man could just stroll out with a spear or club and do the job. He wouldn't get near or he'd be trampled to death.

In order to kill the bison, the tribe had to 'think' like the bison. The bison was their life; their life came from the bison. They were one and the same thing. Cave paintings were a place of worship where man was at one with the animal. In front of the bison's image they became the bison.

This is magic: the identification of yourself with an object that represents your life through a symbol of that thing. Eventually, in this desire to identify, the cavemen took it further. Through draping bison skin around themselves or wearing the animal's horns, they would absorb the animal's strength and knowledge. Bingo! Man just invented clothing. The Bison tribe started to look like the bison. With all this wearing of animal bits going on and different tribes worshipping different animals, it's easy to see how you might wander back to your cave and go ugging on about how you were sure you'd just seen a creature that was half-man half-antelope: mythological creatures were born.

Of course, as many millennia moved on, the identification of humans with the bison, or other animals, weakened but was replaced by equally strong symbols that governed their lives. When farming came in, they had to figure out the weird lights that revolved above their head at night: the stars. In them were patterns they symbolised as star signs. The pattern of their appearance was recorded by cutting the year into 12 animal signs, vital in telling when the right time came to plant or harvest. The strength of this relationship faded too, but it is still alive and kicking in horoscopes – we still identify the date of our birth with it.

As humans evolved and languages were formed, this need to identify remained just as strong. Cave paintings evolved and became our mascots, which represent our allegiance to something or someone that we believe will give us life. The men in sandals explained life everlasting, symbolised by the cross, to Britain's here-today-gone-tomorrow warlords. It was the thing the warlords craved and so the cross took on massive significance for centuries. Nations formed as people identified with eagles and bears; men go to war hoping to draw on the courage of the lions and hawks painted on their tanks and aircraft.

Oakwell, like any football ground, is little more than a cave that is home to a tribe. By wearing our red shirts we become part of the team: we are the players, the players are us, all of us are tarn. The tyke who ate blades of grass that afternoon was just strengthening this magical bond. And because our bond was formed underground, it's far stronger than any other. Many may while their time away with solitary surfing, but could it be that only a tyke crew are equipped to hunt in the dark void of cyberspace?

Stranger things have happened, like a blue whale coming to tarn. So now we turn to ask 'why'. Why did the whale resurface when it did? Chance . . . or something deeper? For the answer, I think we must return to tarn in the '60s.

Cheese and Cornflakes

IN LATE 1968 A BRILLIANT WINTER MOON SHONE DOWN ON THE black-wooded silence of the Worsborough Valley in much the same way it had done since Wyrc looked down from his hilltop stronghold. Rockley Wood, at the valley's bottom, had been trampled through long before the Vikings stormed in. Even at the height of that century of mining, the countryside around tarn changed very little.

Nothing seemed to have changed that night, but everyone knew it had. That Christmas Eve, a static-clouded voice came from the dark side of the moon, the Lord's Prayer echoing to Earth through a quarter of a million-mile void. No matter how hard I squinted, I still couldn't see them sitting in their tin can. It didn't matter.

There were men up there! For the first time man was circling the moon!

Apollo 8 blasted the rocket-launching, planet-circling adventures of our comic books out of science fiction and into reality. There was scarcely time to draw breath before mankind took a giant leap onto the next summer moon. We needed no travellers to relay the news of change; tiny tykes were allowed to stay up late to watch fuzzy images beaming back from the lunar surface as Apollo 11's Eagle landed. *Men on the moon!* Saluting flags. Playing golf. A slight disappointment that it wasn't made of cheese, but so what? Anything seemed possible: space-stations, moon-bases. Next stop Mars! We would boldly go where no man had been before.

School projects were tackled with star-struck enthusiasm. 'Seas of Tranquillity' were squidged together from washing-powder-dusted swamps of papier mâché ready for egg box and silver foil lunar landing craft. Fuelled with pocket money, young tyke space pioneers blasted off for Woolworth's on May Day Green to Airfix the future together.

But you had to be careful: very careful indeed. There was so much future around in '68 there was no tyke had enough pocket money to buy it all. The space missions alone would have been more than enough to captivate us, but there was more, much more. In the end, like many others, I had to resort to cornflakes.

While older tykes may have put flowers in their hair and taken their first puff of cannabis in the late '60s, I became a thiamin, riboflavin and vitamin B junkie, crunching my way through a technological revolution. Frantically gobbling bowl after bowl, with eyes glued firmly to the back of the packet, I knew this was the way to get my hands on the shape of things to come. With the required number of box tops diligently collected I sat back and waited. Come the great day, graceful, white delta wings were snapped onto the slim needle body and there she was: my very own Concorde.

Rolled out to an admiring world in the last days of '67, she lifted off just before the moon landing. 'Wizard flight', the test pilot told us. A whole new world of travel lay ahead. Even more powerful craft were on the drawing board. Soon supersonic speed would shrink the globe: London to Australia in a matter of minutes. Probably.

No sooner had I gorged myself on one new flying machine than another would appear. From America an aircraft twice as large as anything seen before – so big it was dubbed a 'jumbo' – took to the air and fell into our cereal bowls. Next came the 'Harrier', a bird of prey that could actually hover like a helicopter above the breakfast table.

Magical craft of the high seas were also buried deep in these oceans of corn. In 1968, a giant sea creature burst into life and slid into the English Channel. Thundering forward on an invisible cushion of air she left mere ferries floundering in her wake. Dover to Calais in a lightning 30 minutes – had man ever been propelled across the seas so swiftly? Up on Clydeside a new queen of the ocean, the *QE2*, had rolled down the slipway and now readied herself for a maiden voyage to New York. It seemed to go on and on and on.

Christian Barnard caused a greater sensation than 'Dr Griffin' as he completed the first human heart transplant. No tyke tried to emulate this feat however – well, not that I'm aware of. And if America owned the moon . . . England had the world! When Bobby Moore lifted the Cup in '66 he ensured that playing fields and recs all over tarn were covered with jumpers for goalposts and echoed to the cries of runny-nosed tykes replaying our encounter with the Germans.

In those years of wonder, we lived and breathed never-ending progress. Our fathers had spent their lives underground to give us these machines. All these things were far away from tarn, but it would be our generation that would reach out to take them higher, further, faster.

Out on May Day Green, Jonah spoke to us of the mysteries of his deep world and warned that change was coming, even to tarn. The new American moon of '68 shone down on mysterious goings-on deep in the Worsborough Valley. Nothing seemed to have changed, but everyone knew it had. This was a new age of progress. As young tykes we didn't know that progress always has a price.

Monsters

IF HORACE WALPOLE HAD BEEN FLOUNCING AROUND THE gardens of either of the Wentworth estates in 1968, he would have been appalled. Both houses remained much the same, but the days of the gentry had passed. The 10th Earl Fitzwilliam clung on, continuing to use Wentworth Woodhouse, but its landscaped parkland had been scarred by extensive mining after the Second World War and would never again see its pre-war glory. Wentworth Castle's last owner, Vernon Wentworth, had sold up after the war and the castle became a college.

But it was the monsters that would have caused old Horace to faint clean away. Estates and valley echoed to the most terrifying snarling, not heard since dinosaurs roamed the earth. Often these shattering roars drowned out our lessons, rattling chalk dust from schoolroom windows. Afterwards we'd hurry down to a swaying, rickety stick-bridge to gaze down on an awesome spectacle. It just didn't seem possible. Below had once been quiet sun-dappled woodland, criss-cross mossy paths, trickling streams, butterflies, hidden dens and swings. Now it was a broad river of churning brown mud, the realm of yellow monsters. Monsters that were eating Rockley Woods!

If engineers had set out to design a Jurassic beast they couldn't have done a better job. Young tykes were well used to seeing heavy machinery close up, but this was something else. All they did was eat. Their cavernous-bellied bodies were edged with a steel-toothed mouth that gouged out everything in their way. Up front, steel 'neck' tendons held a belching exhaust stack and bobbing, swaying head, while some unseen engine powered wheels as big as a house. These earthmovers really were Tonka toys on steroids. For weeks, scores of the beasts swallowed childhood dens, relentlessly tearing out a broad brown scar north–south through our playgrounds and the Wentworth estates. Then one day they were gone. Almost silently came the next stage, a long grey river rolling up from the south. Three tarmac lanes thrusting north to Leeds, and three heading south to London. Once more, tarn found itself on the most important trade route of the day, the M1: Britain's first motorway.

Such a marvel had never been seen before. Leeds even went so far as to proudly call itself 'Motorway City' in the early '70s. So impressive was it that photographers sped north to snap service stations, bridges and barriers. Postcards were printed showing the road dotted with frantic Austins and Morrises winding themselves up to the timewarp speed of 70 mph. These images are now consigned to a book of 'boring postcards', but there was nothing boring about it at the time. This really was our physical link with the future. We young tykes, open-mouthed in wonder on May Day Green, never suspected of course, but the showpeople knew well enough what this new road would bring.

After hundreds of years the magic men would cast their spell over hundreds of market places no more. A heritage of bulls, bears, boxing kangaroos and other magnificent spectacles that graced town centres was coming to a close. England was changing and tarn would be no exception.

One Saturday afternoon, a few years later, Mother Nature summoned up a great gale that whirled market stalls into the air and sent goods spiralling to the four winds. It never opened again: the coming of the whale signalled an end to tarn life that stretched back over seven centuries.

The Crash

NOTHING EVER TURNS OUT THE WAY YOU THINK IT WILL. Journeys of exploration that fired imaginations and transported us to new realms are no more than fragments at the bottom of a cereal packet well past its sell-by date.

Way above us solar winds blow metallic tumbleweed through lunar prairies. The arthritic landing craft's leg creaks beside a moon-dusty, star-spangled flag that still proclaims this forgotten frontier. The chances of anyone going to Mars are a million to one it seems; the Martians sleep soundly to this day. The 'space race' staggered and fell before the second hurdle. Only one dynamic duo gave hope from the depths of space: Wallace and Gromit bravely blasted off to prove the moon was, after all, made of cheese.

Our great white bird spiralled earthbound in flames. The hovercraft, a sad seagull-shat hulk, sits discarded on a forlorn Dover slipway. The smooth tarmac rivers multiplied from M1 to M60, but rather than flow to the future they promised, they're congested to the point of heart attack. Next time you sit watching verge-grass grow by an overheating M25 think about what a really boring postcard that would make.

Weatherworn cobbles on May Day Green were torn away long ago. The new market wasn't so much heart surgery as a total transplant, a two-storey complex dwarfed by an equally featureless County Hall tower. To '60s town planners, concrete walkways and tower blocks were modern, clean and safe, the way forward for every town. Older tykes very much doubted it.

Those who recall the whale in other towns tell similar stories of long-lost market places. Leafy Camberwick Green's had a relief road skewered through its heart, of course. The windmill's been converted into a stockbroker's holiday home; old Windy Miller lost his job as nightwatchman at the Euro-GM-Bakery complex after a mugging and now ekes out a pathetic existence in sheltered accommodation.

The mines may have gone but the miners were only the first. The grocer's daughter turned the country into one vast corner shop and it soon became clear that everything was 'uneconomic': everything had to go in the great closing-down sale. The drive for profit and efficiency was on and the law of the jungle, so feared by a visionary miner, came to pass. Profit-driven accounting machines roamed the country unopposed, cutting costs, slashing workforces, 'atomising' society. No one would be spared the death ray. Steelworkers, engineering, car plants, shipyards, railways: anything that stank of the hated 'society' was to be cleansed in a brave new world of initiative and incentive. By the year of the second coming there really was very little left.

To noisy, disbelieving protests, Dagenham and Welsh steelworks were forced to close their doors.

Business is business, but it's difficult to build the stuff of dreams when they take away the tools. All the things that would fly us to the future fell to earth. At the end of the '60s it all looked like a new beginning, but perhaps it was a last shout of that 100 years of progress.

Now we're on the brink of something even bigger, even better: a whole new world is out there to explore. This is the IT revolution, the age of speed. Things are moving so fast you really shouldn't be reading this in the first place; you'd better be quick and get on board or be left behind. OK! Here I go . . .

Yes! I'm a sort of silver-strandy-surfer, balancing on a surfboard as I speed across the surface of the globe. Come join me – let us surf fearless along the information superhighway into the wonderland of cyberspace. But I'm not doing that at all; in reality I'm just sitting at a keyboard typing. So that's the future then – just sitting on our bums, looking at a glass screen. This is not the trip to Mars I was expecting.

That year of the whale I tried, I really did. But it still looked like a keyboard and a glass screen to me. All around me was a whirl of speed and the endless talking talk of the talky people shouting out that I was wrong: the *real* world doesn't matter, the *virtual* world was the future and nothing's quite what it appears to be. Like all times of great new inventions, no one's really sure what they all mean and how they'll work. It was time to get out, slow down and have a think: time for a holiday.

I'll send you a postcard.

Lindisfarne

SEAHOUSES MIGHT BE A LITTLE PLACE, BUT IT'S GOT A LOT OF restaurants. As soon as I spotted the horned helmet, long beard and war axe of an illuminated, perspex warrior gazing longingly towards Norway, I knew the Viking Café was the one for me: a big enough place, but apart from us and another couple it was empty and quiet. Perfect. At the panoramic window, Caroline and I drank warm coffee, shook off summer drizzle and gazed out over a damp North Sea.

Down below a red fishing boat bobbed alongside the quayside and began loading its quota of squealing pushcairs, blossoming lemon-and-turquoise cagoules and snappy cameras. Hurrying down to the harbour we jumped aboard as the engine chugged to life. Wrapped in wheeling seagulls, the little boat nosed out towards black rocks some three miles distant. After only a few minutes of wallowing through spray and rain all were soaked through. Further out, startled, tubby puffins flapped stubby wings, trying to free themselves from a lumpy green sea. Fat seals plopped up to peer at us through shining coal-black eyes before bobbing back down.

Funny thing, the sea. I mean, what really is down there? Perhaps we'll never know: even now we haven't reached the deepest of the deep trenches. We might think the ogling of eels and octopuses in aquariums a quaint pastime of long-gone people, but we're just the same today. In that year of the whale, I realised that when something weird surfaces even national newspapers brush other stuff aside so we can all have a good look.

Off Australia, fishermen cut their nets in horror when a sea monster got trapped, and what a whopper it was. Weighing in at 32 stone and 36 ft long, this was a relic from prehistory. The giant squid is another elusive sea creature, never having been caught alive. This specimen was dead when towed back and probably just as well: its parrot-like beak was capable of chewing a man's leg off. Once prepared it will, of course, go on display in a Melbourne museum.

One specimen caught closer to home won't, though: a tremendous 15-stone halibut landed off Rockall appeared in the papers shortly before falling to the fish knives and forks of Aberdeen restaurants. Even the smallest make headlines. Dotty the Box Fish pined in her loneliness at some aquarium until she fell in love with a dice dropped into her tank.

Just to prove Sam in Brighton wrong, and to mess up another council budget, a huge cetacean washed up in Sandwich Bay, Kent, that year. The humpback whale was almost 100 years old and exhausted; he had to be put down. They showed his eye on a news report – very sad. Sandwich Council was left 'deciding how to remove the carcass from the beach'.

But my favourite just has to be Barney the Lobster. He's out in the Channel even now and I've got a lot of sympathy for him. Barney wandered into a lobster pot, but on delivery to a top London restaurant the chef decided he just couldn't end up like all the others. He was too big too . . . too . . . well, they just couldn't. Taken to London Aquarium, he was estimated to be about 60 years old. Barney cropped up in the papers a few months later when he was escorted back to the Channel by a couple of divers who took him out and placed him gently back on the sea bed. Nice one, Barney. Even now, he'll be scuttling around, trying to tell his great tale of his journey to another world, and everyone will think he's just codding.

Perhaps the best news of all has only just been splashed across the front pages. Is Brighton's 'White Elephant' a thing of the past? Well, the country's greatest aquarium has just opened in Hull. It's got a glass lift that actually takes you deep down among the swirling rays and gliding sharks. The Deep estimated it needed 800 visitors a day to break even; it was overwhelmed by 4,500. See what I mean? That old fascination never dies.

The skipper cut the engine down and we bobbled alongside rocks that St Cuthbert chose as home. Plump seals washed onto rocky ledges scratched and waved and barked as the saint's own 'Cuddy Ducks' drifted alongside. The Farne Islands: hard black, treeless seagull-shat rock stubbled with scrubby patches of gorse. You really could do a lot of thinking out there; apart from staying alive there'd be nothing else to do on that forbidding rock.

A little later, just up the coast where the road runs into the sea, we waited for the tide before journeying on to Lindisfarne Island. We had no saint-in-a-box and I didn't want to get my sandals wet. The sheep up at St Michael's Bay were still being ruffled by the wild east wind as we walked a scraggy grass and pebble bay guarded by upturned blackened hulls of fishing boats-turned-sheds. It was here the dragon-headed landing craft arrived and stormtroopers hit the beach running to bring the world to its knees. The ruins are still there: the grey veins of St Cuthbert's Abbey run through rich green grass above the beach.

By evening, the sea ran in once more and this remote outpost of Western civilisation settled quietly into its past. Far and away and across the dark evening bay, the roar and snarl of dragons can still be heard. It could be seals I suppose, but who's to know? I promised Caroline I wouldn't be keeping a watch for whales, but I don't think she believed me. By the way, if you do see one in trouble report it to the coastguard, and remember it was designated a 'royal fish' centuries ago, so don't go running off with it.

There was nowhere else to go that year but the borderlands. Inland, the shouting had got louder and louder, and more and more urgent.

The beastwagons were forced to stop rolling, though only for a while. All painted in fine colours and logos they may be, but they are just as terrible as those long ago. I'm sure some expert might disagree with me, but unless that 'expert' happens to be a lamb or a calf then I'm unconvinced.

We sailed north in silence through grim fields filled with yellow machines and men in chemical suits, vast ditches dug and walls of black burning animals. Up past York, the yellow machines were frantically gouging channels, while walls of sandbags were thrown up to dam floodwaters that threatened to engulf whole villages. Why was this all happening? Nobody seemed to know.

No one even knew where it was safe to go on holiday; the only answer seemed to be to talk louder and louder. Odd really. This was supposed to be the 'information age', so why was all the information from millions of glass screens useless? If this was a 'knowledge economy', why didn't anyone know why all these things were happening? Or how to stop them spreading? The experts in talking kept on talking. That would solve things, probably.

Bamburgh

IT WAS RAINING SIDEWAYS WHEN A SEA GALE BLEW US UP THE rockface of Bamburgh's fortress. Dripping across the great halls I once again had the chance to peer into a microscope 'thingy', this time to view the Bamburgh Beast. This fine-crafted sliver of gold no bigger than your little fingernail once belonged to the holy men across the water, long before the Vikings landed.

In upper halls the armoury's dark walls are lined in silver sword, axe and lance, muskets that would have been shaken from their racks, primed and pointed seaward as a monkey aboard the *Chasse Maree* sailed south to Hartlepool. In a glass cabinet I stumbled across an even older weapon: a pitted, dull sword from Wentworth Woodhouse dating back to old Tom Wentworth's days.

Out again into the gale, we barrelled down past iron cannons to a small doorway. Inside there is a cave hung with strange trophies from Northumberland fishermen's nets. Looking closer one caught my eye: a sea dragon. Not a thing of myth or legend – this really was part of a fire-breathing sea dragon, a reminder of one of the strangest events ever to have taken place across this coastline.

Out across the North Sea on a frozen airfield, six young men swung into the belly of an aircraft that minutes later lumbered into the darkness on a westward heading. The six men aboard their bat-winged bomber believed in the crooked cross painted on her tail. But behind her glazed nose she bore another symbol: a shield containing a Viking longship. On Northumberland's coast many heard a dreaded roar coming in from the sea. Over 1,000 years after they first hit that coast, the fire dragons were back. German propaganda resurrected the memory of their north European ancestors in their own search for new land. For that Heinkel bomber was part of KGr 100, a unit that really had taken the role of those longships. They were the Luftwaffe's elite, pathfinders roaming the world from Durham to St Petersburg, Spain to the Suez Canal. And where they led, the 'Great Host' would soon follow. Day after day throughout the Second World War a new generation of sea-raider would stream in from the seas, strafing shipping and hitting north-east industrial targets. Yet on one raid, a surprise lay in store.

Heinkel pilots watched the North Sea slip below and signalled 'enemy coast ahead' to their crews. Tense gunners flicked off safety catches and swung their machine-guns in arcs across the sky, watching for enemy fighters. Thundering across the coast towards their intended target of Durham, they could never have dreamed this island had a defence far more effective than the RAF.

All those centuries ago, the saint-in-a-box northern tour reached its (not surprisingly) miraculous conclusion. Putting the good saint down for a rest, the holy men found that, on trying to resume their trek, the box had become too heavy to lift. Help was called in but the box wouldn't budge. Clearly St Cuthbert was indicating this to be his final resting place. The holy men got the message and proceeded to build Durham cathedral over him.

Heinkels carrying tons of incendiaries, high explosives and land mines, versus the bones of a man who'd died over 1,000 years ago? No contest really. As the aircraft approached Durham, bomb-aimers lying in the Heinkels' glass noses indicated to abort the bombing run. The whole town was shrouded in a thick sea haar.

The Cross 1, the Crooked Cross 0. *Nice one you saint!*

Among the rusting metal legs, rotting tyres and faded photographs at Bamburgh there hangs on a wall a black piece of metal bearing a shield and Viking longboat; the fragment of a fire dragon that later fell to more conventional defences. Or did it?

The '*Skylarks*' of Brighton beach failed to get such saintly protection in those war years. Brass bands and string quartets stepped ashore as marines fitted machine-guns, then set sail across the Channel to Dunkirk. Two never came back, taking hits from dive-bombers off the beaches. When invasion loomed on the south coast, Brighton Aquarium's tropical fish were sent to London, while edible exhibits suffered an inevitable fate. Archie the alligator resisted all attempts at evacuation; I'd have thought he'd have been invaluable as first-line defence but it wasn't to be. The local press showed someone holding a shotgun in one hand and an alligator in the other. At the same time Eric the Finback was carted in his box over the Pennines and buried under Morecambe's roller-coaster.

The Giant-hunter's west end museum took several direct hits from the bat-winged bombers. Thousands of exhibits were blown to fragments, but John Hunter's statue and the Irish Giant survived to stand as prime exhibits near a badly charred hippopotamus skull.

The American entertainer Charlie Kunz defected to join the German Wehrmacht and fought bravely at Stalingrad. Well, actually he didn't, but that's what was claimed at the time: it's a true sign of fame to be singled out for use as propaganda by the enemy. German radio broadcasts during the war also claimed the popular pianist had been imprisoned in the Tower of London as a traitor and performances contained 'hidden codes' used to direct German bombers to their targets.

Yes, that's the thing about crosses and other symbols – you've got to be careful which ones you sign up for because they can be a whole lot of trouble. Some seem attractive to start with, but get twisted around to the point where you realise you're on a pretty dodgy team: often you realise this too late. The swastika itself is an ancient symbol that once upon a time represented 'well-being', though no one will ever look at the crooked cross that way again.

The business world loves manufacturing symbols too; the outwitters spend billions trying to convince you that life's impossible without them. Mobile phones, mountains of fcuking clothing: all it needs is the right logo stitched on and you can really rake it in from the great unwashed. Even a cheap canvas shoe with a rubber sole filled with fresh air is transformed by a small embroidered 'tick' into a precious holy relic that some are prepared to kill and die for.

The old conman must be laughing still.

Hartlepool

MAKING OUR WAY DOWN THE COAST THERE WAS A TINGE OF disappointment on reaching Hartlepool, for me anyway. One of the old docks has been recreated as a port from Napoleonic times, complete with HMS *Trincomalee*. All very interesting, with lots of fusty ship's stores and plastic naval captains doing the old 'har har me hearty' bit, but the main monkey keeps a low profile around there. Perhaps he was hanging around somewhere else and we didn't spot him. I didn't think Caroline would want to go up to the Victoria Ground on the offchance of bumping into H'Angus.

Football's certainly changed a bit since Hartlepool FC signed Forman from Workington for £10 and a box of kippers. I reckon it all kicked off when the fat bloke sang. Three lions roaring out defiance, Gazza blubbering, white shirts holding fast, then Stuart Pearce and Chris Waddle blasting us out of the Italia '90 semis in that heroic penalty shoot-out against the Germans. Pavarotti belting out 'Nessun Dorma'. Ah yes, all the poetry, passion and emotion of the beautiful game. That's when people who'd previously ignored football started to take an interest, as Brinner identified: 'Ten years ago the only people who watched England were people who watched footie generally. Now your mum and yer dad and yer lass and yer gran all watch as well.'

For those sensing a fragmenting of the community, the 11 men took on a new significance. In Euro '96 the nation was gripped by footy fever and another penalty shoot-out, and it wasn't just your nearest and dearest who started to take notice. Celebs, politicians and anyone who was anyone started banging on about how they'd been lifelong supporters of one team or another. I've even heard that one Peter Mandelson's rubbing shoulders with H'Angus these days. New Labour! New Football! New Monkey!

Then there came a bright shining light. Grass-root supporters lifted their eyes to the heavens and verily, they saw a vision of the future. Money fell from Sky like manna from heaven. Pattering onto dull, barren rooftops, it brought forth a rich endless field of satellite dishes. At first it all felt so good. We were hooked on round-the-clock football, never thinking that the only real goal was profit. Business used to be business and now even football's business; everyone studies club share prices more eagerly than league tables.

Accountants applaud swelling profits as terrace fodder's fed through the marketing turnstiles, processing passion into monthly payments. Time to reap the harvest from our satellite fields! I can hear old Barnum cheering from the dugout.

'Roll up! Roll up! Pay per view!'

The corporate tentacles, sad to say, even reached out to the whale hunters. Had I posted my 'whale on a lorry question' only a few months later, it would have gone unnoticed: NTL sank the ship that Tommy tyke, Radders & Co. built.

Many football club bulletin boards have been put together by supporters. The corporate world, of course, knew better than bunches of scuzzy amateurs. NTL paid for the rights to all clubs, destroyed the past and imposed a new future. All boards would be the same: all would be shiny and efficient. From the moment the new board was launched it didn't work. There could never have been any hunt or any conversation on the new board. It demanded codes, passwords and, like some deranged bouncer, wouldn't let you in even if you had them, or threw you out for no reason. There were a few cries of anger and despair in the darkness, but now it's all gone. The old crew have been swept overboard forever.

Now the game's well and truly addicted: more cash injections, more cash injections! Clubs forced to beg for another fix pawn their heritage, rename football stands and even grounds. Terraces are relegated, executive boxes promoted. Players are the new Giants as we're invited to turn up and be wowed by their towering pay packets.

Perhaps it's gone even further: Posh and Becks have been elevated to superhuman status. A couple of artists depicted them as Hindu goddess Parvati and god Shiva – even Brooklyn got a look in as Ganesh, the elephant god. I don't think they're quite there yet; if a mysterious sea haar blankets the England goalmouth I might be prepared to believe, though.

But as Jonah's tour showed, you should never ever underestimate the stupidity of the business world. Cable, dish and digital calculations done in speed and greed assumed everyone who had lived, and ever would live, would spend their entire lives watching football. Fortunes were spent and now – surprise, surprise – not enough's coming from the dodgy products. The money's running out and it's the monkey that's having the last laugh.

Advertising's now become little more than entertainment and everyone loves the cheeky sock-monkey on TV. I've even heard of someone who taped all the ads to watch when they're feeling down. A successful ad, then? Not if you're the company who commissioned it. Everyone bought the monkey but no one bothered much about the product. As the corporate debt begins to mount it looks like a spectacular own goal, but it's worse than that.

When football was a game, the losers would be back to fight another day. Now that it's a business, the losers are simply destroyed: winner takes all. Still, I suppose we can look forward to watching Man United v. Man United in coming seasons. Impossible? Not really: the married men can play the bachelors.

Goathland

THERE'S A WINDSWEPT VIEWING POINT ON A ROAD THAT spirals up and up to the giddy heights of the North York moors. Up there seagulls must sense they're better equipped to deal with gales than we are. The one that hid by a litter bin as I ordered from the tea and coffee van, then chased me squawking across the lay-by, certainly was. As wind whipped coffee clean from my cup we settled on half a kipper-pâté roll each.

It's a breathtaking view up there, even without the breathtaking wind. I felt, but was told I didn't look like, Heathcliffe. Up there it was as far away as it is possible to be from the new revolution. No trace of it anywhere, but somewhere over the horizon it was all going on.

Massive migrations of people were on the move, creaking grey-faced and angry along collapsing rail networks and jammed roads monitored by staring cameras. Filing into offices they began a daily grind of sorting and sifting and sending e-mails to other people who are sorting and sifting and sending the same, all dull-eyed in the knowledge that this will go on hour after hour, day after day. This, so the ads tell us, is the future, forever and ever amen. But from the number of distant funeral pyres and red-and-white taped-off pathways, all the information being gathered informed no one of anything.

Funny things, computers, when you think about them: are we working at a machine or are we becoming part of the machine? Million upon million of us, weaving the web of meaningless information that's smothering the globe. Everyone likes to think they're some vague thing called 'middle class'. But if the information age makes us get in earlier and leave later and leaves no time for anything else, then isn't everyone part of a new 'working class'?

Luckily the bright wind blew the cobwebs away; we swooped across the winding windy moor towards a broad North Sea sparkling in the sun. Turning off the main road we dropped down steeply into a mossy green world of twisty one-track lanes that no mapmaker had managed to master. Little villages and farmsteads huddled in gullies and wooded ravines well away from the wind. I couldn't even find them again if I tried, but the names round there seemed familiar: Battersby, Easby, Mickleby, Barnby, Aislaby and the fantastically named Ugglebarnby. The original settlers must have felt well at home here. OK, so they may have been a little over-enthusiastic with the old war axe, but at least you knew where you were with the Vikings: 'So tell me, what is it exactly you do for a living, Mr Skullsplitter?'

One of the rules of the new revolution is that nothing should have a name that indicates in any way what it does: Consignia, Thus, Nimbim, Egg, Concentrica, Blomten, Enron. Anyone would think they had something to hide. (By the way, I think I made some of those up, but I can't be sure which.)

Parry Jones would recognise the way they go about their business, though.

'Merciless to their own class, the workers and the community . . . their only goal is gain.' Actually they've got more than a little in common with old Dark Age warlords: out in the corporate world it's war! Great leaders demand blind loyalty from underlings and in return promise to axe job after job if the millions don't keep flowing into their bulging 'war chests'. It's the language of war: first strikes, campaigns, killer applications. Of course, you never hear all this; it's left to us chickens to clothe these worldwide warriors in a reassuring cloak of care, commitment and 'customer service'.

The top men rarely visit the real world – not without a well-rehearsed, fork-tongued script anyway. But from time to time one does break free in an ill-advised moment of zealous enthusiasm to reveal the inspiration for their life's work. A computer software chief-exec left readers of the *Financial Times* in no doubt who it was he admired when he dribbled enthusiastically about his new strategy: 'It's rather like heroin dealers who give away the drug for free, and once people are hooked, they sell them on to the higher-grade stuff.'

It's nice to have someone to look up to I suppose, but following his plan to its conclusion I fear we'll all look forward to being targets for corporate drive-by shootings if we don't buy his stuff.

By the time we reached Goathland, I realised that this naming business was where everything had started to go wrong. Some very, very strange things were going on at Goathland. There's a little station that runs trains down to Pickering through the densely wooded Newton Dales. The steam engines are quite incredible. *They're alive!*

Muscular, snorting, steaming bulls that, even at rest, exude an intense, primeval power. They look like they could thunder on for mile after mile, crushing leaves and snowflakes under their mighty wheels: mile after mile, year after year, forever and ever. The feeble, rotting tissue boxes stuffed with commuters that rattle and fret into London would be swept aside and faint dead away if they ventured anywhere near these mighty beasts.

It's a bit of a tourist thing, of course; I know you couldn't run a real railway with these engines, although we used to. I suspected some of the men in Goathland used to work on those old railways – silly sods would never get a job on a proper railway today. Instead of tapping mobile phones, they were tapping the rails. Is that a way to run a business? There was very little incentive or initiative about the whole operation as far as I could make out. Staff in the tearooms smiled and called me 'love' and there were real flowers on the gingham-covered tables.

The surreal rail system may be little more than the top half of an accountant stitched to the bottom half of a lawyer, but the private companies did make one big mistake in the naming of the parts. Take Railtrack and Southwest Trains for example. Where were the image consultants when they came up with names like that? If only they'd gone for proper names like 'Butterfly' or 'Biscuit Tin', perhaps everything wouldn't have gone off the rails.

Whitby

I STOOD UNDER THE WHALEBONE ARCH UP ON WEST CLIFF looking out across the craggy little fishing town towards East Cliff and St Hilda's ruined abbey. From up here, women scanned the horizon, waiting for the safe return of their men who months before had sailed into treacherous Arctic waters. Up here children danced and sang, 'spelling' a good wind for their fathers' return: 'Suther Wind suther, an' blow mah father heeam t'mah mother.'

From up here came the first cries of joy as needle masts of ships were spotted and all strained to see if a whale's jawbones were lashed on high as a sign of a successful hunt. Back then the whole town below would have wallowed in the thick stench of whale. Unlike the Nantucketers, the Whitby whalers brought blubber home to be melted down to the precious oil that accounted for almost half of Britain's needs.

William Scoresby and his son are the most famous of the Whitby whaleship captains. Never heard of them? You might have heard of another captain who learnt his trade in the wild Arctic wastes, a young seaman called Horatio Nelson, who made quite a name for himself in the navy. Whitby whalemen's seamanship was unparalleled and made them a prized target for naval press gangs, yet they weren't absolutely fearless. Like all who ventured into new worlds, they had their strange superstitions. A drowned dog or cat and a woman whistling were most definitely to be avoided, but seamen feared one object so much that they couldn't even bring themselves to speak its name. Instead the humble egg was referred to as a 'roundabout'.

I doubt they had a problem with kippers though. I vainly tried to pick out the blackened smokery tucked away among the fishermen's cottages that wind under East Cliff. Years of curing herring have turned its old stones oily: a place that's become half shop, half kipper. It's a bit different to most shops: it doesn't have any advertising, fancy signs, loyalty cards, slick promotions or money-off deals; it gets by with a white card in the window that says 'kippers'. You have to get there early, but it's well worth it. They sell the best kippers in the whole country and for that reason I'm not telling you how to find it.

Looking down onto fishing boats bobbing from the stone harbour out to sea, I remembered my meeting with Harry Brookes. I eventually managed to track down the elusive tarn market expert: he remembered Jonah, of course, and even Eric, but really couldn't tell me much more. He did suggest I try the *Chronicle* or Barnsley Library; they'd know something for sure.

I glanced around at Harry's paintings, proudly displayed on the walls. He'd turned his hand to woodlands, mountains and seascapes, but it was the ship that caught my eye. The *Endeavour*, he told me proudly, nodding at pale canvas on canvas: a small sailing ship approaching Whitby harbour carrying home the ghost of Captain Cook.

If the spirit of tarn market lives anywhere, it's in Harry's small front room. He unfolded careful typewritten pages and faded photographs telling a tale of colourful characters and day-to-day tarn life far more vividly than I could ever hope to. He would have got along with Sam down in Brighton. As Sam spun his yarns, Paul whispered 'to tell a story you have to have lived it'. And I had no doubt Harry and Sam had lived their lives to the full. Their voices seem faint echoes of a long-gone country: tales of sharks and matchsellers, lifeboats and bulls.

Today millions of us leave the same glass screens in the same offices to drift into the same crappuccino bars to sip the same identikit froth and shout into the same mobiles that we don't have time to be where we are. We might not have a life, but who cares? The outwitters are slobbering to sell us a lifestyle.

We're all individuals in a world where being an individual involves striving to be much the same as everyone else. We're free to choose, but the only thing is we've got no choice because everything's the same. The only way to really express your 'individuality' is with a different snap-on cover or ring tone. Wild. In years to come, what stories will come from our dull grey offices? *Memories of a Mobile Phone Salesperson*, or *Tales from a Marketing Consultant?* Gripping stuff. I can hardly wait.

Perhaps it's only on this borderland of sea and earth that anything actually is different any more. Strange to think that it was from way over the horizon that it all started with our tyke ancestors in their longships. One of the old crew's still out there. Knut's a Norwegian Barnsley fan, which I suppose makes him the most authentic tyke out of all of us. And the northmen just keep coming; only recently another great Norse leader came ashore. This 'son of Eric' was fortunately a little more mild-mannered than his forebears and arrived at our invitation in the hour of great need. Strangely, he achieved victory not through shouting, but by quietly whispering tactics that proved as sharp as old Sven's harpoon.

Of course, it's from those faraway Norwegian waters that great Jonah came. No one knows how many are left for sure: possibly only 1,000 around the Arctic region and 5,000 worldwide. Whale oil and coal; liquid gold and black gold. For all that century of progress there were some who had to pay the price. We still know relatively little about those great mammals, but in the year of the hunt it was discovered that some live to be over 200 years old. And what do any of us know compared with the wisdom of two centuries?

Somewhere out in broad oceans it's likely there's another great whale that first sang alongside its mother as tykes marvelled at all the inventions so long ago. On and on he swam, beyond the harpoons; on and on through all the revolution and war and strife of mankind, through all the vain hopes and proud boasts; on and on he swam as great men were born then crumbled to dust. And perhaps one dark, fateful night he skirted a great iceberg and a mighty vessel and shed silent tears for all the folly of men.

Up on West Cliff I followed the great captain's eyes out to sea, then turned inland to a house on the banks of the River Esk where, as a boy, Cook learnt his trade. Visit that house on Grape Street and you can stand on the very spot where a young boy dreamed of launching into the unknown. 'I can be bold to say that no man will ever venture farther than I have done,' Captain James Cook wrote much later. He was right. Captain James T. Kirk's pledge to 'boldly go where no man has ever been before' remains but fantasy.

Whitby: the launch pad for Cook's blast-off in search of new worlds. The base of his statue bears inscriptions of thanks from those that followed . . .

'*To strive, to seek, to find and not to yield . . .*'

At least the captain would have understood my voyage.

And so it appeared the hunt was over. I should have known better. Staring out over the North Sea, little did I suspect that Jonah had not quite finished with me. Far had I roamed in my search for the meaning of his Second Coming, but now it was time to leave my coastal musings far behind; too soon they would count for nothing.

We must now set a final course west, some 70 miles across the flatlands to the only place our voyage could ever have ended. Ahead the past, present and future are set on a collision course in a final, terrifying encounter with monkeys and mayors and bones and arches and towers – and the great whale himself.

Tarn

Dream tonight of peacock tails
Diamond fields and spouter whales
Ills are many, blessings few
But dreams tonight will shelter you.

Thomas Pynchon

Bones

JUST HOW LONG CAN A 200-YEAR-OLD MYTHICAL ANIMAL survive? You might well have thought the hanging on a Hartlepool beach an obscure oddity that belongs way back in folklore. Yet as we've seen, the monkey's new football career brought wider fame today. Amusing perhaps, but surely the end of the story?

I really don't know how the indestructible simian hit upon the idea. Did he tire of flicking peanuts into the crowd? Or did he, during some tedious, sea-haar-shrouded, 0–0 draw recall his long-ago meeting on the sand with the Mayor of Hartlepool? Whatever the reason, H'Angus, Hartlepool FC's mascot, decided to stand for the position of mayor in the local elections. He'd got it all well planned as well. Touring the town in blue-and-white strip, he chattered out his campaign pledge of 'free bananas for all schoolchildren!' No other candidate took him seriously, of course. He was just a looney in the mould of the legendary top-hatted Screaming Lord Sutch.

And so to that stormy electoral evening in Hartlepool, as the assembled press and delegates gathered to keep a sharp lookout for the winner. As silence fell and the results were read, confusion reigned as all present relived the utter terror of those long-gone fishermen. This was yet another case of mammal mis-identification! There, standing on the platform, was a man!

H'Angus wasn't a monkey after all!

Stuart Drummond leapt free of his monkey suit and swung to a historic victory. The Hartlepool Monkey that wasn't actually a monkey (but a man who'd been voted in under the guise of a monkey) was now the world's first monkey mayor – or man-monkey mayor, depending on how you look at it.

Naturally, candidates who'd been hung out to dry that day objected. No one likes to be beaten by a 200-year-old mythical animal, I suppose. There was a lot of tut-tutting from politicians about the democratic process being made a monkey of and quite rightly too. I mean, what would things come to if people were allowed to vote for whoever they wanted? Clearly, the people of Hartlepool made up their minds there was no point voting for yet another monkey in a suit when they had a chance of voting for a man in a monkey.

Yet that election victory still seems strange to me. For so many years local people had tried to shrug off the mocking cry of 'monkeyhangers'. And now they'd brought the object of this ridicule into the world's spotlight. Perhaps Hartlepudlians had tired of the same new policies, the same new promises, the same new initiatives, that seem to lead to the same old business parks, the same old shopping malls, the same old retail chains. Perhaps they'd tired of being 'represented' by those who didn't seem to 'represent' the locality at all, but were committed to a process that's banishing the last traces of regional identity as it reshapes high streets from Hartlepool to Hereford into identical consumer-processing alleys. Did the town strike back to reassert its identity with its unique symbol? Because the monkey doesn't represent the town: *he is the town.*

By now the mighty simian's power knew no bounds. Victorious in Hartlepool he may have been, yet he went further, journeying south on a new mission. No one could ever have detected the monkey's silent presence in a meeting room in Barnsley. But it was here that he would appear, all St Cuthbert-like, before R Kid, bearing an electrifying message that would set us on our final heading.

R Kid works for a construction company that builds things like supermarkets. He once supervised the building of a supermarket in Kingston that's very, very close to the station. So if you find yourself in there, tread carefully: you may just be stepping over the old bones of a long-dead elephant. That particular morning the meeting no doubt followed its usual course of costings and timings, but once over, mention was made of a job in a north-eastern town: a place where, apparently, locals went by the tag of 'monkeyhangers'. Talk turned to monkeys and hanging and then, because the Hartlepool Monkey's story had now become inextricably linked with Jonah's, to whales.

There was the usual disbelief, the inevitable laughter, but in that room there was one who remained silent. Deep in thought, links were made and silence turned to a sudden rush of excitement: 'You mean . . . like . . . the whalebones? The whalebones! The whalebones on the A61!'

Come evening, cross-country airwaves were jammed with excitement. Just to the north of Barnsley there were whalebones! Charts were consulted, frantic raids carried out on the library. We had to be sure . . . whalebones at the side of the road! And this was no coastal road: the A61 runs from Sheffield, up through tarn and on to Leeds. I fixed a position on my charts and could scarely believe what I saw. Rothwell: not far from Wakefield and not far at all from a furnace that once stood at a place called 'Soot Hill'.

This, beyond all reasonable doubt, could mean only one thing: we'd found him! The last mortal remains of Jonah! They had to be. But what, exactly, was there? A great whale deboned and left at the side of the road? My mind's eye conjured up a mouldering skeleton, half-concealed by undergrowth, invisible to traffic rushing by. But wouldn't it have been stripped by souvenir-hunters after all this time? Or carried off by foraging dogs? Thinking about it, though, it would be a mighty big dog that could trot off with a whale rib. I endeavoured to set sail as soon as possible, yet R Kid lay at anchor much closer; he would set a northerly heading the very next evening.

The following day dribbled by in never-ending impatience.

The appointed hour was near as my tube rumbled out of London. I sat tenderly cradling my despised mobile, now transformed into a vital link to the conclusion of the inland whale hunt. Minute after minute I fretted the sleepers away, urging the clanking train on. I had to make it home before it rang.

It rang.

At the other end, muffled confusion and tyres on gravel.

'R Kid . . . R Kid . . . you're goin' to have to be quick!'

The mobile's red eye blinked at me in contempt and gave out a mocking bleep of warning.

'R Kid are you there . . . is it him?'

'*We're just pulling up . . . it's here! It's massive! It's . . .*'

The mobile died.

Bastard.

The Arch

I CAN ONLY SUPPOSE THAT FATE PLACED ME FOREVER IN THE borderlands. Walking south from my parents' house you'll reach the top of the village in a couple of minutes. At a bend in the A61 there's a sandstone obelisk dated 1775; no one seems to know exactly why it's there. The only clue is an arrow pointing west towards the Worsborough Valley, along with an inscription: 'Wentworth Castle 3 miles.'

My parents used to pay rent to the Earl of Strafford; some neighbours are still tenants of the estate, the last remnant of a way of life that spanned centuries. It may be that the obelisk was the lord of our manor's signpost to make sure his visitors weren't confused with the other Wentworth, because cross the road at that point and you are on Wentworth Woodhouse land, the A61 marking where the two great estates meet. Right in front of you used to be miners' cottages, on a lane that led to my grandfather's pit. There's no trace of Rockingham colliery now; it's a business park.

Look further east toward rising ground and you'll see 'Hoyland Law Stand', an old stone folly built by the Marquis of Rockingham. Wentworth Woodhouse is further away to the east. It's still the country's biggest private house and the only one with two 'fronts': the East Front (which is the front) and the West Front (known locally as 'The Back Front'). Yes, confusion still reigns supreme in these parts. Like Wentworth Castle it spent some time in the hands of an education authority, but it must have been mighty expensive to keep going. It's now in private hands once more: I spoke to the owner. Understandably, he wasn't too enthusiastic about a crazed whale hunter trampling through the great house, but he told me of a very cold day back in the '50s on London's South Bank, when he took a stroll through the belly of an enormous whale.

How far had word of the whale travelled in those endless months? Jack from The Cow, on his travels from Dallas to Uzbekistan, had spread the word in Russia and Holland; no one knew anything. Hardly surprising really: a Pole questioning Russian air-traffic controllers in St Petersburg about a whale on a lorry in England was a bit of a long shot. Gary, setting sail from tarn to the gaming tables of Las Vegas, had more luck though. There he met up with a cousin from Tokyo who recalled a faraway May Day Green: 'My father only took me out twice when I was a kid, and once was to see that whale.'

Yet for all our worldwide roaming it would be from here, this village of my childhood, that I would voyage along the tarmac umbilical cord that connected me with the whale. Turning north, I swept along the A61 under old Wyrc's stronghold. Far out west the razor-sharp Pennines were shredding the sky into angry black squalls, dazzling white candy-floss and flashes of high, brilliant blue that tumbled across old Strafford's rolling deer park and gardens. I plunged into the valley, then climbed steadily into tarn, dripping through the Dearne Valley, then on and on still further north. Beyond Wakefield the A61 shrugged itself free from the procession of sandstone and red-brick villages and climbed gently to open grassland. I knew well enough what lay at the bend ahead.

I stared up in wonder at twin whalebones; this was like no arch I'd ever seen. At a push you can reach up and touch the apex of the Whitby Whalebones. The bones in front of me soared skyward to puncture sodden clouds. How big must this creature have been?

The Fenton family were once wealthy coal owners around here. The family home used to be somewhere near where I stood. Exploring new markets well over 100 years ago, one Fenton sailed to America, where he was very much taken by a pair of whalebones. On returning home, they were erected as a gateway to the Fenton home and hung with a lantern. But whalebone doesn't last forever, especially if exposed to the elements and an over-enthusiastic horse-and-carriage which did for the original pair. Hazel found only fragments in tarn library but we knew that the A61 bones had been replaced two, possibly three, times and the last time was in the '60s: the late '60s.

Surely, surely . . . this must be . . . determination soured into an unfamiliar, desperate anger.

Michelle and Linda rallied to the cry of a windswept mariner who blew across the building site, shaking hail into Rothwell library and crying out in his madness.

'The whalebones . . . the whalebones!'

Urgent clippings and cuttings were unearthed, messages sent and tea brewed.

The sky rolled a dull grey shroud over me as I returned to stand silent once more under the great arch. Wind and water swirled and spattered off the old bones. Grey wood. They looked a lot like grey wood, but peering closer, there was the unmistakable honeycomb structure of a once-great living animal.

I reached out.

As I touched the whale I recalled a storm a long, long time ago and cries of anguish across the cybersea.

'But Statis, I saw it . . .'

'It's an early memory, possibly the earliest I've got . . .'

'It couldn't have been . . . I wasn't born until later, '67.'

1967: the year that almost tore us apart and sent Ahab on his remorseless quest. I took away my hand and peered up through the rain, at the bones of a finback whale, a 75-ft female caught in the Antarctic in 1965 and brought to Rothwell in 1967.

It wasn't him, but it hardly seemed to matter. I stood in the rain there for some time, surrendering to a sinking feeling of overwhelming dread. In truth there seemed nowhere else to go that day. For this was the day our never-ending talk of speed ended in a shuddering halt. Standing under that whalebone arch I knew I hadn't found Jonah but, through my fear, I sensed he'd summoned me to this place, on this day, to witness another.

Way beyond the boiling wake of the Pennine sky, out across wide waters, a monstrous creature had risen, tearing open the sky to embark on a voyage that even now cast his never-ending shadow across the face of the earth. Leviathan: the symbol of unmitigated evil and a terrible warning to mankind.

Only the day before, the future had shone proud on a small island just off the mainland. Here lived the self-proclaimed 'masters of the universe'. Superhumans who'd created a symbol of a religion that would endure for all time. There was no past, only this new beginning. With a cry of 'forget the history, buy the mystery', these gods would lead us to a future where the world would speak with one tongue, the language of eternal profit.

No matter where you were that day, you'll have known exactly how it felt to be in old Alcuin's sandals. History turned in from the friendly skies and struck a hammer-blow into the heart of civilisation. Was this the end? Fire dragons roaring in from the sea: a world sure of its own destiny rocked back on its feet. Shock waves around the globe.

No superman flew in to save the day. Once-empty churches were crammed, candles were lit, prayers wept. Humanity turned away from the glass screen, forgot grey mountains of information and hunted down symbols and signs and meaning and connections: Nostradamus; numerology; the Bible; the Koran. And all the while, the mighty whale cast his cold, relentless shadow across the earth: 'He maketh a path to shine after him . . . when he raiseth himself up the mighty are afraid . . . for he is king over all the children of pride.'

Onward my friend, into the darkness.

The Tower

THE HIGHEST HILL IN BARNSLEY OFFERS A FINE VIEW, EVEN better if you climb to the top of the glass tower that's built there. From up there you get a panoramic tarnscape.

Mid-winter might not be the best time to admire the view, though. While I was up there, daylight was thin: a few short hours where the lansdscape woke under a flat grey sky that gave up a spat of freezing drizzle or a few watery rays of sun before fading back into the impenetrable moorland night. Despite the gloom I could make out another black hill to the north, defined by a sprinkling of orange-and-white pinpricks. Up on its summit there used to stand an old Norse stone cross that's still remembered to this day in the village name: Staincross. Beyond that summit, the A61 weaves its way out of Barnsley, north to Wakefield and whalebones. Looking out west to Emley Moor, the blackness was slashed by a snaking red/white river flowing north–south between Motorway City and London.

Beyond, I could just make out where the rolling valleys and hills, on which tarn and its surrounding villages stand, come abruptly up against the hard granite of Pennine peaks. An ancient coastline where many, many millennia ago, water swirled through dense, forested swamps and lapped against the country's backbone. Tucked deep into one of those unseen valleys, the farmstead of the Danes still shelters from bleak Pennine weather.

The descendants of those wild Norsemen have long since hung up the war axe. Nowadays they prefer to take on all-comers with a pastry-cutter. The residents of Denby Dale make exceptional pies – and make no mistake, I mean exceptional.

No one knows how it all started, back when Barnsley prepared for its great expansion, but the decision was taken to bake a pie to celebrate the King's recovery from a bout of madness. The event was a huge success and, though George III's brush with sanity proved temporary, commemorative pies did not. When Wellington whupped the French at Waterloo, the ovens were busy with an even finer pie. To say it was large would be an understatement: it contained two sheep and twenty fowl. At each event the Denby Dale pie grew by staggering proportions. Not all were a success, however. The cutting edge of monster pie technology is a hazardous place to be, as hungry villagers discovered while contemplating the gargantuan specimen baked to celebrate the Golden Jubilee of Queen Victoria. At 8 ft wide and 2 ft deep, and stuffed with a selection of game, poultry, rabbit, veal, mutton, pork and 40 stones of potatoes, it caused more than a stir when the crust was cut. Midsummer was no time to tackle such an ambitious pie: the stench of stale meat spread over the village as horrified Dalesmen and women hauled the offending giant to be buried in lime at a nearby wood.

Yet the pie-making continued and examples such as these are looked back on as mere vol-au-vents. Denby Dale's crowning glory was baked in the year of the Second Coming of the whale. The Millennium Pie weighed in at a record-breaking 12 tons and was enough to feed 50,000 people. I often used to wonder how they came by a dish big enough to hold it. R Kid told me that his company's construction expertise won them the contract for that mother of all pie dishes. And as for transporting such a heavyweight? Strange to think that interest in a 'big whale on a lorry' was regarded as a sign of madness that year, but had I asked about a 'big pie on a lorry' no one would have batted an eyelid around Barnsley.

Deep in that winter tower I had a new job. It wasn't one I had sought, but I had no option. The glass tower itself was much the same as any other, stuffed with PCs and technology I couldn't understand. A few people fussed around, others idled the days away. Everyone stayed on late into the night. Some didn't go home at all – sad. Time passed unmarked as lengthening nights slowly squeezed daylight into scarcely noticeable smudges of grey. I had more than enough time to think.

Sometimes I'd drift back to my idling in that summer tower by the Thames. Back then, everything looked so bright, so sure, so confident. 'The world is changing,' they shouted. So it had, although not in a way anyone could have predicted only three short winters ago. The white-hot heat of progress was growing cold.

Few of us even pretend to understand how the wise men who spearhead our information revolution go about their business. Everyone just assumes they must be mighty clever. After all, you'd have to be very, very smart to make money out of just talking. The electronic bulls and bears and stockmarkets and financial gibberish were beyond anyone's understanding, including, as it turned out, those doing all the talking. But did it all really matter? Theirs was a world that has little do with any of us. Actually, unfortunately, it does.

For the last few years we, the unwitting outwitted, had been invited by the outwitters to a grotesque show pitched on the global market place. This was, so the adverts told us, the greatest show on earth, and perhaps it was. Novelty followed novelty. We watched in wonder as the magic of money tranformed all it touched. We gasped in amazement at bizarre celebrities, grotesque lifestyles, deformed egos, obscene wages, all paraded for our entertainment as we cried out for ever-freakier freaks.

But these were mere sideshows, the glitz that would distract us from the only game in town. Drunk on entertainment, we gladly handed over our money to the smooth-tongued outwitters for the greatest con of all. Barnum laughed as he raked it in: 'Yes . . . you sir! See how by sleight of hand I will return to you a fortune . . . simply by talking!' We held up our mobiles and cheered. But cheers turned to gasps of amazement, then cries of horror, and now sighs of despair. It had indeed all been an illusion: we'd been suckered.

The show's over. Everyone complained; no one got their money back.

The outwitters laughed, melting into the shadows with the takings. The talking talk of the talky people is fading into the night. Shares are plummeting, ripping the icing off corporation after corporation to reveal the turd beneath. It became clear that a future founded on hot air is no future at all. And now, as pensions shrivel before our very eyes, we might well come to know what old Parry Jones meant when he feared that in order to exist, thousands of the thrifty would have to eat up what 'they had stored for their children's education and provision for old age'.

Things will continue as they have done, of course, for a while at least. The deception and denial that fuelled the new revolution isn't easily stopped. I knew that far to the south many other towers would be full even at this late hour. They'd be careering around strip-lit chicken runs all night, dementedly crowing out 'customer satisfaction' till dawn.

I preferred to get my 'customer satisfaction' from a place that's been offering it, unadvertised, for hundreds of years. Just half a mile south of my winter tower I could find everything I needed on tarn market. If the money really does run out, it's the best place to be for a fantastic bit of salmon, Barnsley chops, bacon and the best lamb shanks around, not to mention black pudding. There's probably a stall with a five-legged, green elephant with a glass eye too, if you look hard enough.

Yes, the confidence of that profit-fuelled future seems long ago. There's always hope, of course, although moneymen tend to find it in the most unlikely places. Out beyond black moors another storm was brewing that winter. Runway lights flared: an afterburner crackled orange, then another, then another. Urgent soundbite reports rap out a warning.

War, boys! This is war!

Spreadsheets and hedge funds are thrown aside in a scramble for F-16s and fatigues. Out in the darkness Terror roams the earth. Trembling newscasters told the truth: 'The bloodstained devil could be anywhere! He incites his hell hounds to execute his vengeance with chemicals, rocket-launchers and bombs!' Vigilance is the watchword as we all strive to imitate those fishermen and root out the spies. And strangely enough, despite all the information we've amassed, we're still not sure what the enemy looks like.

None but the truly insane would welcome the way the world's started to tremble under Leviathan's shadow. Yet the insane are up for it. Crazed financial fundamentalists look forward with glee: a good war; a just war; a decisive war! This would be just the thing to rally the markets! No matter that their greed, speed and incompetence had brought the walls tumbling down, slaughtering someone – anyone – will soon get us back on track. With their deeply religious belief in the infalliblity of money, any conflict will be, for them at least, a holy war.

But cheer up. There's always football. The faithful will always file down Bala Street to Oakwell the way they've always done.

Or will they?

How dark can the darkness be?

In that year of the Second Coming I'd taped a photograph to my PC: I spent more time looking at it than the screen. Day after day I smiled back at myself, pausing to pose framed by Twin towers. Red shirt, red-and-white chequered flag held high as the red sea flooded up Wembley way – a great day. As the referee blew to start that play-off final no tyke could have imagined how much would be at stake over the following 90 minutes.

We filed from that match dejected but defiant. The vision of the whale appeared to me as we tykes contemplated yet another assault on football's summit. There was no joyous return to the top flight that year. Optimism remained strong and we all gazed resolutely towards heaven, but all the while we were falling, unsuspecting, into a hell no tyke could have conjured up in their deepest, darkest nightmare.

The following season fingernails had been chewed right off before Norwich journeyed once more to Oakwell. It was the penultimate game and we had to, just had to, get something from it. Because if we didn't . . .

We didn't. The final whistle consigned us to the Second Division.

The last match away at Wimbledon saw a futile Reds victory, but by then the whole game was losing big time: no one more than our protesting hosts that day. The south London club had years before moved from their Plough Lane home to ground-share with Crystal Palace, but worse was to come. Financial considerations resulted in new owners uprooting the club and moving it to Milton Keynes. So was Wimbledon really 'Wimbledon' any more? Surely, if the team played in Milton Keynes, they were 'Milton Keynes' . . . weren't they? This was groundbreaking stuff in every sense. Business is business and now it was really getting down to business. A sense of identity forged in the last revolution seemed to be undergoing the final stages of destruction. Money had destroyed communities and now, victorious, was destroying the symbols of the vanquished.

We hunkered down at Oakwell but few could escape. The promised Nationwide League money never came: a pity, because much had already been spent. Some blamed ITV Digital; some blamed lack of planning; some blamed players' wages; some blamed lack of vision. No one, of course, took the responsibility. To our horror the team spiralled down the Second Division. Could it get any worse? It could. Preedy's dream began to die before our eyes. Amid rumour, half-fact, accusation, speculation, threats and counter-threats, Barnsley Football Club went into administration.

Out in the darkness beyond my tower the war of words reverberating around tarn was bloody and prolonged. Survival hung in the balance. Some said there might not even be a club at all: we might be sold off as a supermarket. No one knew what the future held or what to make of all the denial, deception and disinformation that always surrounds business deals these days. All I do know is that if your mascot hangs up his boots then things are pretty desperate. Toby Tyke confided in Nicholas that he was leading a dog's life down at Oakwell; he'd be sticking with the scissors in future.

I now knew for certain that, for all my searching for meaning in the Second Coming of the whale, it was all too clear – in football terms at least – what that meaning was. Jonah appeared to us as a silent warning that the fate of his kind and ourselves might well be intertwined.

Yet amid the destruction and darkness that winter there was hope. I don't feel too sad at the loss of the old board and the crew. NTL might have destroyed the board but all is not lost. Blind corporations are very like dinosaurs: big, noisy and dangerous, but slow, stupid and easy enough to give the slip. Business loves to control and thought it could control the Internet. It couldn't, of course. The dream of ensnaring us all in the web, of turning it into a global worldwide supermarket to wring never-ending profit from obedient consumers, is a long way off yet. Because what jargon-gibberish-spouting businesses are blind to is that 'consumers' are in fact 'people', and people can just walk away.

There's no crew to look at 'strategically targeted' advertising on the NTL board. Thousands of potential consumers just drifted away. We're still out there though: the red flag flies high over a new board built by Tommy Tyke and Radders. I didn't join them that winter, but I knew well enough that if in this fight for their beloved club there was the slightest suggestion of deception, old Norse blood would boil once more. The cybersea would blaze with a fierce passion: we still never take anything too seriously until, that is, we talk of justice and right.

Parry Jones would have understood. He told of a time long ago when our forefathers would gather each day at a certain meeting place deep underground before journeying to their work, a place of debate and discussion.

> To the outsider it would be a revelation to hear the varied subjects dealt with there. Politics, philosophy, psychology . . . take first place; then comes football and all branches of sport; and following in their wake current events of the day.

The name given to such meetings: 'The Spell'. Centuries may pass and technology change, but the old ties are not easily broken. Those born and bred may be scattered to the four corners of the world, but the old spell is still as strong – and perhaps even stronger than we imagine. Yankee tyke's never set foot in tarn, possibly never even visited the country, but her whispering late one quiet night shows that even those not 'born and bred' can lay claim to be as much 'tyke' as the rest of us. Those great movements of people that set in motion the last revolution reverberate still.

> One set of my great-grandparents was from Wales. They settled into the Barnsley area about the turn of the century . . . Great-grandma loved it there and when they settled in the States, she always told her

kids that they were going back there to live. She
never made it . . . Barnsley has always been kind of a
magic place to us, the place she loved.

Could it be that the Internet will strengthen ties such as these?
A far cry from plans for the new technology drawn up by
business basketcases, to be sure. Their feverish struggle to
connect people with e-mail and mobile results in ties, but just
how strong are they? Flimsy strands too easily formed and
broken. In its preoccupation with shallow glitz at the surface,
business has no time to gaze into hidden depths, where deeper,
much deeper than many of us imagine day to day, there runs a
spirit more powerful. Could it be, as we voyaged deep for the
whale, Jonah showed that whatever may change, and whatever
the storms, there lie bonds so strong they can never truly be
broken? Could it be our hunt was proof that the heart of our
community beats as strong as ever, that the spirit of our
forefathers – the very spirit of tarn – is something that can never
die? I hope so.

Of course much has changed, on the surface at least. The
dense forests fell to give us a landscape rich in layers of black
gold, but reminders of Barnsley's century of change are hard to
come by. Glowering slag heaps that once formed unwelcome
new hills and valleys have been levelled or grown green, pit-
heads demolished and tracks torn up. The winding gear of
Barnsley Main colliery still stands as a reminder but the
blackened stonework around Barnsley has been scrubbed. Some
remains, though, if you look hard enough.

The biggest house in the country must be mighty difficult
and expensive to clean. Horace Walpole would have been
appalled by towering, blackened columns and soot-crusted
pediments. Yet I think old Rockingham would approve of this
lasting reminder of the vision of his successors and their valiant
attempts to impose some order on that turbulent century:
'There cannot be a more false or dangerous doctrine than that

the interests of employer and employed are opposed to each other. Their real interests must always be one and the same, and they must stand together or fall together.'

I can hear Parry Jones cheering and a greengrocer's daughter spitting at the 6th Earl Fitzwilliam's sentiment from over 100 years ago.

Yes, it's almost all gone; the men of the underworld, praised in time of disaster as worthy of a cross for valour, have no memorial. Off Doncaster Road, above the site of the Old Oaks colliery, the Angel of Mercy spreads his golden wings to keep watch over miners of old. He guards only Parkin Jeffcock and his rescue party though; hundreds of others remain nameless, forgotten.

Perhaps, one day soon, it will all be forgotten, on the surface at least. Amazing plans have been drawn up to tranform Barnsley into . . . wait for it . . . a walled Tuscan town complete with its own lake. The proposals have even been displayed in Venice complete with a halo of light in the night sky that will mark out tarn for miles around. And in that future tarnscape, whatever it may be, many will know nothing of their forefathers and the underworld. Only a while ago Hazel heard a little tyke turn quizzically to her mother in the market place and ask a question that seems quite incredible.

'Mum . . . what's coal?'

There are many others in Barnsley trying to forget too, who still rankle at the endless mantra of 'flat caps and whippets and strikes and mushy peas'. True, it's a strong image. But it's one created by those who looked no futher than the surface, those who had a vested interest in making sure the miners were never given their due. The Mayor of Barnsley, Joe Jones, was a mining engineer. He once lectured at Oxford University where he listed the many products made from coal, ending his speech with the wry observation, 'you can get anything from coal except a decent wage for the miner'.

George Orwell, who stopped over in Barnsley on the road to

Wigan Pier, saw beyond the surface. 'Society stands on the shoulders of the miners,' he wrote. I don't think he was far wrong. Old stories spun by image-makers would have us believe wars were won and the British Empire born on the playing fields of Eton. But they weren't. The millions of men who poured underground, and into foundries and steelworks, were the builders of Empire, men who journeyed day after day to a hazardous, unforgiving world to hack out millions of tons of raw materials for furnaces that built great machines. Without such men, nothing would have been possible.

So think on whippets and flat caps if you will. Yet the whale taught me that truth is rarely found at the surface. Way down in the silent depths, there are other stories to be told, if only we take the time to slow down and listen. And so, my friend, farewell. Our voyage is at an end: for you at least. I had a little further to go that deep winter, but I cannot take you there.

The winterworld slowed in much the same way it does every year. Out in the darkness the tarnscape shone with jewelled trees, raised amid old tales of peace on earth and goodwill to all men. My prayer in that cruellest of all winters was that out in those dark streets there still shines an everlasting light, of a spirit that will never die. For my vigil in that tower was drawing to a close and alongside me were those who will never forget the men of the underworld.

We'd worked shifts that winter: my brothers, my mother and me. Staring into never-ending darkness while the old men drank tea and ate biscuits deep into the night. My father was among them.

For a quarter of a century Jan blasted passages through solid rock, deep below the earth's surface: a 'ripper' working with explosives, waist-deep in black, freezing water. Few jobs were more hazardous: 'hell', he'd told my mother.

Many times through those silent nights Orwell's words came back to me. 'Society stands on the shoulders of miners.' Well, if society stands a little shaky on its feet these days it's because old shoulders grow tired. These men had left the mines long ago, but the mines would never leave them: emphysema, oxygen, bronchitis, hopes and prayers.

And so the old men talked quietly into the night. Brief flashes of laughter, faint smiles of recognition at recollections of long-gone mines and mates. But soon, all too soon, talk began to fade; soon, all too soon, the time for talking would be over.

We waited on our father, deep into the night.

Way up high on old Wyrc's hill
An old miner sleeps sound 'neath a stone
That bears an eagle and a crown
And the red and white flag of a land far away
Not born or bred,
But as true a tyke as any.

Do widzenia.

Onward

THE WHALE HUNT'S FAR FROM OVER. THERE'S STILL MUCH TO be discovered. For latest sightings, climb aboard at www.bigwhaleonalorry.co.uk. But don't spend too much time in front of that glass screen. Take a few voyages of discovery out in the real world. I've flicked through the old whale hunt logbook and come up with some ports of call.

Cap House Colliery: inject yourself into the earth. The National Coal Mining Museum of England, Overton, near Wakefield. Tel: 01924 848806. Open daily 10 a.m.–5 p.m. (except 24, 25, 26 December and 1 January). On the A642 between Huddersfield and Wakefield. www.ncm.org.uk.

Wentworth Castle: the house and grounds that won the first Style Challenge. A lottery grant and a lot of hard work are being put into restoring the grounds and garden to all their former glory. Follow in a frilly-cuff's footsteps around the castle's gardens at Lowe Lane, Stainborough, Barnsley, South Yorkshire. Tel: 01226 731269. Opening times vary, so check first. M1, Junction 36 then left at the obelisk on the A61 towards Barnsley.

Wentworth Woodhouse: home to the biggest billionaires. View the biggest private house in the country. You'll reach the stable block first; don't mistake this for the house! From marked footpaths you can stroll through the grounds and find the follies. Don't forget to explore the village too. Tel: 01709 835904. M1, Junction 36. Find out more at www.wentworthvillage.net or Rotherham Tourist Information.

The Elsecar Heritage Centre: discover what people did before staring at screens. The Earl of Fitzwilliam's mine workshops are now home to the Newcomen Beam Engine centre, national bottle collection, museums, arts and crafts, and lots of other stuff. Elsecar steam railway and various special events. Elsecar Heritage Centre, Wath Road, Elsecar, Barnsley. Tel: 01226 740203. Open seven days a week except Christmas and New Year period. Signposted at M1, Junction 36.

Locke Park: the navigator's park and fading follies of Victorian England. Don't miss Locke Park Tower – hopefully renovated soon for spectacular views over the Worsborough Valley. For special events, tel: 01226 773633. M1, Junction 37.

Barnsley Market: for whale hunting it's your first port of call . . . not to mention Barnsley chops, salmon, black pudding and the rest. Go hunting for Sailor Sid, George the Sockman, Morris's Coats, Renee and her roundabout, Mitchell's fish stall and much, much more. Right by May Day Green, so why not ask if anyone remembers anything abart that whale that came t'tarn? Barnsley town centre. Tel: 01226 772239. Tuesday: second-hand market; Wednesday, Friday, Saturday: market days; Sunday: car boot sale. M1, Junction 37. www.barnsley.gov.uk (click on tourism).

Barnsley Football Club. Well at the time of writing we're still in business. The 2002–03 season's penultimate game saw us needing a point against Brentford at Oakwell to avoid relegation to Division 3. With the score at 0–0 and the clock ticking past full time, few knew that as other results went against us we needed a win. If Jonah prophesied our fall, then I can only hope it was another prophet set us on a new course that afternoon; a goal from Isaiah Rankin in the 93rd minute saved us. For more nail-biting action take your seats at: Barnsley Football Club,

Oakwell Stadium, Barnsley, South Yorkshire, SJ1 1ET. Signposted from Junction 37 M1. Tel: 01226 211211, or climb aboard at www.Barnsleyfc.net. You might just meet some of the old crew.

Brighton Fishing Museum: all aboard the *Skylark* and the *Sussex Maid!* 201 King's Road Arches, Brighton, West Sussex. Open all year round 9 a.m.–5 p.m. Tel: 01273 723064.

Brighton Sea Life Centre: gawp and gape at new monsters of the deep. Marine Parade, Brighton, West Sussex. Tel: 01273 604234, www.sealife.co.uk.

The Red Cow: all nationalities welcome. Pop in for a pint: talk to the locals or just talk to yourself. The Red Cow, Public House, 59 Sheen Road, Richmond, Surrey. Tel: 0208 940 2511.

The Walter Rothschild Zoological Museum: see Mick the Miller, and Mexican fleas through a microscope. Akeman Street, Tring, Herts. Tel: 0207 942 6171. Mon–Sat 10 a.m.–5 p.m., Sun 2 p.m.–5 p.m., www.nhm.ac/museum/tring.

The Hunterian Museum: meet the Irish Giant! Unfortunately it's closed until late 2004 for refurbishment, but it's well worth waiting for. The Hunterian Musuem at The Royal College of Surgeons, 35–43 Lincoln's Inn Field, London WC2. Tel: 0207 405 3747.

And finally, get out and about and ask around in your hometown. Because chances are that once upon a time, a big whale on a lorry sailed there too. Someone will remember him. Won't they?

Shipbuilders

Thanks to all those who worked so hard behind the scenes long before we set sail.

Alliot, Gerald, *The Vanishing Relics of Barnsley*, 1996, Wharnecliffe Publishing

Barnaby, David, *The Elephant who walked to Manchester*, 1988/1989, Basset Publications/Hyperion Books

Barrow, Tony, *The Whaling Trade of North-east England*, 2001, University of Sunderland Press

Bryant, Arthur, *Set in a Silver Sea – A History of Britain and the British People*, 1985, Book Club Associates by arrangement with William Collins Sons & Co

Cooksey, Jon, *Barnsley Pals – The 13th & 14th Battalions York and Lancaster Regiments*, 1986, Wharnecliffe Publishing

Carwardine, Mark, Fordyce, R. Ewan, Gill, Peter and Hoyt, Erich, *Whales and Dolphins*, 1998, Harper Collins

Daykin, John, Dennis, Brian and Hyde, Derek, *Barnsley Football Club – The Official History 1887–1998*, 1998, Yore Publications

Devey, Joseph, *The Life of Joseph Locke*, 1862, Cox & Wyman

Elliot, Brian, *The Making of Barnsley*, 1988, Wharnecliffe Publishing

Elliot, Brian, *Aspects of Barnsley 2,* 1994, Wharnecliffe Publishing

Elliot, Brian, *Aspects of Barnsley 3*, 1996, Wharnecliffe Publishing

Elliot, Brian, *Aspects of Barnsley 4*, 1998, Wharnecliffe Publishing

Elliot, Brian, *Aspects of Barnsley 5*, 1998, Wharncliffe Publishing

Elliot, Brian, *Aspects of Barnsley 6*, 2000, Wharncliffe Publishing

Hogben, Lancelot, *From Cave Painting to Comic Strip*, 1949, Chanticleer Press

Howse, Geoffrey, *Around Hoyland*, 1999, Sutton Publishing Limited

Ingham, Bernard, *Yorkshire Millennium*, 1999, Dalesman Publishing Company Limited

Ingram, Arthur, *The Story of Pickfords*, 1993, Roundoak Publishing

Kellet, Arnold, *The Yorkshire Dictionary*, 1994, Smith Settle Limited

Kurlansky, Mark, *The Basque History of the World*, 2000, Vintage

Marseden, John, *The Fury of the Northmen*, 1996, Kyle Cathie Limited

Melville, Herman, *Moby Dick*, 1994, Penguin Popular Classics (first published 1851)

Parry Jones, T.J., *The Other Story of Coal*, 1925, Unwin Brothers Limited

Payne, Fred, *Whaling and Whitby*, undated pamphlet, Elsom Cook

Philbrick, Nathaniel, *In the Heart of the Sea*, 2000, Harper Collins

Taylor, Warwick, *South Yorkshire Pits*, 2001 Wharncliffe Publishing

Young, Roy, *The Big House and the Little Village*, 2000, Wentworth Garden Centre

I am also indebted to Harry Brookes for kindly sharing with me his notes and memories of life on Barnsley Market. They're not published. But they should be.

Acknowledgements

The hour is late and the fire burns low: just enough time for a word of thanks to all those who made this whale hunt possible.

The tyke crew you've already met. Although it's perhaps unfair to single out anyone, I'd like to thank my second-in-command, Big 'n' Daft, for his (nearly) unfailing enthusiasm and the course headings that sent us in search of a monkey and fleas. During the voyage there were so many others who contributed. It proved impossible to include all the cries of support but if you were on board during that summer of the whale, you know who you are. Thank you. No captain could have wished for a finer crew. And thanks from the crew to Dr Vanessa Toulmin of the National Fairground Archive for the 'first sighting' of Jonah.

Thanks to Georgina Widdrington, Adele Lang and Anne Dewe: without your patience with Old Ahab and his ravings, this story would never have been told; to Gaz Gerrard who corrected my failing memories, although all lapses are my own. Thanks also to Clive Priddle at Fourth Estate, who listened long and hard to help shape this cyberseafarer's tale – a nice enough chap, but a little too interested in a pike caught on Wimbledon Common, which exploded in the back of a van – apparently. And of course, all hands on deck to salute Bill Campbell at Mainstream Publishing, who believed in an old whaleman's dream.

Many heard the tale of a whale but few believed. Thanks to the few who did and helped spread the word: John Peel and Jackie Smith at BBC Radio 4, Keith Arthur of Talksport Radio, Tim Grohne, Gary Grainger, Debbie Cass, Jack Sosnierz.

Thank you to everyone who sent in memories from across

Europe. Without you perhaps there would have been no tale to tell. Special thanks must go to Anne Turner in Cumbria, without doubt the most passionate 'whale believer' of them all.

Love to my mother Audrey and brothers David and Andrew and thanks for support in the darkest of hours: the spirit lives on. To Hazel for her unquestioning, tireless research at the bidding of a madman and to Caroline who waited patiently ashore for near three long years as I sailed for the far-flung reaches of madness.

To those who gave their time and enthusiasm to bring this story to life: George Logan for photography; Mark Mangla, Ann Statham, Emma Shepperdly, Chris McAlees for design.

But perhaps the greatest thanks of all goes to the many who never believed. It was their laughter that hardened my resolve, their accusations of madness that strengthened my determination – to go on in pursuit of a big whale on a lorry.